AGENCY AND RESPONSIBILITY

Agency and Responsibility

A Common-sense Moral Psychology

JEANETTE KENNETT

CLARENDON PRESS · OXFORD
2001

OXFORD

UNIVERSITY PRESS

Great Clarendon Street, Oxford OX2 6DP

Oxford University Press is a department of the University of Oxford.
It furthers the University's objective of excellence in research, scholarship,
and education by publishing worldwide in

Oxford New York

Athens Auckland Bangkok Bogotá Buenos Aires Calcutta
Cape Town Chennai Dar es Salaam Delhi Florence Hong Kong Istanbul
Karachi Kuala Lumpur Madrid Melbourne Mexico City Mumbai Nairobi
Paris São Paulo Shanghai Singapore Taipei Tokyo Toronto Warsaw

with associated companies in Berlin Ibadan

Oxford is a registered trade mark of Oxford University Press
in the UK and in certain other countries

Published in the United States
by Oxford University Press Inc., New York

British Library Cataloguing in Publication Data
Data available

Library of Congress Cataloging in Publication Data
Kennett, Jeanette.
Agency and Responsibility : A Common-sense moral psychology /
Jeanette Kennett.
p. cm.
Based on the author's thesis (Ph. D.)—Monash University, early 1990s.
Includes bibliographical references (p.) and index.
1. Ethics. 2. Will. 3. Self-control. I. Title.
BJ45 K46 2001 170'.1'9—dc21 00–060671
ISBN 0–19–823658–1

1 3 5 7 9 10 8 6 4 2

Typeset in Times
by Graphicraft Limited, Hong Kong
Printed in Great Britain by
T.J. International Ltd.,
Padstow, Cornwall

PREFACE AND ACKNOWLEDGEMENTS

This book began life as my Ph.D thesis at Monash University in the early 1990s. I was very fortunate to have Michael Smith as my supervisor throughout my candidature. From Michael, in seminars, in discussions, in his comments on my work, and through work we have done together, I have learned a very great deal about doing philosophy. His rigorous criticisms, advice, and encouragement, both then and since, have been invaluable. His influence on the shape and the arguments of this book should be obvious. My greatest intellectual debt is to him and I thank him.

During my time as a Ph.D student, John Bigelow, Richard Holton, and Rae Langton gave me particularly helpful comments on draft chapters and material presented at departmental seminars. Alan Crooke's meticulous proofreading of my thesis back then saved me from many errors that must otherwise have delayed me at a later stage. I would like to thank them and more generally everyone in philosophy at Monash who, as fellow students and teachers then, and as colleagues now, have provided a stimulating and supportive research environment.

John Campbell (La Trobe University) and Susan Wolf wrote very thoughtful examiner's reports on my thesis which assisted me greatly in preparing the manuscript for publication. I also had the pleasure and benefit of conversations with John during a period of study leave at La Trobe University in 1997, and more recently he generously read through and commented on revisions to Chapter 4. Thanks to them both.

Special thanks are due to Brad Hooker, Al Mele, and, in particular, Jay Wallace, who read the manuscript for Oxford University Press and provided me with extensive and careful comments and criticisms, and made many useful suggestions for improving the manuscript. I have tried to accommodate their concerns in this final version, though I fear I have not always succeeded. The shortcomings which remain are all my own work.

I thank Peter Momtchiloff at Oxford University Press for his consistent encouragement and for his patience and understanding when adverse circumstances slowed the pace of revisions. Thanks also to T. W. Bartel for his careful and sensitive copy-editing of the final manuscript and to Charlotte Jenkins for guiding me through the final stages leading to publication.

Finally, any work in moral psychology needs to be responsive to everyday life and to the pushes and pulls and complexity we find there. To my close friends and family, and especially to my children, Christopher, Simon, Jeremy, and Catherine, thank you. You have been the heart of my life and the best of teachers. This book is for you.

CONTENTS

Introduction: Moral Psychology and Common Sense

> Dr Johnson shunned to-night any discussion of the per-
> plexed question of fate and free will, which I attempted
> to agitate: 'Sir (said he), we *know* our will is free, and
> *there's* an end on't.'
>
> (Boswell, 1791: ii. 82)

1. Scepticism about Philosophy

Philosophy and common sense have in many areas been at
odds with one another. From Berkeley's denial of the existence
of external objects to Paul Churchland's (1988) and Patricia
Churchland's (1986) eliminative materialism regarding the
inner states of belief, desire, sensation, and emotion, their positions have been met with immediate disbelief and sometimes
ridicule from those who take common sense as their touchstone.
It must sometimes appear to those ordinary folk as though

> Whatever has the air of a paradox, and is contrary to the first and
> most unprejudiced notion of mankind, is often greedily embraced by
> philosophers, as showing the superiority of their science, which
> could discover opinions so remote from vulgar conception. (Hume,
> 1739: i. 71)

This is not quite fair to philosophy and philosophers of
course. Common sense *has* had its defenders among philosophers, notably Thomas Reid (see Dalgarno and Matthews,
1989). And in any case the deliverances of common sense should
not be beyond question and examination, since they may be
inconsistent, incomplete, biased, or confused.

The common-sense picture of the world must be capable of philosophical vindication if it is to have any authority for us. This essay is intended as a defence of common sense in the area of moral psychology. I suggest that in this domain, at least, philosophers ignore common sense at their peril. Moral psychology is centrally concerned with the folk-psychological categories of belief, desire, emotion, evaluation, and decision; it therefore needs to be informed by and sensitive to the accumulated wisdom about human motivation and human action which common sense offers. My task is to show that the distinctions made by a common-sense moral psychology can be systematically articulated and defended against the attacks which philosophers have made on them.

In the remainder of this brief introductory chapter I will say what I think common sense is and what I think it is not. I will outline the claims made by common sense about moral motivation, moral success, moral failure, and moral responsibility. And I will indicate what it is about these claims that have led philosophers to be sceptical of them.

2. Intuition, Convention, and Common Sense

In some quarters common sense has had a very bad press. It has been mistaken for convention, confused with intuition, and used to defend excesses of religious bigotry, misogyny, and the like. Mary Wollstonecraft for example sees it as allied with instinct and opposed to reason. She says:

A kind of mysterious instinct is *supposed* to reside in the soul, that instantaneously discerns truth, without the tedious labour of ratiocination. This instinct, for I know not what other name to give it, has been termed *common sense*, . . . and, by a kind of *indefeasible* right, it has been *supposed*, for rights of this kind are not easily proved, to reign paramount over the other faculties of the mind, and to be an authority from which there is no appeal. (Wollstonecraft, 1790: 30)

Wollstonecraft is a passionate defender of the role of reason in regulating human affairs. But she need not be concerned to defend reason from the intrusions of common sense. The 'mysterious instinct' which she describes is not to be confused with common sense; it is rather the faculty of moral intuition, whose stoutest exponents are to be found among those philosophers, such as John McDowell, who are most opposed to the conclusions of a common-sense moral psychology.

A more troubling possibility is that what passes for common sense is just popular or conventional opinion. For then common sense would frequently be bland, trivial, arrogant, and even obnoxious in its pronouncements, and it is puzzling why anyone would want to defend it.

In so far as common sense is self-satisfied, requiring for itself no better support than social convention, I will not defend it. I do not deny that some part of what is thought to be common sense is purely conventional. However, popular conventions and opinions may also be questioned by common sense, which suggests that the two are conceptually distinct. In any case the part of common sense that I will be defending has little to do with the conventions or popular opinions current in any particular society. Common sense at its best is, as I have suggested, the distillation of accumulated human wisdom about common human experience; it is the very embodiment of reason. And in the area of moral psychology it has hardly wavered in its conclusions despite the efforts of Socrates and philosophers since his time to revise them.

3. What does Common Sense Say?

Every day at about four in the afternoon Jane leaves her office and goes to the cafeteria to buy cream cakes. She knows that eating cream cakes is bad for her: her family has a history of heart disease and her doctor has advised her to lose weight. Yet each day she lines up at the cafeteria and buys and eats not one but several cakes.

Now, the ordinary or common-sense view recognizes at least three different ways in which a story like this can be filled out. It says that Jane may be either reckless or weak or compulsive in acting as she does. As the allocation of moral responsibility is in large part determined by whether we think of

Jane as reckless, weak, or compulsive, deciding among these alternatives is of great practical significance.

First, consider the case of recklessness. While there are several varieties of recklessness which will be discussed at length in Chapter 6, here it is sufficient to say that Jane is reckless if, despite being aware of all the considerations which weigh against the desirability of her eating cream cakes, she ignores them in arriving at a judgement in favour of eating cream cakes. Jane thus makes a culpable error in reasoning: she makes a judgement that she would not have made if only she had paid more attention to the reasons available to her. Let us further suppose that had she made the judgement that she should not eat cream cakes she would not have eaten them. Common sense tells us that when the case is detailed in this way Jane is fully responsible for what she does. For she apparently freely chooses to eat the cream cakes while knowing the consequences.

Next, we come to the case of compulsion. Jane is compulsive if, despite judging that it would be best if she did not eat cream cakes, she eats them anyway because her desire to do so is irresistible. An irresistible desire is (to postpone many questions) a desire that an agent cannot control. Such desires are discussed in Chapter 6. In this case the ordinary view holds (with some provisos) that Jane is not responsible for what she does. Though she knows the consequences, she does not freely choose to eat the cream cakes.

Finally, we think that Jane might be weak-willed in eating cream cakes. When we develop the story in this way we imagine a case intermediate between the two just described. For we imagine that Jane eats cream cakes despite judging that it would be best if she did not. But unlike the case in which Jane is compelled we imagine that here, as when she is reckless, her desires are not irresistible. We imagine that she has the capacity to control what she does, but she does not exercise it. She just gives in to temptation. In this case common sense tells us that Jane is responsible for what she does; since her actions are under her control, her choice to eat cream cakes is free.

These common-sense distinctions between recklessness, weakness of will, and compulsion have been the targets of much philosophical attack. The problematic category has been held to be weakness of will. Philosophers from Socrates to Davidson have questioned whether it is ever possible for an agent to act freely and intentionally against her better judgement. If it is not, then the common-sense distinctions collapse, and weakness must be assimilated to either recklessness or compulsion. Such an assimilation would not be without its price. A dissolution of the common-sense distinctions between recklessness, weakness, and compulsion challenges other central tenets of common-sense moral psychology and threatens to demand a significant revision of our ordinary moral practices. If we assimilate weakness to recklessness then, though we hold on to the idea that the weak-willed are responsible for what they do, we must think that they do not really judge to be best the actions that they say they judge best. We must conclude that in addition to judging badly, weak agents are often insincere in their public pronouncements. On the other hand if we assimilate weakness to compulsion then, though we retain the idea that the weak really do judge it better to act in one way while in fact acting in another, we must then think that the weak are not really responsible for what they do. Both alternatives are costly.

It should also be apparent that there is no place for the idea of self-control in a moral psychology which does not admit the possibility of an agent's choosing to act against her better judgement. Such an omission is an affront to common sense. Common sense does not hold that simply knowing what is best is sufficient to ensure that we do what is best. The ordinary view recognizes that Jane may have a struggle on her hands if she judges that she ought not to eat cream cakes yet desires, albeit not overwhelmingly, to do so, and it does not think any the worse of her for that. The revisionary accounts cannot make sense of Jane's struggles at all since they cannot, or cannot fully, acknowledge that they occur. This has far-reaching consequences, not least for the picture of value and evaluation that emerges from such narrow theories of moral motivation. I will suggest that a common-sense moral psychology which is faithful to common experience must embrace a theory of valuing that can explain how it is that agents may be motivated contrary to their practical judgements, and can recognize the plurality of desires and values which is required to ground a complete account of moral successes and moral failures.

4. How is Common Sense to be Defended?

It is doubtful whether any philosophical analysis could ever force us to surrender the common-sense distinctions we make, like those between recklessness, weakness, and compulsion, which seem so accurately to reflect settled features of common moral experience. But these distinctions have lacked a comprehensive and vigorous philosophical defence and so the question must arise as to whether any such defence is to be had. Do the common-sense distinctions mark real differences: differences that can be systematically articulated?

As it is weakness of will (or akrasia) that is the main target of the sceptics it is weakness of will that must be shown to be possible. If the common-sense view is to be vindicated we must make sense of the akratic conflict, and to do that we must establish both the general possibility of desiring in opposition to judgement and the possibility of Jane and those like her exercising self-control. In arguing for the common-sense conclusions I will of necessity sometimes appeal to common experience and ordinary examples to support my case. But I have already said that I regard sensitivity to ordinary experience as a virtue rather than a defect in moral psychology.

The order of proceeding will be as follows. The next two chapters are primarily devoted to a critical examination of some classical and modern views of reasons for action and motivation for action which tend, sometimes despite themselves, to assimilate weakness to recklessness or compulsion. Chapter 2 focuses on Socratic accounts, Chapter 3 on Humean accounts. The critical shortcoming common to these different accounts is in their failure to distinguish between explanatory or motivating reasons, and justificatory or normative reasons. The distinction between the explanation and the justification of action is part of common sense. While a close examination of the shortcomings of Socratic accounts, which equate virtue with knowledge, tends to push us towards accepting a Humean account of the *explanation* of action, I argue that the conceptual resources available to the Humeans are too thin to enable them to adequately address the issue of *justification* and so to explain and distinguish the various failures of agency that are our main concern.

Chapter 4 is pivotal. In it I describe Gary Watson's Platonist view of human psychology and the account of weakness which he derives from it. While sympathetic to the distinction he draws between wanting and valuing, I conclude that his account leaves the connection between evaluation and motivation obscure. With respect to the distinction, I claim that we should think of evaluations as conclusions about our reasons for action and I argue that such reasons may have a variety of sources. I point out that Humean theorists who assert that all such reasons are desire-dependent do not escape the problem, faced by those who argue in favour of the existence of desire-independent reasons for action, of explaining the link between our evaluative conclusions and action. There is an inescapable normativity to reason. Once this is recognized, the view that all practical reasons must have their source in desire, and the related scepticism about the possibility of agents acting contrary to their better judgement, should seem less compelling. I then examine response-dispositional theories of value and argue that a suitably modified version gives us a plausible way of cashing out the ordinary connection between judgements of value and action and leaves us better equipped to understand and explain failures of agency. By the end of Chapter 4 we are in a position to defend the common-sense distinctions between recklessness, weakness, and compulsion and provide persuasive accounts of self-control and moral responsibility. The rest of the book is devoted to these tasks.

In Chapter 5 I present a taxonomy of agent-control which lays out in some detail what self-control is and how it may be exercised, and I draw a distinction between autonomy, as self-rule, and orthonomy, which is right rule. I interpret right rule in broadly Kantian terms as the rule of reason. In Chapter 6 I argue, against Watson, that those who have the capacity for self-control need not always exercise it. I outline criteria for determining whether agents are weak or compulsive, and distinguish three varieties of recklessness. I then consider how the accounts of evaluation, orthonomy, and control, and the distinctions between recklessness, weakness, and compulsion, underwrite common-sense allocations of moral responsibility. In the seventh and final chapter I test the account I have developed by considering the pressures placed upon ordinary notions of moral failure and moral responsibility in the case of agents whose actions are extraordinarily evil.

2

Classical Theories of Reasons
and Motivation

In this chapter I outline Socrates' view of moral psychology as presented in Plato's *Protagoras*; in particular, the role he gives to knowledge and pleasure in the production of action, and his consequent explanation of weakness of will. I then look at a recent analysis of moral knowledge and moral motivation given by John McDowell (1978, 1979), which is in many respects Socratic in postulating a necessary connection between knowledge of the good and desire, and which yields a Socratic account of incontinence as a kind of ignorance.

I will suggest that the cases covered by their explanations do not include many of those commonly held to be central to weakness of will. The posited strict connection between perception of the good and motivation that underpins the explanation leaves both continence (self-control) and compulsion problematic, and collapses the common-sense distinction between recklessness and weakness. Furthermore, McDowell's account, at least, presents an unrealistic and rather unattractive picture of virtuous agents. This is too high a price to pay for the hypothesized strict connection between evaluation, desire, and action. I conclude that we must look for a looser connection at a lower cost to common sense.

1. The Socratic Account

In the *Protagoras*, Socrates offers a revision of the common view that in weakness of will the agent's knowledge of what is good is overcome by pleasure. The common view reflects a misunderstanding, he thinks, for pleasure and goodness are really the same thing. The mistake of thinking some pleasures bad or evil arises because some pleasures, notably the sensual pleasures, give way to or cause subsequent pains. Such pleasures are not evil in themselves, Socrates suggests, since if their indulgence were to have no bad consequences we would not be inclined to call them bad merely on account of their hedonic quality. They are evil for no other reason than 'that they end in pain and rob us of other pleasures' (*Protagoras* 354a). Conversely those goods which we are liable to see as painful (such as exercise or medical treatment) are called good not because of the immediate suffering they impose but because of the pleasure and absence of pain which is their end.

According to Socrates there is no other measure for good and evil than pleasure and pain.[1] Knowledge of the good is therefore motivationally powerful since all men necessarily desire their own happiness:

if the pleasant is the good, nobody continues to do anything with the knowledge or belief that some other thing would be better and is also attainable, when he might do the better . . . no man voluntarily pursues evil or that which he thinks to be evil. To prefer evil to good is not in human nature; and when a man is compelled to choose one of two evils no-one will choose the greater when he might have the lesser. No-one willingly goes to meet evil. (*Protagoras* 358b ff.)

Knowledge of the good therefore cannot be overcome by apprehension of greater pleasures or pains, for good is the greatest pleasure. Apparent akrasia, i.e. the case where we choose the lesser pleasure over the greater pleasure, is only explicable if our knowledge is incomplete. Socrates explains our ignorance of the good as akin to an optical or auditory illusion. Just as an object which is close to us appears larger than a distant object of the same size, so too do the pleasures at hand appear greater than pleasures which lie further in the future. The akrates

---

[1] Gerasimos Santas (1966: 7–8) points out that Socrates is aware of the limitations of his argument: weakness may be possible if the good is different from pleasure. And, of course, the hedonism here is not matched in other Socratic dialogues. However I am not here concerned with whether or not the views Socrates expresses are consistent between dialogues. It is the *Protagoras* which has powerfully influenced the debate about weakness of will.

suffers from a *temporal* illusion and mistakenly chooses *as best* that action which is really worse.

Her mistake is just a failure to measure accurately enough the pleasures and pains to be gained from each course of action and to weigh them properly against each other. Her salvation, Socrates thinks, lies in the art of measurement, which is a particular branch of knowledge. Done properly, such measurement yields knowledge of which action is best, and, given Socrates' assumption of psychological hedonism and his equation of goodness with pleasure, that knowledge will be sufficient to ensure that the agent performs, or at least tries to perform, the best action.

This picture of human psychology is, surprisingly, closer in some ways to Hume than it is to Plato or to Aristotle. Reason facilitates fulfilment of the natural desire for pleasure by discovering where the most pleasure lies. Reason is not seen in the *Protagoras* as an independent source of motivation; it is not something that might compete with the desire for pleasure. However, the desire is not an independent variable either. It is not something which an agent might fail to have or might have only weakly—scenarios which are perfectly conceivable on a Humean account. There is a necessary connection between knowing or believing that a certain course of action is *best*, i.e. most pleasant, and desiring *most* to perform that action.[2] Reason thus determines the intensity of the desire for any

---

[2] Compare the following schematic picture of Socratic practical reasoning, which is roughly that offered by Norman Gulley (1968: 108), with the Davidsonian schema (in Davidson, 1969). They are remarkably similar, though Davidson does not of course attribute an intrinsic desire for pleasure to all agents, or equate goodness with pleasure.

    (i) To make a judgement that some action will yield a greater balance of pleasure over pain than any possible alternative actions is to judge (or believe) it best to perform that action.

    (ii) If an agent judges that a particular action is best, then her desire to perform that action is stronger than her desire to do anything else.

    (iii) Agents will do what they most strongly desire to do.

Both accounts hold (ii) and (iii), but Gulley (along with Socrates) specifies, as Davidson does not, the content of better judgement which makes clear the connection of such judgements to motivation. However, Davidson attempts to evade the scepticism about weakness of will which Socrates embraces.

particular object or action by its estimation of the good to be obtained therefrom.

It is clear that on this view of human psychology and practical reasoning apparent cases of weakness of will can *only* be explained as cases of ignorance. Indeed all moral failings must be the result of ignorance. They are to be explained by the fact that human beings are frequently instrumentally irrational. We all want pleasure most but we often choose the wrong means to it. Now, sometimes of course this ignorance is not *culpable*. Children, for example, may be excused for not knowing their desires well, for not knowing how to satisfy them, and for not discerning which pleasures are enduring and which may turn to ashes in the mouth. But weakness of will is presumably culpable ignorance, and herein lies a problem. The Socratic explanation of weakness looks to be exactly the same explanation as we ordinarily give for recklessness. The common-sense distinction between the two collapses. The weak agent, like the reckless agent, does not take sufficient care in forming her judgements of what is best. She fails to weigh properly the evidence available to her, and does so in circumstances where her failure cannot be excused by factors such as illness, tiredness, or the unusual difficulty of the task. The judgement she makes is not just erroneous but obviously so.

This assimilation may be resisted by defenders of common sense on the grounds that it is just manifest that people who act wrongly are *not* always in a state of ignorance about what is right. After all, the people concerned often express judgements about what they should do which are in direct opposition to what they actually do. Many smokers for example readily concede that smoking is bad for them and that it would be best for them if they did not smoke; indeed this is taken to be a paradigm case of weakness of will. How can their failure be seen as a cognitive failure, such as marks recklessness? The ordinary view is that it must rather be a failure at the conative level, a failure of the will.

The Socratic response must be to deny that such agents can really believe or really understand what they are saying, since if they did they would necessarily be motivated to act accordingly. They are merely paying lip service to a standard they do not share; in Aristotle's words, 'the fact that men use the language which flows from knowledge proves nothing . . . we must suppose that the use of language by men in an incontinent state means no more than its utterance by actors on the stage' (*NE* 1147ª18).[3] On this interpretation there may be a slight difference between the akrates and the reckless agent but it is not what we thought. In addition to being a bad judge of what is best the akrates is often insincere in her public protestations. Contrary to the common-sense view, it then turns out that the akrates is somewhat more culpable than the reckless agent.

Now, no doubt there are cases which are appropriately described in this way, but it is not credible that in every case an agent who expresses judgements of value which are at odds with what she actually does is either insincere or ignorant of the import of her words.

John McDowell (1978) gives a more subtle response which does not impute any insincerity to the akrates. He agrees with Socrates in denying that the akrates' perceptions of a situation match those of the virtuous person; he agrees, that is, that the failure is cognitive rather than conative. But he suggests that the posited difference in perception may not be capable of expression in words. In some respects the akrates' perceptions do match those of the virtuous person; their failure to match them exactly may be manifest in their deeds rather than in their words.

We might immediately wonder why such subtle differences in perception lead to quite unsubtle differences in desire and action between the weak agent and the virtuous agent. McDowell's position is discussed in more detail in the next section of this chapter. Here we should note that *his* account does leave room for some distinction between weak agents and reckless agents: there is a difference in the magnitude of the perceptual error. Reckless agents, unlike weak agents, make gross and obvious errors of judgement.

---

[3] In Aristotle, of course, the incontinent state is a state of passion: a state which alters our bodily condition, and overcomes knowledge, just as sleep, madness, or drunkenness do (*NE* 1146ᵇ33 ff.); whereas for Socrates the incontinent state is more accurately described as one where we are misled, not by pleasure as such, but by its proximity, into forming a wrong judgement. In both cases, however, the assertion of a contrary judgement is empty.

Sophisticated defenders of the Socratic view might well be able to elaborate on the cognitive differences between the two types of agent. Walsh (1963: 94) suggests that continence might be analysable as an epistemic power to hang onto correct beliefs. So while the reckless agent blatantly disregards the facts in arriving at a judgement, the weak, incontinent agent experiences difficulty in keeping them in view. She fails in skill or perseverance at the cognitive level.

There is some truth in broadly Socratic accounts of weakness and in what is implied by them for any analysis of self-control; nevertheless it represents a considerable narrowing of the common-sense account. It denies the central cases of clear-headed weakness of will, concentrating instead on those cases which occur around the margin, where weakness shades into recklessness. Weakness of will is not the only folk construct to be shifted or erased from the moral-psychological map by this view of reasoning and motivation. Socratic models require a wholesale realignment of moral-psychological phenomena to accord with the single dimension of explanation that they allow for failures of practical reason. Weakness, if not quite assimilated to recklessness, is moved a lot closer to it, while psychological compulsion disappears altogether from the map. There are no irresistible desires according to Socrates, who argues that 'knowledge is a noble and commanding thing, which cannot be overcome, and will not allow a man, if he only knows the difference of good and evil, to do anything which is contrary to knowledge' (*Protagoras* 352c). The only kind of compulsion that Socrates acknowledges is external compulsion; he recognizes that we may be coerced by others, but denies that we could be similarly coerced by our own desires and alienated from our proposed actions by them.

Perhaps Socrates might at least concede this, which I take to be the Aristotelian opinion: that a desire may chronically interfere with one's ability to distinguish good from evil, pleasures from pains. So the *genesis* of the agent's ignorance may differ somewhat between compulsion and what we call recklessness; there may be a continuum of culpability on which we may situate carelessness near one extreme, and grossly distorted vision near the other.[4] But this is a doubtful interpretation of Socrates' view, since it gives an unwanted primacy to desire in the explanation of some wrong actions, whereas for Socrates it is knowledge or belief that is primary, and the strength of the desire for a particular end is dependent (in fact, entirely dependent) upon knowledge or belief. In any event even this modified view would deny inclusion as instances of compulsion to many cases which we usually understand in that way. We might include, say, obsessive handwashers who are ignorant of the source of the attraction that certain actions have for them, and who may even be unaware of what they are doing for much of the time, but we must exclude unwilling heroin addicts, along with clear-headedly weak smokers and chocolate eaters.

The failure of the Socratic view to recognize many instances of weakness and compulsion is not all. What account could be given of self-control or continence? Perhaps the virtuous person will turn out to be the talented and skilled measurer of the good, since for Socrates wisdom and temperance are one and the same (*Protagoras* 333b). 'Continence' or 'self-control' will then be the label for the less talented person's conscientious application to the task of measuring competing goods so as to choose the action which will maximize pleasure. The securing of instrumental rationality is certainly an aspect of self-control, and it is to be discussed at length in Chapter 5. But there are other ways of exercising self-control which the Socratic account, with its one-dimensional account of failures of practical reason, cannot recognize. It precludes a full analysis of the capacity for self-control and will only incidentally fit with the ordinary person's grasp of when self-control is called for and how it is exercised.

Here is a rather mundane example which should suffice to show that we take into account more than a person's state of knowledge and level of skill in determining whether she needs to exercise, or whether she has exercised, self-control. Imagine

---

[4] Some agents will also fail to act for the best because of natural deficiency of intellect. They may simply have no talent for this type of measurement.

three people shopping for Christmas presents. The first is especially good at working out just what the recipients will like. She has a flair for selecting gifts that will charm and delight her loved ones while staying within her budget. Her ready insight allows her to complete her shopping trip smoothly and swiftly. The second shopper does not share this flair, though she shares the first shopper's concern to maximize the recipients' pleasure. Consequently her shopping trip takes five times as long, as she walks from store to store to compare merchandise and wrestle with budgetary considerations. She ponders each item carefully and puzzles over its possible reception. Her enthusiasm for the task at hand never flags, however, and in spite of the practical difficulties she encounters it never even occurs to her to give up and go home before it is completed. The third shopper also lacks the flair that makes shopping easy. After a time her feet begin to hurt, her head aches, and she begins to think longingly of her armchair. Her enthusiasm for getting the right thing falters. She is strongly tempted to buy the next thing she sees, or to go home empty-handed and disabuse her children of their fond belief in a benevolent Santa Claus. But, somehow, she struggles on and completes her shopping with due care.

The first case parallels the Socratic description of virtue. Given the description of the cases we may immediately wonder why virtue is so much more *morally* praiseworthy than continence, but I will defer consideration of that issue to the next section, on McDowell's views. Now, both the second and the third shopper lack the talent of the virtuous shopper. But it is only in the third case that we would say that the shopper needed to, and did, exercise self-control to complete her task. This must be explained by her disinclination, a feeling that cannot wholly depend upon her lack of knowledge or skill at the primary task of choosing the right presents, since it was not shared by the similarly unskilled second shopper and since it is not unimaginable that this feeling might on occasion be had by the more skilled shopper. It is the disinclination—the conative state—which renders self-control necessary for the third shopper and which makes the description of her as one who is exercising self-control, in carefully completing her shopping, appropriate. The shopper who was all eagerness to do the job might yet fail to do it well because all the care and all the trying in the world could not compensate for her lack of insight into other people's wants. But on the face of it this is not a failure of *self-control* and, though she fails through ignorance to maximize the good, in this case the pleasure of the recipients, we do not properly call such an agent weak or reckless or compelled.

It looks as though we cannot rely on the single dimension of knowledge or the lack of it to capture and explain all the phenomena that common sense permits. It may be that common sense needs revising, but it is not at all clear that it should be revised along these lines. We need some further argument before we should be prepared to trade in the richness of the folk theory for the unity and explanatory simplicity of the Socratic account.

2. McDowell's Account of Moral Motivation

So far I have suggested, against Socrates, that it is not at all unimaginable that an agent should know and judge something to be good, or better than the alternatives, and yet fail to desire it, or desire something else more. Such an agent is not necessarily ignorant of something relevant in her situation which if revealed would shift the focus of her desire. The clear-headed smoker knows of all the deleterious effects of smoking; she may even know them better than the lifelong nonsmoker, since she knows some of them by acquaintance as well as by description. If she *is* ignorant her ignorance does not rest on any obvious factual error or error of measurement. (Such errors would presumably lead to or support a different judgement from the one she makes.) The explanation for her weakness must be rather more subtle. It is now time to consider in detail McDowell's variation on the Socratic theme that perception of the good determines desire, and his particular characterization of the ignorance that afflicts the less than perfectly virtuous. His argument is presented in two papers, 'Are Moral Requirements Hypothetical Imperatives?' (1978) and 'Virtue and Reason' (1979).

McDowell suggests, uncontroversially, that to explain an action in terms of the agent's reasons is to 'credit him with psychological states given which we can see how doing what he did, or attempted, would have appeared to him in some favourable light' (McDowell, 1978: 14). He goes on to argue that this favourable light is not to be *identified* with desire (though in many cases the light will be shed by some desire), since in cases of prudent action and virtuous action any desire which we ascribe to the agent in acting will be entirely consequential on the agent's seeing the proposed action in a favourable light. While it is fitting to ascribe a desire to him in acting, the motivating power of his reason does not depend upon the presence of an *independent* or antecedent desire; it simply flows from his particular view of the facts.

This is a view of the facts which, McDowell claims, could not be shared by someone who is not so motivated. So expressed, the claim borders on fiat and is, I will argue, insupportable. Somewhat more moderately, McDowell suggests that it is *not* the case that someone could share the virtuous person's conception of the circumstances but fail to see reason for herself to act as the virtuous person does. In so far as we are disposed to agree with this second way of putting the point, though, we are responding to a separate claim. On the face of it the first version of McDowell's claim is much stronger than the second and would gain little support from the truth of the second. The claim about what we have reason to do is ambiguous and, unlike the first claim, does not rule out the possibility of clear-headed weak-willed action. The ambiguity rests on a distinction between two senses of the term 'reason' which McDowell does not embrace.

In ordinary discourse we recognize a difference between what is reasonable and justifiable and what is merely explicable. That a person buys and eats an ice-cream is a perfectly explicable sequence of actions, given that she desires to eat ice-cream and knows how to go about getting one. Her desire must constitute a reason in McDowell's terms, because it does reveal to us how doing what she did appeared in a favourable light to her. It provides an explanation of her actions in terms of her purposes. But of course we need to know more if we are to move to the rather different conclusion that what the agent did was reasonable. It might not have been. Her buying an expensive ice-cream might mean her children go hungry that night. Or it might fly in the face of medical advice. And surely she might be aware of these things at the time that she buys and eats the ice-cream. Then, even by her own lights, her action is not one that she has reason to perform—in the justificatory or normative sense of the word—though it does appear to her in *some* favourable light which serves to motivate and explain her performance.[5]

It seems clear from this example that the two kinds of reasons may come apart. So it appears, contrary to the first version of McDowell's claim, that someone could share the virtuous person's beliefs about what is justified or required in a particular situation without sharing the virtuous person's motivations. Properly explicated, the common-sense distinction between explanation and justification permits and supports the idea that there *can* be clear-headed weak-willed actions.

Now, if we accept this distinction between explanatory and justifying reasons, there is a reading available to us on which we are able to agree with McDowell when he says that the virtuous person's conception of the facts cannot be shared by someone who *sees no reason* to act as the virtuous person does. This claim is persuasive if we read 'reason' here exclusively in the justificatory sense, since the facts of a case are often cited in support of claims about what would be reasonable or justified, and it might indeed reveal a certain sort of ignorance, the sort characteristic of recklessness, if an agent just did not see that the facts in a certain case were such as to justify or recommend a particular course of action. McDowell acknowledges a justificatory component to reason. If one accepts that one has reason to do something, one should in principle be able to cite 'the appropriate specific consideration which one takes to justify the view that one should act in that way' (1978: 14). But of course McDowell is also making the

---

[5] Whenever we talk of reasons being 'good' or 'bad' or 'stupid', we must also be talking about how well or how badly they serve to justify a course of action that they may also explain. For more discussion of this distinction see Woods (1972); also Williams (1981*a*) and Smith (1987).

stronger, more comprehensive claim: a claim which is thoroughly Socratic in shrinking the moral-psychological map.

In his discussion of virtuous action McDowell is asserting a unity or at least a necessary connection between certain kinds of cognitions and motivations to act, and what is more, he is asserting the motivational supremacy of these states over any antecedent desires of the agent. In the domain of virtue, at least, there is no distinction of the kind described above to be made among reasons.[6] If an independently intelligible desire is needed to explain an action then according to McDowell that action does not manifest virtue. He agrees with Thomas Nagel (1970) that within the domains of virtue and prudence, a conception of the facts, a view of how things are, 'constitute the whole of a reason' for action, not just, as we might have thought, the whole of a justification for action (McDowell, 1978: 16).[7] It is not clear in McDowell precisely how a view of the world can, by itself, motivate agents in a particular way. At one point McDowell suggests that the world itself is not motivationally inert. If this is the case it would seem that you don't acquire a motivation *as a result* of your perception

[6] In one place McDowell appears to accede to the view that the agent's belief about how things are is ordinarily combined with an independently intelligible desire to explain the action performed. He says that 'A full specification of a reason must make clear how the reason was capable of motivating; it must contain enough to reveal the favourable light in which the agent saw his projected action. We tend to assume that this is effected quite generally by the inclusion of a desire. (Of course a reason which includes a desire can be specified elliptically, when the desire is obvious enough not to need mentioning; as when we explain someone's taking his umbrella in terms of his belief that it is likely to rain.)' (1978: 14–15).

Here all McDowell denies is that 'the motivating power of all reasons derives from their including desires' (15). However, he thinks it makes just as much sense to construe the case in purely cognitive terms, as 'a colouring of the agent's view of the world' (24).

[7] Elsewhere, he says it is not enough that the agent's motives and action appear to conform with the requirements of virtue; an action manifests virtue only if the agent's conception of how to live is capable of 'actually entering our understanding of the action, explaining why it was this concern rather than any other which was drawn into operation' (McDowell, 1979: 344). This appears to rule out (for example) an antecedent desire for a friend's welfare partly explaining an action manifesting the virtue of friendship. Plausibly, such concerns may shape or influence our conception of how to live but this does not sit well with McDowell's purely cognitive construal of virtue.

of how things are; rather, to have the perception *is also* to be motivated in a particular way. The favourable light emanates from the world, not from the agent. On this distinctly Platonic reading the special attribute of the virtuous person is her capacity to apprehend certain facts out in the world, facts that are in themselves motivationally compelling.[8] That is what virtue amounts to. The less than virtuous agent, then, is presumably the agent who has not had direct access to these unusual facts. These moral or prudential facts are facts which she only 'knows', if she knows them at all, in the attenuated sense pointed to by Aristotle, just as 'those who have just begun to learn a science can string together its phrases, but do not yet know it; for it has to become part of themselves, and that takes time' (*NE* 1147^{a}18). In the matter of virtue, knowledge by acquaintance would appear to be essential. It is clear and direct apprehension of the good that is motivationally compelling.

At other points McDowell appears to suggest that an appropriate desire is *entailed* by the virtuous agent's view of what is required. On this reading, as on the first, the desire which is ascribed to the agent is a consequence of her cognitions. It doesn't play any independent explanatory role in disposing the agent to act in one way rather than another. The explanation here, however, focuses more on facts about the agent than on facts about the world and speaks rather of a 'colouring of the agent's view of the world' (1978: 24). McDowell says:

[8] The Platonic view that knowledge of certain features of the world is by itself motivationally compelling is criticized by John Mackie in his argument from queerness (1977: 38–42). There he suggests that such features would have to be 'entities or qualities or relations of a very strange sort, utterly different from anything else in the universe. Correspondingly, if we were aware of them it would have to be by some special faculty of moral perception utterly different from our ordinary ways of knowing everything else' (38).

This he finds completely implausible. McDowell openly embraces the intuitionist line in his essentially unanalysable characterization of the virtuous person's special way of seeing things. My criticisms of McDowell arise out of phenomenological concerns, rather than from the metaphysical and epistemological problems raised by Mackie. However I am assuming, on the basis of Mackie's argument, that the burden of proof lies with McDowell when he claims that, notwithstanding all other evidence of similarity of perception and judgement between two agents, a difference in what they actually do is invariably confirmation of a difference in perception, not merely of a difference in desire.

The desire for the good of others is related to charity . . . not, then, as a needed extra ingredient in formulations of reasons for acting. Rather, the desire is ascribed . . . simply in recognition of the fact that a charitable person's special way of conceiving situations by itself casts a favourable light on charitable actions. (1978: 20)

In spite of his insistence that we must stand in the right place if we are to take in the view, McDowell does not canvass the possibility that a desire for the good of others may play *some* role at the ground floor in constituting an agent as charitable and thus sensitive to the considerations which recommend charitable behaviour.[9] Here he takes himself to be talking about a purely *perceptual* capacity which when exercised yields essentially *cognitive* states. He denies that invitations to see the facts in a particular way, e.g. as the charitable person would or as the shy and sensitive person would, are invitations 'to feel, quite over and above one's view of the facts, a desire' (McDowell, 1978: 22). One's view of the facts, if taken from the right perspective, will be motivating on its own.

In 'Virtue and Reason', McDowell argues that virtuous people see the facts differently from the non-virtuous. Their special conception of how to live governs their perceptions. The interaction between their conception of how to live and their knowledge of a particular situation yields 'a view of the situation with one . . . fact, as it were, in the foreground' (McDowell, 1979: 345). This is the salient fact of the situation and it both draws the appropriate concern into operation and silences all other concerns, thus ensuring that the virtuous agent acts virtuously and wholeheartedly. The virtuous person's perception of certain facts as *salient* distinguishes her from others who are apparently in possession of the same facts.

These others—the merely continent agent, the akrates, and, presumably, the compulsive agent—have their view of 'the noble' clouded or blurred by 'a lively desire' (McDowell, 1979: 345). They may at one level share a view of the facts with the virtuous agent since, as McDowell concedes, they do know what virtue demands. But there is a subtle difference in what they perceive, analogous to their experiencing something as differently coloured, or perhaps as being more or less

---

[9] I consider this kind of possibility in Ch. 4. See also fn. 7 above.

intensely coloured; and this is a difference which does not always emerge in a verbal report on what is perceived (McDowell, 1978: 28). Even when the perceptions of a certain situation by a virtuous and a non-virtuous agent differ in no other respect, they must differ in patterns of saliences, in the way in which the facts these agents perceive are organized in their over-all conception of the situation. The virtuous person, says McDowell, 'conceives the relevant sorts of situations in such a way that considerations which would otherwise be reasons for acting differently are silenced by the recognised require-ments'. The attractions of alternative courses of action are 'insu-lated by the clear perception of a silencing requirement', and do not engage the will at all (McDowell, 1978: 28). As David McNaughton explains it in his discussion of McDowell, once the virtuous person 'has fully attained the correct conception, once she has perceived what morality requires, she will be unmoved by competing attractions because she will not even see them as attractions' (McNaughton, 1988: 116).

So on this view it is constitutive of virtuous action that the virtuous person is free of conflict and in no danger of being motivated contrary to her view of what is required. Self-control is never necessary for such a person. McDowell sees mere continence as very much second best to virtue: indeed it is a form of moral weakness on his account. The absence of a sufficient desire to do what is seen as best or the presence of contrary motivations, i.e. the very occurrence of conditions in which self-control might be called for, are for him clear evid-ence of a failure of sensitivity and awareness. There is, then, no concession from McDowell that self-control might be a valu-able capacity in its own right, one that even virtuous people should possess, and little indication of how it might be exer-cised. The continent agent differs from the weak-willed agent and the compulsive agent only in the closeness with which her view of the situation matches that of the virtuous agent. In her case it is sufficiently close to motivate her to perform the right action but it is not close enough to render her action virtuous, since she still feels the pull of competing concerns.

This view of continence seems counter-intuitive. Certainly it is against one traditional view of virtue in action, which gives the highest honours to those who have to struggle against recalcitrant motivation to do the right thing but do it none-theless.[10] However, in a sympathetic reading of McDowell, McNaughton argues that the two ways of understanding moral weakness that are available on this cognitivist picture of moral motivation are both plausible and recognizable and provide for an adequate account of continence. The weak individual may share just enough of the virtuous person's conception of a situation to recognize the moral requirement but fail to see it clearly enough to silence the attractions of some other course of action. Just as I might recognize that a piece of music is very good without yet being able to pick out all the features which contribute to its excellence, so the weak individual has yet to reach a full appreciation of the force of the moral requirement. Or perhaps the weak agent did at some point share the moral vision of the virtuous person and remains convinced of the rightness of a particular course of action but her view has since been clouded by desire. As McNaughton says: 'It is one thing to see the wrongness of adultery when there is no prospect of it, and quite another to keep a grip on that conception when the occasion presents itself' (McNaughton, 1988: 129). The less than virtuous agent is prone to 'falling back' into a more limited view of the facts in situations of temptation. From this more limited view the course of action which is still judged to be worse looks more attractive and so one is in danger of acting wrongly.[11] The cure for weakness on both readings is to become more attentive and sensitive to certain aspects of the situation before one and allow these to assume their proper weight in one's overall conception of it and of what is to be done. In the case of adultery one should presumably be more attentive to the act of betrayal and all that it would involve both for oneself and one's spouse, rather than to the

---

[10] I take up this point in more detail below.

[11] So expressed, this explanation of weakness is similar in structure to that given by Donald Davidson (1969), which is examined in the next chapter. Both claim that the weak person does not act without a reason and that explanations of weakness of will must show how the incontinent action could come to seem more attractive than the action the agent judged she had most reason to perform. For both of them strength of will must involve the capacity to keep a grip on the broader set of considerations which led to the original judgement.

pleasure and excitement of the adulterous liaison. Once one's conception of the situation is corrected, motivation falls into place. McNaughton (1988: 131) thus appears, like Walsh (1963: 94), to analyse strength of will in terms of an epistemic capacity to keep the facts fully in view in circumstances where it is hard to do so. If an agent fails to sustain the right conception of the facts she is in danger of acting weakly.

McNaughton accurately describes some perfectly ordinary and recognizable ways in which it may come about that we fail to do as we ought, as well as some important ways of overcoming these failures. The question to be asked is whether this picture is complete. The failings are recognizable, they are on the moral-psychological map, but are they properly called weakness of will? The first way of characterizing weakness leaves it unclear why such a failing should be considered culpable. The ignorant agent might reflect in good faith, but, through no fault of her own, lack the skill or experience needed to reach a full appreciation of the respective values of the available actions. If the thought is that she fails to properly appreciate the good through inattentiveness or carelessness her fault is more naturally cast as one of recklessness. The second way of characterizing weakness fits better with common-sense conceptions of weakness of will but does so only in so far as an important explanatory role is given to desire in the construction of the conflict. On this reading it is not clear whether McDowell's conception of weakness really does differ significantly from traditional accounts in which desire and judgement are at odds. Either way it does not appear that these understandings of weakness and continence represent an advance on Socrates. Indeed in some respects the Socratic view, in postulating a necessary desire for pleasure, is more coherent than McDowell's avowedly cognitivist view of both evaluation and motivation.

3. *Three Problems with McDowell's View*

What reason do we have to accept either McDowell's entirely cognitivist view of moral motivation or the ideal of the virtuous agent he presents? Though a cognitivist account of moral *judgement* seems to me to be substantially correct it is not clear, given some plausible assumptions about the complexity of the moral universe we inhabit, that the process of judgement described by McDowell supports his central claims about moral motivation and the nature of virtue.

There are three problems peculiar to McDowell's proposals regarding reason and motivation besides the general failure of Socratic accounts to differentiate weakness, recklessness, and compulsion.

(i) The use of the notion of salience does nothing to advance or support McDowell's claim that the difference between the motivations of virtuous agents and the motivations of others *does* have its source entirely in cognition, since McDowell himself seems to acknowledge a distinction between what is motivationally salient and what is salient in deliberation. He does not establish that the difference between cases of virtue and weakness is not simply, or at least primarily, one of motivational salience, a conative difference.

(ii) The pattern of motivation ascribed to virtuous agents, in whom other motivations are silenced, is hardly exclusive to their case or to virtuous action, and it is stretching credulity to suggest that unclouded cognition is the key to understanding motivation in the other cases as well. Indeed the sensitivity ascribed to virtuous persons by McDowell may reasonably be supposed to permit and even require that on some occasions other motives are *not* silenced.

(iii) McDowell's characterization of virtuous motivation and his dismissive attitude towards self-control raises a normative question: does virtue really exclude self-control?[12] Or should self-control be seen as valuable in its own right, or as a necessary concomitant of virtue?

I will discuss these points in turn.

---

[12] Indeed, as described by McNaughton, it is not clear how continence differs at all from virtue, since both involve attaining the right view of the

(i) Salience

McDowell introduces the notion of salience to answer the obvious objections to his claim that beliefs of a certain kind *necessarily* motivate those agents who hold them. In need of some way of overcoming the apparent counterexamples to his thesis that a difference in action is always at root caused by a difference in perception, he turns to the idea of salience to evoke that difference. But this cannot save his position, since the old objections arise all over again in the new context.

When we deliberate about what we should do, we are, I think, chiefly concerned to find reasons of the justificatory kind. We may take some of our desires into account in various ways during the process of deliberation, but there are no good grounds for thinking that we take them all into account. There are no good grounds for thinking that the process of coming to an all-things-considered judgement involves registering all of our desires, and counting them all as providing reasons for action, albeit defeasible reasons.[13] McDowell *does* interpret these all-things-considered judgements as such registerings and weighings of desires, and so he rejects the idea that the incontinent person is one who fails to act on them. For if this is what is meant by an all-things-considered judgement, he thinks it utterly mysterious that we could be moved by a desire that has already been taken fully into account and outweighed.[14] Why, he asks, 'is its ability to move one not exhausted by the weight it is pictured as bringing to the scale?' (McDowell, 1979: 345). By contrast, he maintains that the virtuous view does not take alternative attractions into account at all. So the motivating

situation, which is acknowledged to be a difficult achievement. Perhaps the difference is meant to be that the continent individual, unlike the virtuous, may have some underlying character flaws. To use McNaughton's example (131), an individual may be naturally cowardly and this makes him prone to assess situations with a view to avoiding danger. But then it is hard to see how virtue can be a higher achievement than continence.

[13] I develop this point in Ch. 4 in my discussion of Bernard Williams's sub-Humean account of deliberation.

[14] Donald Davidson (1969) uses the picture of judgement that McDowell rejects, and attempts to show how an agent can be motivated contrary to such a judgement. His treatment of the problem will be examined in the next chapter.

potential of these attractions is unused, and remains capable of influencing action unless insulated by the clear perceptions of virtue.

Now, there is here, in McDowell's own account, an uneasy recognition that there is some distinction to be made between what is motivationally salient and what is salient in deliberation, at least for non-virtuous agents. The picture of judgement that he rejects is rejected apparently *because* of its failure to recognize the separation of motivation and deliberation that permits weak-willed behaviour. It appears that the weak-willed person, the self-controlled person, and perhaps even the compulsive person, might all reason in the way that the virtuous person does: that is, they take the same considerations to be important and for the same reasons, and they reach the same conclusions about what should be done on the basis of just those considerations and no others. The problem is that what is *motivationally* salient to them is not always what is salient in their deliberations. They have rogue desires. Now, there is nothing unusual in holding, as McDowell does, that what is distinctive about virtue is that for the virtuous person judgement and desire go hand in hand. This view is held by many theorists on the subject, including Philip Pettit and Michael Smith (1993), and Gary Watson (1982*a*). The questions in front of us are how this harmony is achieved, and what goes wrong in the other cases. McDowell's contention is that the difference between what is motivationally salient in the actions of the virtuous agent and the actions of continent or weak agents rests solely on a difference in the clarity with which they perceive the salience of certain facts in deliberation. He thinks that motivational disparity is in fact clear evidence of such a difference, which overrides anything the agents concerned might actually be able to say. But this is all just reiteration of McDowell's original claim, not a reason for accepting it. So what, if anything, is there to say in support of the claim?

McDowell's assertion borrows its plausibility from the commonplace observation that our deliberative judgements are usually given effect in action. Most often our beliefs and desires do march in step, and changes in what we desire to do seem in fact to reflect changes in our practical judgements, and in the beliefs which support them. Moreover we are convinced that this harmony between our beliefs about what we have reason to do and our actual desires and actions is no accident. McDowell is concerned to press this point: that the connection between our evaluative judgements and our desires is a non-accidental function of perception. He contrasts the necessary desires he postulates with desires that are merely independently intelligible, and finds such fortuitous accord between judgement and desire unsatisfactory as an explanation, at least of virtuous action. But of course these are not the only possible positions. If we could discover a connection that was neither fortuitous nor necessary this would surely suggest a more plausible position to adopt.

I argue throughout this book that weakness of will and compulsion are very robust phenomena, which defy all attempts at redescription or assimilation. They are *not* properly represented as the behavioural outcomes of an interference with the reflective and perceptual processes themselves, and one moreover which skews its conclusions in ways too subtle for report. Culpable distortions in practical reasoning are surely a different kind of failure; we recognize them as problems of recklessness or self-deception. But, like Socrates, McDowell subsumes all of these failings under a single heading and places them squarely within the province of cognition.[15] This, I think, evades the real challenge that phenomena such as weakness and compulsion present. They constitute a distinctive problem in moral psychology just because their occurrence so clearly violates the norm of practical reason which requires that, other things being equal (i.e. that we are awake, not bound or paralysed, etc.), we will be motivated to act in accordance with our practical judgements. If we wish to retain the norm, that practical reasoning *is* practical, and to recognize all of the common-sense phenomena, we must presume that the ordinary

---

[15] I acknowledge that certain moral failings, such as wishful thinking, have both conative and cognitive elements. Perhaps one could argue that the full explanation of all moral failings will turn out to be mixed, though with desire playing a more prominent role and reason a much less prominent role in cases of weakness of will than in cases of recklessness. I think that the traditional categories do mark important distinctions of kind.

connection between judgement and action is a defeasible one. The challenge then is to locate and describe such a connection. Before this is attempted, however, there are some further normative questions to be dealt with in relation to McDowell's account.

(ii) Silencing

I have not suggested that the notion of silencing is incoherent, or that it does not capture a significant part of our experience, both as moral agents and generally. But it is not at all clear that this pattern of motivation, where all other considerations are silenced, bespeaks unclouded perceptions in the person who is so motivated. Nor is it clear that there are any significant conclusions to be drawn about the path of virtue in action from an examination of this phenomenon of silencing.

According to McDowell the interaction between the virtuous agent's conception of how to live and her knowledge of a particular situation yields 'a view of the situation with one . . . fact as it were in the foreground.' This is the salient fact of the situation, which McDowell says constitutes for the agent 'a reason for acting which silences all others'. He thinks that the virtuous agent will not even feel the pull of competing concerns; she will apprehend her reason 'not as outweighing or overriding any reasons for acting in other ways . . . but as silencing them' (McDowell, 1979: 335).

This story about silencing may derive from the evidential model of practical reasoning to be found in Davidson (1969). It is true that if a piece of evidence is trumped by the general evidential considerations then it loses all weight for us.[16] Suppose I want to know whether my friend has done well in his exam. Initially I take his gloomy expression as evidence that he has done badly but, when I check the results posted on the notice board for myself I know better. I don't think that there is still *some* reason to believe that he has done badly. His gloomy face is not evidence for that at all. Is it equally true, though, that what we initially took to be reasons for action are not

---

[16] Philip Pettit brought this point to my attention.

reasons at all, once we have decided that some other action is, in McDowell's words, 'the thing to do'?

Now, certainly, a conception of how to live and the individual evaluative beliefs which make up that conception influence our perceptions and mould our responses to particular situations. But this is not exclusively a fact about the way virtue operates, as McDowell himself acknowledges with his example of the shy and sensitive person (McDowell, 1978: 21–2). It is a matter of common observation: if I value benevolence, and you on the other hand value self-reliance, we may perceive very different requirements in the same situation of poverty and need, and derive from it very different motives for action. Just as certainly, it is sometimes correct to speak of any reasons or motives we might have had for acting in other ways as having been silenced, or better still eclipsed, by a particularly powerful consideration. We can agree with McDowell that, on occasion, the perception of a particular requirement in our situation quite properly silences the other obligations and accompanying motivations that we would normally have. No one thinks, for example, that you have *any* reason to stay at work and attend a weekly staff meeting when the hospital has phoned to tell you that your loved one is critically injured and asking for you, though it is undeniable that you do ordinarily have such an obligation. Here it *would* be quite inaccurate to speak of other considerations as having been outweighed, for they did not count at all.[17]

But it is not always so appropriate that our contrary motivations are silenced. How then is this kind of psychological state, where all considerations but one are silenced, to be tied to the notions of clarity of perception and virtuous action? A person who desired maximal power over others might find all other motivations silenced by the perception that here was an action which would increase her influence. Someone addicted to heroin might have all other considerations (including moral ones)

---

[17] In more everyday non-morally loaded cases, practical considerations, such as that it's time to pick up the car from the garage, or to take the pot off the flame, regularly move us to act without conflict and fortunately so, since daily life would be impossible if we were constantly tugged by the alternatives to each and every action.

silenced by the perception that here was a way of getting some heroin. And an ambitious athlete might not see the neglect of family responsibilities as any kind of sacrifice, even one which is outweighed by the benefits of more training.

Now, the agents in these cases have each perceived one fact very clearly (namely that a certain course of action will enable them to obtain power, heroin, success), but it appears that they have ignored or not noticed other factors, including some which we may think ought to have weighed with them. The focus of their attention has been exceedingly narrow, and this narrowness may well be because their desires for success, power, and heroin have obscured their view of other things, just as McDowell suggests. But broadening their focus and increasing their sensitivity and awareness of their situation is likely to complicate these agents' motivations. New perceptions will bring into play desires which compete with and perhaps conflict with each other, and with the respective desires for power, heroin, and success. If this is true it calls into question McDowell's idea that it is *unclouded* perception which guarantees the silencing or insulation of contrary motivations. Such single-mindedness seems to be more accurately described as the result of *narrow* perception. There is little evidence to suggest a conceptual connection between virtue, which for McDowell seems to amount to a special sensitivity and clarity of perception that surely must include attentiveness to all the facts, and the phenomenon of silencing. Indeed, far from it being the case, as McDowell argues, that the presence of contrary motivations constitutes a taint on virtue, such a silencing sometimes suggests an insensitivity on the part of the agent, which detracts from a claim to virtue.[18]

[18] Perhaps McDowell does not think that silencing is a marker or enhancer of virtue. He might say that it just so happens that clear perception of the facts does this to you; it doesn't play any role in constituting the action as virtuous. And so perhaps he might agree that this kind of perception is not exclusive to virtue. A wine connoisseur may have just such finely tuned flavour perceptions. However, the clear inference is that, in the moral case at least, the absence of silencing is evidence of a failure of perception. And this is just another restatement of the original brute claim. Why should we accept that a clear perception of the facts does this to you? My argument is that, on the contrary, it often militates against the uncomplicated motivational state that McDowell ascribes to the virtuous agent.

There are many situations where our conception of how to live, allied with our actual circumstances, does not provide an easy or unambiguous answer to the question, 'What should I do?' But McDowell's account must assume that the virtuous person at least will find no intractably conflicting requirements on action when she looks at the world. This is surely false. We think we may sometimes quite properly be in two minds about what to do, and reflection on the situation will often confirm rather than dissolve the initial conflict. In such a case we realize that, whatever we do, something important is left undone. Where one course of action is eventually chosen over the other we think we have acted as well as we can even if we continue to feel the pull of the forgone course of action.

For example when, after consideration, I decide that my obligations at work must take precedence over attending a parents' morning tea and performance at my daughter's kindergarten, I do not think that my decision to act one way saps the reason to act in another way of its force. I will keenly feel my daughter's disappointment. The reasons I had for going to the morning tea have not been silenced at all. But in this instance my actions were guided by another value, and McDowell offers us no argument to show that they were only imperfectly guided by that value, or that they were flawed in any way by my continuing sense of conflict and regret. On the contrary, the example suggests that we have reason to hope that we will *not* always be wholehearted about the decisions we will have to make. For surely the person who feels bad about missing her child's performance at the morning tea is much more appealing to us than the person whose wish to see the performance has been silenced by the perception that some other action is required of her.

McNaughton suggests that where one obligation must give way to another, the lesser obligation is transmuted into something else. In light of the weightier obligation at work I do not have an obligation to attend the performance. I do, however, have an obligation to make amends to my daughter and attempt to compensate her for her disappointment. These two requirements do not conflict and so perhaps the conflict I feel when I contemplate the situation is a result of faulty perception.

But this is too shallow a response to my situation, since I do already recognize the need to make amends and this does not replace the reasons I have for going to the performance. In any event, it is a response which will not work in more difficult and also quite common situations.

Many families have a child with a physical, intellectual, or psychiatric disability. Some such children can be very demanding of a parent's time and energy, to the point where the well-being of other children in the family is seriously threatened. What is the good parent to do? Whose interests are to be compromised? We are to imagine here a situation in the real world where support from external agencies is limited. The parent cannot adequately meet the important needs of all her children for *her* time and attention, yet she has equally weighty duties to each of them. Each of her children will be damaged by neglect and she knows it. Most such parents will not be helped by a clearer appreciation of the situation. They are already acutely aware of their dilemma and it is not one which is likely to be dissolved by more information and reflection.[19] The idea that one silencing consideration will emerge from a complete and rounded view of such a situation or that the competing demands will fall into a neat hierarchical ordering is surely a damaging fantasy. The harm done to the child whose needs go unmet is uncompensated for by an apology. The parent's obligations to her are not transmuted by the needs of her sibling into something lesser and nor should the parent think that they are. The problem here, as in many other situations, is not that the parents are lacking in virtue but that they are human beings with finite capacities in a morally complex world which often enough throws up conflicting requirements on action.

It appears then that the silencing of contrary motivations is neither sufficient nor necessary for virtuous action. It is not evidence of clear moral vision. Indeed it may on some occasions be evidence of the opposite.

---

[19] What could such information be? Suppose I find out how things will turn out in the future. Even if I find out that my disabled child will die in three years it does not lessen my dilemma now.

(iii) Virtue and Self-control

McDowell acknowledges that his view of virtue is highly idealized. He writes: 'the best we usually encounter is to some degree tainted by continence. But in view of what genuine virtue is, idealisation is not something to be avoided or apologised for' (McDowell, 1978: 28). In Chapter 5 of this essay I put forward a full-blown account of self-control. Here I just want to prefigure something of the position developed there. Self-control is not, or not always, a second-best response to the perception that some action is required of you, and it is valuable not just instrumentally but intrinsically. This is not a radical position: on the contrary it is in accord with some of our deeply held moral intuitions.

The description McDowell gives of virtuous agents suggests that their motivations are stable and secure. The akratic struggle cannot arise for them because their desires are necessarily in harmony with their judgements concerning value. I have argued that there is no such strict connection. Such stability cannot be relied upon; moreover an insufficiency of desire, or the presence of competing desires, need not be indicative of any moral shortcoming. For one's motivational state must be partly dependent on what Williams calls incident luck (Williams, 1981b: 25), and virtue surely should not be dependent on this kind of luck. Suppose tragedy or disaster were to befall a virtuous agent. It would be more than a little odd if her desires still marched uninterrupted to the tune called by her values; yet it would cast doubt on her claims to virtue, if, upon losing the appropriate desire, she simply ceased to act in accordance with her judgements. There may be no reason for an agent to alter her judgements of value, even in circumstances where we would see the loss of the relevant desire as completely appropriate, and would be repelled to discover that in this respect it was business as usual. In extreme circumstances, and indeed in merely difficult circumstances, it is reasonable to expect that a person will have to struggle to act in accordance with her judgements of value. Her perceptions of what is required will not instantly bring forth a single, strong, and sufficient motive, and she may have to use some technique of self-control if she is to be successful.

Consider for example a person whose spouse has died suddenly. In her grief she may lose much of her previous warm interest and concern in her children's education, the problems of a friend, and her work. She doesn't feel like doing anything in these areas, though she believes she should.[20] Often she can only bring herself to act by reminding herself that this is her duty or by telling herself that this is what her spouse would have wanted: that is by calling upon motives that are not connected directly to the values she seeks to serve. But surely such exercises of self-control do not detract from our estimation of her character and virtue. The readily apparent fact that we actually prefer this person to the person whose everyday motivations are unaffected by such a loss suggests that the unwavering motivation which McDowell claims as essential to virtue does not constitute an unequivocal ideal.

McDowell could no doubt concede that unabated enthusiasm for one's usual pursuits would betray a certain insensitivity in some circumstances without giving up on his main point. He might say that though the widow's view of the world will, appropriately, be coloured by the sadness she feels, in so far as she is virtuous she will experience no motivational barriers in doing as she perceives she ought and thus have no need of self-control.[21] His view of virtue in action is thus very different to that adopted by Kant, who says of the sympathetic man

---

[20] This example is taken from Kennett (1993: 266). Alfred Mele (1996: 734–7) uses a similar example to argue against internalism. If these examples are at all plausible McDowell's strict internalism is in trouble.

[21] Such a move might hold dangers for McDowell's cognitivism however. If in general it is affective states that colour one's view of the facts or organize one's perception of salience then the virtuous person needs to be in the right emotional state to perceive the facts rightly. So there must be a non-cognitive state, though not a desire, underpinning the reflections of the virtuous, and it may be this which explains both the differing perceptions and the subsequent differences in desire between the virtuous and the weak. It is not at all implausible to suppose that mood does influence one's perceptions—if I'm in a whimsical mood I'm likely to see, and even to have, reason to do things I would not see or have reason to do if I were sad. But though this seems a natural way of understanding what is meant by a 'colouring' of perception I do not think that McDowell would wish to make use of affect to explain the alleged difference in perception between the virtuous and the non-virtuous.

that it is only when sympathy fails and he must drag himself out of 'dead insensibility' to perform a benevolent act out of duty alone that his action displays true moral worth.

Now in suggesting that continence is a part of, rather than a falling away from, virtue I am not going to the Kantian extreme of suggesting that to display true moral worth an action must be performed, against inclination, from duty alone. But I am suggesting that McDowell's view of virtue is unduly narrow and rigid. For note that he is clearly committed by his position to judging even the Jesus of Christianity as a man of tainted virtue. Remember he says of the continent person that 'Their inclinations are aroused, *as the virtuous person's are not*, by their awareness of competing attractions: a lively desire clouds or blurs their focus on "the noble"'[22] (McDowell, 1978: 28, my emphasis). Christ *qua* human is supposed to have been seriously tempted in the desert and again in the Garden of Gethsemane. According to McDowell's position, he was at those times to be distinguished from an ideally virtuous person. Yet it surely enriches our perception of his moral character (and his humanity) to imagine him as one who sometimes had to struggle to do what he believed was required of him, rather than as someone for whom competing motives were invariably silenced.[23] We see him as someone who actively chose and carried out a course of action, as a committed individual rather than as the passive instrument of his divine nature. I do not think we find his struggle indicative of any moral deficiency.

4. Conclusion

The appeal of Socratic accounts of virtue and weakness, which postulate a necessary internal connection between perception and desire, may lie in their simplicity—in their lack of

---

[22] The implicit claim here, that the virtuous person's focus will be on 'the noble', is questionable. A focus on 'the noble' seems, for the most part, irrelevant to everyday moral requirements and actions. A person who was overly concerned with 'the noble' might overlook the more everyday, mundane moral requirements on action and might fail to possess the virtue of humility.

[23] I thank John Bigelow for suggesting this example to me, in very helpful comments on Kennett (1993).

grey areas. But our psychology is not really so simple or so co-operative. The presence of a justificatory reason, however clearly perceived, does not guarantee the presence of a corresponding appropriate and exclusive motive. Indeed when we hold a value we take it to offer us reasons for acting which are importantly distinct from our desires of the moment. It is this separation of reason and desire, or perception and desire, which permits the occurrence of those states we are most interested in here: weakness and compulsion. Where there is a gap between reason and desire, some so far unanalysed exercise of self-control may be necessary to establish a connection between judgement and action.

Accounts of the relation between value and action which insist on a perfect match between judgement and desire cannot capture the commitment that rational agents must have to acting on their reasons as they perceive them. And without such a commitment we must doubt whether an agent even has values, let alone whether she acts on them on a particular occasion. For the harmony McDowell describes is sometimes a matter of luck, and is at other times positively undesirable, since it may militate against the agent coming to a full appreciation of her reasons. We expect that rational agents will experience conflict from time to time, even when it is clear to them what they should do. And we expect, by and large, that a person who is sincere in her adherence to some value or principle will act accordingly, even when luck fails and temptation intrudes. In so far, then, as the capacity for self-control reflects a rational commitment to action in accordance with evaluation, its exercise is not an inferior response to the recognition that our values require our action. In Chapters 4 and 5 I will explore the nature of this rational commitment.

3

Humean Accounts of Reasons and Motivation: Davidson and Decision Theory[1]

Donald Davidson in his paper 'How is Weakness of the Will Possible?' (1969) is concerned to show that incontinence, conceived of by him as clear-headed action against our better judgement, *is* possible. However, his approach throws into sharp relief a problem which surfaced in my discussion of McDowell. This is the problem of construing just the right sort of connection between an agent's judgement and her actions: the sort of connection which gets broken in cases of weakness and compulsion. The structure of the conflict as broadly defined by Davidson accords nicely with common sense, but there is in his account an explanatory shortfall. Accounts like Davidson's attempt to situate the phenomenon of weakness of will unequivocally within a causal theory of action, according to which actions are events with a particular kind of mental-event history. Such accounts need to explain how all-things-considered judgement sometimes causes (appropriately) an action in accord with that judgement, and sometimes does not. Is there a role for judgement *qua* judgement in such theories? If not, can we extract from them explanations of weakness, compulsion, self-control, and responsibility which are credible, and acceptable to folk theory?

First I will describe Davidson's distinctly Humean account of reasons for action, and examine his characterization of practical reasoning and weakness of will in the light of this. I

---

[1] This chapter is based on my paper 'Decision Theory and Weakness of Will' (Kennett, 1991).

aim to show that his reflections on akrasia bring him up against a problem which he does not resolve, or even explicitly recognize: that of reconciling a Humean view of motivation with a normatively loaded conception of better judgement. I then consider the possibility, argued for by Jackson and by Bigelow, Dodds and Pargetter, that the akratic conflict is not what the folk theorists thought it was, and thus that the problem does not arise. I conclude, however, that the alternative constructions of akrasia offered by these decision-theorists, with their explicitly reductive view of evaluation, do not succeed in capturing the phenomenon they set out to explain. We are returned to the problem of finding a secure connection between what still appear to be the distinct states of evaluation and desire, a connection which both accommodates and explains weakness, continence, and compulsion.

1. Davidson's Account of Incontinence

(i) Primary Reasons for Actions

In 'Actions, Reasons and Causes', Davidson argues that an agent's reason for doing something yields a particular kind of explanation of an agent's actions (Davidson, 1980*a*). Reasons *rationalize* action by indicating what it was about the action, when it was proposed, that appealed *to the agent*. We can contrast this kind of explanation, which takes the agent's purposes as central, with explanations which focus, for example, on historical, cultural, or socio-economic factors, or which look at neurophysiological goings-on. According to Davidson there are two components of an agent-centred reason. The agent must have some sort of desire for, or 'pro attitude' towards, some feature of an action or its consequences. And the agent must have an associated belief that the projected action or sequence of actions will have the desired feature or consequence. Davidson's view of the structure of reasons for action is thus straightforwardly Humean.[2]

[2] Hume, *Treatise*; see II. iii. 3 and III. i. 1. For example: 'It has been observ'd, that reason, in a strict and philosophical sense, can have an influence on our

Of course the mere existence of such a belief–desire pair cannot guarantee that the indicated action will be performed, though it does offer some reason in the sense of being latently explanatory of it. But for any action an agent actually performs, an explanation can be constructed which is composed of such a pair, and which constitutes, Davidson says, her *primary reason* for acting. He further claims that the primary reason for an action is its cause. Reasons, as Davidson describes them, motivate action. For John Bishop (1989),[3] who also embraces a causal theory of action, all action, whether continent, weak-willed, reckless, or compulsive, will thus be at least minimally explicable in terms of the agent's beliefs and desires. It will become clear that actions which accord with an agent's values are, on this theory, simply actions with a particular kind of mental-event history.

The view that all intelligible actions can be given a primary-reason explanation is, as far as I can see, a part of common sense.[4] Now writers such as McDowell and Nagel (1970) think that desire is not essential to action explanation; they think that in the case of prudential or moral action, belief does the whole job of motivating an agent and explaining her action.

conduct only after two ways: Either when it excites a passion by informing us of the existence of something which is a proper object of it; or when it discovers the connection of cause and effects so as to afford us means of exerting any passion. These are the only kinds of judgement, which can accompany our actions, or can be said to produce them in any manner' (III. i. 1; pp. 190–1).

On the face of it, it would seem that Hume would have a difficult time producing any account of continence, weakness, or compulsion, given this restricted view of the role of reason. Thomas Hobbes in the *Leviathan* expresses a similar view. He says: 'the Thoughts, are to the Desires, as Scouts, and Spies, to range abroad, and find the way to the things Desired: all Stedinesse of the minds motion, and all quicknesse of the same, proceeding from thence' (1651: ch. 8; pp. 53–4).

[3] Bishop's purpose is to show that the natural and moral perspectives on action are compatible, and that moral autonomy is a natural possibility.

[4] I concede that common sense is not wholly unambiguous here. Sometimes people will say of an action that they did it in spite of not wanting to at all. The Humean will insist that there is *something* the person wanted (say to avoid a parent's disapproval) to which this action was a means. This needs further examination. However the prominence that an excess or deficiency of desire plays in everyday explanations of agency failures suggests that something like the Humean view of motivation is embedded in ordinary thought.

Desire may accompany the action but does not play any explanatory role. Rather, it too must be explained by the evaluative or prudential belief. However, our discussion of McDowell casts doubt on this claim since it appears that the weak agent and the virtuous agent may converge in their moral or prudential beliefs but not in their actions. If so, belief cannot do the whole job, even in the case of virtuous action.

Let's accept for the moment, then, that desires and associated means–end beliefs are mental states whose onset, in appropriate conditions, causes the behaviour which counts as action. The question that I am interested in is whether this Humean account of the antecedents of action is able to give us all the resources we need to understand and explain weak or compulsive action, and to distinguish these from each other and from continent action.

Now, in accepting this we have agreed that all actions of the above kinds are amenable to primary-reason explanations. One person accepts a cigarette because she has a strong desire to smoke and she believes that, among other things, taking the cigarette is a means to satisfying that desire. Another person, or the same person at another time, refuses the cigarette because she desires good health and she believes that not smoking is one way of protecting her health. We can guess that the first action is reckless, weak, or compulsive, and that the second action is temperate or at least continent; but we may be wrong. Focusing solely on the primary reason for the action cannot resolve the matter. And, even if we are told that the first action is weak and the second is continent, the primary reasons don't tell us *why* this should be so. Something more is needed to explain the difference between weak action and continent action.

(ii) How Weakness is Possible

It is obvious that we have very many beliefs and desires, not all of which issue in action, or contribute even secondarily to the causation of action. Davidson interprets the terms 'belief' and 'desire' very broadly. Believings are 'knowing[s], perceiving[s], noticing[s], or remembering[s]'; desires or pro attitudes include 'wantings, urges, promptings, . . . goals and values' (Davidson, 1980a: 3–4). However, he cautions against interpreting pro attitudes as convictions that an action is 'worth performing, or is, all things considered, desirable' (4). Indeed it is just this distinction between all-things-considered judgements and pro attitudes *simpliciter* that Davidson exploits to explain weakness of will.

In 'How is Weakness of the Will Possible?' Davidson distinguishes between an agent's all-things-considered judgements and her unconditional practical judgements. An all-things-considered judgement of desirability is a conclusion reached by deliberation on all of the factors taken by the agent to be relevant to the decision to be made. The agent's set of principles, opinions, beliefs, and desires becomes, in effect, the evidence on which a judgement that, *prima facie*, it would be better to do *A* than *B* is based. This is a *conditional* judgement and Davidson points out that reasoning which stops at such conditional judgements 'is practical only in its subject, not in its issue' (1969: 110). It is, Davidson thinks, equivalent in form to other kinds of probabilistic judgements, such as those we might make about tomorrow's weather, and like them it doesn't commit us to any stronger conclusion. An *unconditional* judgement that *A* is better than *B* issues in or presents the agent with what we have been calling a primary reason, i.e. it issues in the reason on which the agent acts. These judgements *are* practical in their issue; for if the agent judges unconditionally that *A* is better than *B* then, according to Davidson, he wants to do *A* more than *B* and 'he will do A if he does either A or B intentionally' (1969: 110).

What is the connection between the two types of judgements? How does the first kind of judgement, the deliberative judgement, get to be effective in action? Davidson argues that there is no *logical* connection, for ' "A is better than B, all things considered" surely does not entail "A is better than B".' Akrasia is thus not to be explained as 'a simple logical blunder' (1969: 110). The conditional or *prima facie* judgement (and the reasons on which it is based), though, may constitute the reason the agent comes to accept as her reason for judging unconditionally that *A* is better than *B*. As the agent's reason for *doing*

A rather than *B* will, according to Davidson, be identical with
her reason for *judging* that *A* is better than *B simpliciter*, she
acts here in accordance with her conditional judgement of
desirability. So if her unconditional judgement has the right
pedigree her act will be continent. But as the agent's unconditional judgement is not indefeasibly connected to her conditional or *prima facie* judgement, it may not come to constitute
her reason for holding unconditionally that some act is best,
and so may not become her reason for acting as she does.
Davidson thinks an unconditional judgement cannot logically
conflict with a *prima facie* judgement, so akrasia, characterized here as intentional action against one's better judgement
—that is, an all-things-considered judgement—is possible.

2. Problems with Davidson's Account

Davidson's account is susceptible to several criticisms. According to Davidson, akrasia is located in the gap between the
agent's judgement that some action is all-things-considered best
and her judgement that some action is best *simpliciter*. He suggests that the agent always acts on her judgement of what is
best *simpliciter*. Given these constraints his explanation of
akrasia can be shown to be very limited in its application, a
consideration which brings these constraints into serious
question.

First, while Davidson holds that the incontinent agent acts
irrationally, 'for that is surely what we must say of a man who
goes against his own best judgement' (Davidson, 1969: 112),
it appears that he does not fully appreciate the degree of irrationality which would be manifest in many instances of failure
to move from an all-things-considered to an unconditional
judgement. According to his account, the evidence serving the
unconditional judgement can be a subset of the total relevant
evidence on which the all-things-considered judgement is based.
The agent, he says,

does x for a reason r, but he also has a reason r₁ that includes r and
more, on the basis of which he judges some alternative y to be better
than x. (Davidson, 1969: 111)

Here it seems that the agent has simply altered the focus of her attention between judgements. This is of course possible, but it covers only a minority of the cases we commonly recognize as akrasia. In the cases where we do *not* lose sight of the original all-things-considered judgement it would appear to be strikingly irrational to move to a contrary unconditional judgement without further evidence, and so, given the claimed strict connection between unconditional judgements and action, akrasia will be less common than we had thought.

Christopher Peacocke points out that an agent may be in possession of all the relevant evidence when she makes an all-things-considered judgement that A is better than B. She may not believe that any further evidence exists which could cause her to modify her judgement. That is, she may judge both that

pf(A is better than B, E) and E is the total set of available reasons

and that

$\sim\exists P(P$ is true and pf(A is not better than B, E and P)). (Peacocke, 1985: 61)

In such a case the move from the conditional judgement to an unconditional judgement that A is better than B *is* mandatory; not to make the move would be evidence of serious irrationality, and so, given the tight connection in Davidson's account between best judgement, wanting most, and action, it must be that a rational judge in possession of all relevant evidence cannot fail to act continently. So clear-headed akrasia is impossible; akrasia can only be explained as the outcome of a cognitive or logical failure: a failure to draw the obvious inference. This interpretation of Davidson's account places it close to the Socratic view in its apparent assimilation of weakness to recklessness.

Now, we should note that the objection just made holds only if 'judgement' has its usual cognitive implications and if the terms 'better than' and 'best' are held constant in meaning as we move from conditional to unconditional judgement. As Davidson describes it *both* judgements sound evaluative: the agent judges that A is best for a *reason*. But the apparent assimilation of best judgement and intention in Davidson suggests a bending of ordinary meaning at this point: if best judgement is non-evaluative in the theory, if it is simply equivalent to the formation of an intention, then there is no inferential or cognitive lapse in failing to make the move from conditional to unconditional judgement. Quite apart from any complaint we might wish to make about inconsistency of usage, however, it is now hard to see what kind of failure in *reasoning* weakness of will could be on Davidson's account. We will return to this problem shortly.

Alternatively, if we hold the meanings of the terms constant but think of 'better than' as relative, throughout the account, to the agent's desires, as denoting 'more attractive than' or 'more strongly desired than', there is still a second problem (which we saw raised by McDowell) in relation to explaining akrasia via such a model of all-things-considered judgement. If the primary reason on which the agent acts has already been taken fully into account in deliberation and outweighed, how can it then re-emerge and take charge at the level of an unconditional judgement? It was outweighed by a reason with just the same constitution as itself. If the deliberative process is just the process of the agent counting the attractions of alternative courses of action, it is difficult to see how the agent can be swayed by a reason which has already been outweighed on this score while holding fast to the all-things-considered judgement. This suggests that such an agent must be distracted from or must forget the original judgement (or else must experience a diminution of the endorsed desire, or a surge in strength of a competing desire, which on this model would presumably render the original judgement obsolete). This reinforces the conclusion that on Davidson's account clear-headed weakness of will is not possible.

David Charles (1982–3) raises a third problem for Davidson's account. In criticizing Davidson's location of the akratic break in the gap between conditional and unconditional judgement, he argues that the move from all-things-considered judgement to unconditional judgement, and thence to action, is but one possible sequence of events in practical reason, and in any case leaves out a crucial step. First he notes that the agent's conditional judgement, i.e. the judgement that an action *appears* best on the basis of the evidence, may issue in action without any judgement being made to the effect that the action *is* best. Charles then argues that the agent may not feel justified in making the move from the conditional to the unconditional judgement, since she may not think the evidence supports the stronger claim. She may come to act directly on the basis of the conditional conclusion, or she may be akratic in the light of it. Charles further claims that, where we do move to the stronger judgement, it is perfectly possible to be akratic in relation to *it*. There is an extra step between the judgement that a certain action is best and the action itself, which is the formation of an intention to act.

Peacocke agrees that the conditional judgement is not the special case that Davidson thinks it is. He argues that both conditional and unconditional judgements are 'purely intellectual . . . in the sense that one can make [them] without forming any particular intentions' (Peacocke, 1985: 62). Thus the crucial move is not from '*A* is better, all things considered' to '*A* is best', but from '*A* is best (better)' to '*A* is to be done'. According to Charles, the intention is not itself evaluative. He writes:

Intention may be characterised as the acceptance of an unconditional, non-valuational, sentence, whose semantical value is satisfaction with the unconditional aim of satisfying the desire or requirement it expresses. (Charles, 1983: 211)

The problem apparently is in getting the unconditional non-valuational sentence to accord with the evaluative sentence expressing the agent's better judgement, and in just the right way. The acceptance of the non-valuational sentence must be a consequence of the evaluative one being accepted, otherwise the resulting act will be incontinent.

If Charles's amendment is accepted we can see that the gap Davidson notes between all-things-considered judgements and unconditional judgements of what is best is only one point in the process of practical reasoning at which akrasia can occur, and not the most central. There are different types of akratic failure, according to Charles. The gap between conditional and unconditional judgements might be lent to self-deception; or an akrates may, as already noted, 'lose sight of which of his desires are important'. But it is common for people to act akratically without displaying this degree of irrationality. In the central cases the agent acts clear-headedly, as in Charles's example of Abel the akratic, who reminds himself as he accepts a cigarette that nothing has happened to alter his previous judgement that it is best that he not smoke. What is important according to Charles is that the akrates 'violates a principle special to practical reasoning' (Charles, 1982–3: 210).

What is this principle? Charles suggests that it tells us to aim at maximal satisfaction of important desires, by which I take him to mean the desires which are approved by evaluative judgement. They will not be satisfied if they do not move us to action, so the principle must either be or entail an internalist requirement. Davidson expresses it thus:

A judgement of value must be reflected in wants (or desires or motives) (1969: 98),

or more strongly:

If an agent judges that it would be better to do x than to do y, then he wants to do x more than he wants to do y. (1969: 95)

Davidson does not think this principle is violated by akratic action. In his terms it cannot be, for the principle refers only to unconditional judgements, not to all-things-considered or *prima facie* judgements. But then the principle is analytic, it does not govern any *connection*, since, echoing the Socratic accounts, there is no space between *best judgement* and *wanting most* in Davidson's account. Of course if intention is non-valuational, as Charles contends, then we do need a principle to govern its connection with better judgement, otherwise there will be no such thing as acting *on* our better judgement. That is to say, the reasons given by our better judgement will neither contribute to action nor explain action.

This difficulty is obscured in Davidson because of some equivocation in his argument. As already noted, terms such as 'best', 'judgement', and 'reason' are ambiguous. Gary Watson points out that there is no univocal interpretation of these terms according to which all of Davidson's principles will turn out to be true (Watson, 1977). When all the terms are disambiguated, and given the interpretation that will make the principle in which they occur true or at least plausible, it becomes apparent that even on Davidson's account akrasia flouts the internalism requirement—the very requirement on which practical reason is predicated. When Davidson talks of better judgement he appears to be talking evaluatively; he does not signal any shift in meaning when he moves to talking of best judgement, but as we have seen it is not clear that here the terms are evaluative in the same way. In ordinary discourse better judgement has a normative dimension. It draws a conclusion about the agent's reasons for acting; it recommends an action in terms of the *justification* that the agent finds for performing the action. *Best* judgement, as characterized by Davidson, though it may favour the same action, has no such dimension; it is in fact equivalent to Charles's characterization of intention. Accordingly, when the agent acts akratically, her action, like all other actions, is rationally intelligible in the light of some belief–desire pair; it is purposive, so she acts, as Davidson points out, on a reason, but without the additional rational justification which would be provided by her all-things-considered judgement.

It is clear then that there is a leap required, on both of these accounts, from an evaluative state to a non-evaluative state; from a judgement of value to an intention to act. This is a much bigger shift than is required in the case of theoretical reasoning, where the move is from a judgement about what one has reason to believe, on the basis of the evidence, to belief itself. The irrationality of believing against the total evidence, *when the agent herself* accepts that this supports some other belief, is striking. The reckless agent may be irrational in just this respect. But the irrationality of the akrates is usually less obvious, since the reasons for acting that she has available to her fall into two distinct kinds, which are asymmetrically related. Normative (or justificatory) reasons connect with action through motivating reasons, but motivating (or explanatory) reasons do not need the backing of normative reasons in order to be effective.

The distinction made in the preceding chapter between justificatory reasons and explanatory reasons allowed us to give a diagnosis of the akrates' problem, and that diagnosis holds good here. The weak-willed person need not, and typically will not, be suffering an inferential failure. In the central cases of clear-headed weakness of will she does not suffer any kind of cognitive failure at all. Rather, it is just that her justificatory reasons and her motivating reasons have come apart. What is not yet clear is the nature of the ordinary connection between the two kinds of reasons.

Davidson does not explicitly acknowledge or exploit any such difference of kind between reasons in his explanation of weakness. The difference he picks out is, as we saw, just a difference in the scope of the evidence used in reaching the separate judgements. In fact, however, he is not committed to taking the actual strength of desire for a particular course of action as a decisive factor in deliberation, and this suggests some kind of implicit recognition of a division between normative reasons and motivating reasons. Davidson says that 'a reason that is causally strongest need not be a reason deemed by the actor to provide the strongest (best) grounds for acting' (1980*b*: xii). The force of the parenthetic 'best' is obscure, given his Humean account of reasons; perhaps he would agree with Charles that some desires are somehow more important than others. But what gives a desire this special status? Davidson does not say.

Charles argues that the considerations which underpin an all-things-considered judgement are privileged. They are not all the considerations available. It is the agent's practical beliefs and commitments which enable him 'to represent some of his present desires as more important than others' (Charles, 1982–3: 209). These commitments support judgements of the type: 'It is most desirable that *A* is to be done.' The desires that are thus endorsed are the desires that our intentions should be consistent with.

Unfortunately the nature of the agent's practical beliefs and commitments remains unanalysed at this point. Nevertheless it appears that any account of weakness which makes use of the notion of deliberative judgement must invoke some kind of distinction between the reasons attended to in deliberation and those that actually succeed in motivating action. In so doing, such accounts take on the burden of making that distinction explicit and of explaining the nature of the ordinary link between judgement and action.

3. *Scepticism about Practical Reason*

The need to clarify the nature of deliberation and evaluation is pressing in any discussion of practical reason if we are to evade scepticism about its possibility. Episodes of weakness provide confirmation that intentions are influenced by factors other than deliberative endorsement, most notably by the actual strength of the agent's desires, which, it appears, practical reflection is not obliged to take into account.[5] *Strength* of desire might not form part of the evidence for an all-things-considered judgement to the effect that some action is best or most desirable, but it does seem to direct intention far more consistently and predictably than such judgements.

In fact, one must wonder whether anything besides strength of desire, opportunity, and ability can be relevant to the formation of intention. Is practical reasoning of the kind outlined by Davidson, and modified by Charles, truly practical at all? Surely not, unless there is some structural link between its conclusions and our intentions. There could be *some* link, in the Davidson–Charles model, in so far as practical reasoning draws upon actual desires and means–end beliefs, since the belief–desire pair approved of by judgement may turn out to be the causally efficacious pair. But without some further story this concurrence of judgement and action seems purely fortuitous. The judgement itself, that a course of action is better or best, is doing no work.

This is also a problem in Bishop's account. According to Bishop the causal chain leading to action may pass through 'mental events of the kind that constitute practical reasoning'. He observes that typically, i.e. in non-deviant cases, the

---

[5] I argue directly for this view in Ch. 4.

sequence 'proceeds to an all-things-considered judgement in favour of a certain course of basic actions, and culminates in a basic intention to carry out these actions' (Bishop, 1989: 135). But he seems not to notice that in clear-headed akrasia we have an exactly similar sequence of mental events constituting practical reasoning; a sequence which ought, on his account, to result in the formation of a basic intention consistent with the all-things-considered judgement. Instead, with no hint of causal deviancy (which would rob the resulting behaviour of its status as action), the intention formed is contrary to judgement and the resultant action is akratic. In akrasia the causal chain bypasses deliberation. Once again, practical reasoning and all-things-considered judgements appear as mere frills on a process which is affected by no more than an agent's desires and means–end beliefs.

In their respective discussions of causal deviancy, Bishop and Davidson are rightly concerned to show that mere consistency between the agent's intentions and her behaviour cannot constitute the behaviour as an action; actions are done for reasons and Bishop in particular analyses most thoroughly the connection that is required for action, and so for agency itself. We need a similarly thorough analysis of the connection between evaluative conclusions and intention, if we are to make headway towards understanding weakness of will and compulsion as failures of that connection in a way relevant to the moral standing of the agent.

The principle Charles offers—'aim at maximal satisfaction of important desires'—might seem to provide a non-fortuitous link between better judgement and action by fixing on the *normative* element of better judgement. But merely stipulating a principle does not establish any connection.

Certainly we *think* more is involved in practical reflection than the three factors acknowledged by Davidson as being influential in bringing about action: strength of desire, opportunity, and ability. After all, as McDowell and Charles have both noted, we often deliberately exclude some desires and beliefs from influencing our deliberations concerning what it would be best for us to do. In so doing we assume that some kind of rational principle governs our reflections and conclusions. But it is not out of detached hypothetical interest that we engage in practical reasoning: we are not simply interested in knowing what course of action *would* be better in rational terms; we expect that our conclusions will be translated into action as appropriate; and we expect that the process will make a *difference* to what we do. In short, we distinguish between practical reasoning and mere prediction. But perhaps akrasia just gives the lie to our intuitions in this area. Given that better judgement *is* valuational, how do we reconcile this normative aspect with its supposed practicality? What might the normative force consist in, and how does intention come to respond so imperfectly to it?

If we cannot show that the normative (or justificatory) aspect of a reason does not merely ride piggyback on its motivating force, instead of, as we might have hoped, contributing to it, then we have a bigger problem than we started out with. Identifying akrasia as a failure of practical reason, rather than as a failure of perception or of inference, brings us back to questions about the nature of practical reason itself. The very notion of practical reason is called into question; we are beset by what Christine Korsgaard calls 'doubts about the extent to which human action is or could possibly be directed by reason' (Korsgaard, 1986: 5). This in turn leads to scepticism about weakness, compulsion, and continence as genuine and interesting phenomena.

Although Davidson, Charles, and Bishop each give accounts which offer the otherwise satisfying and intuitively correct picture of akrasia as essentially involving a mismatch between judgement and desire, leading to an action not in accord with the judgement, it looks as though their work does not in the end serve to illuminate common-sense observation. There appears to be no more here than the fortuitous alignment of desire and all-things-considered judgement that McDowell found so unsatisfactory as an explanation of virtue. For all that these writers have offered, the nature of the presumed connection between judgements and desire has yet to be established.

But perhaps the difficulty of describing the connection can be avoided altogether. I now want to focus on two decision-theoretic accounts of weakness of will, one offered by Frank

Jackson (1984) and the other by John Bigelow, Susan Dodds, and Robert Pargetter (1990), and consider whether either of them adequately characterizes the akratic conflict. Can akrasia be explained as a conflict among one's desires without reliance on any normative conception of judgement such as has been used so far? If decision theorists can succeed in meeting our intuitions about akrasia with greater economy of explanatory apparatus, their accounts must be preferred.

4. Decision Theory and Weakness of Will

(i) Jackson's Account

Gary Watson points out that, on the Humean model of practical reason accepted by decision theorists, reason is a purely neutral faculty which merely 'computes probabilities and expected desirabilities' (Watson, 1982*a*: 99). It has nothing to say about the worth or importance of the desires it operates on. 'Value' in decision-theoretic terms just means the final numerical value assigned to a prospective action as a result of the computations of reason. It carries no normative implications, and decision theorists take it that every intentional action can be entirely explained without having to resort to any irreducibly evaluative concepts.

We might think that these basic premises about the nature of reason and its relation to desire would leave decision theorists with nothing to say about weakness of will. However, Frank Jackson, in his paper 'Weakness of Will' (1984), attempts to counter the sceptical view that weak-willed action is just like any other action; that all there is to be said is

that if the agent adopts the course of action this proves his desire for the appealing feature is greater than his desire to avoid the unappealing feature. (Jackson, 1984: 5)

Jackson does not think that weakness of will is so general as to threaten every action where our desires are not in harmony and choices must be made. He tries to show what is specific to cases of weakness of will, and to give some content to the classical idea that it involves the agents 'acting against the dictates of their reason'. It is important to keep in mind, though, that Jackson uses 'reason' in a Humean sense. The term does not connote better judgement, for Jackson explicitly argues that acting against one's better judgement is neither necessary nor sufficient for weakness of will. He claims that action against one's better judgement may be reckless or compulsive rather than weak, and that in any case we can be weak-willed while doing what we judge best, as when a raped woman gives in to her religious scruples and does not proceed with an abortion.[6]

Jackson proceeds to give an account of incontinent action which evades the *direct* conflict which we might have supposed central to the phenomenon. His explanation arises from a comparison between rational and irrational changes in desires, and the notion of change is pivotal in them.

He begins with the intuitive idea that, in weakness of will, appetite and bodily feeling play 'an unduly significant role in causing actions' (1984: 2), and he defines undue influence as influence greater than the agent's reason would allow. He does not thereby endorse the view that weakness of will involves any sort of a battle between reason and desire, for this is impossible on the Humean conception, which sees reason as the servant of desire. Rather, there is an incongruity between the two, evidenced by an irrational reversal of the agent's strongest desires. Consider the following example, adapted from Jackson. At time t_1, the agent wishes not to smoke even if he should crave a cigarette. The desire to abstain being his strongest desire, he does not smoke. At time t_2 the agent is struck by a craving for a cigarette. Notwithstanding his earlier situation, he now wishes to smoke more than he wishes not to smoke, and does so. Such a change in the agent's values will be akratic, unless it is fully consequent upon changes in his beliefs.

An agent's desires are conditioned by his beliefs. On Jackson's analysis, the value that we accord any activity derives from the values we give to the states of affairs which we think are likely to obtain if we undertake the activity. Thus

[6] Jackson seems to me to misunderstand this case, to which I return in fn. 10.

the overall value we give to smoking may depend on how likely we think we are to get cancer if we smoke.

Now, the probability function in determining the value of an action can be affected by the available information. If the probability changes as a result of receiving information, the overall (or derived) value will also change. If, for example, Jackson's smoker learns that smoking does not cause cancer in persons of his physical type, this information may result in him coming to value smoking over not smoking. Jackson would consider this a rational change in value. But where there is a change in value not fully accounted for by a change in probabilities—where there is a gap—we have an irrational change, and it is this change which Jackson picks out as akratic. He says that if the onset of the passion or craving

> does more than can be got from prior values and posterior probabilities [the agent] is rightly said to succumb to passion or whatever in the way characteristic of weakness of will. (Jackson, 1984: 9)

When an agent demonstrates by his actions such an apparent change in values we are entitled to wonder if he is being weak-willed. If we see him with a cigarette in his hand two days after he vowed never to smoke again, we suspect incontinence, and we are usually right. The actions of the weak-willed are typically inconsistent with each other and with the agents' proclaimed values, hence the appeal of Jackson's account. But we need to ask to what extent such accord with our intuitions as Jackson's account achieves is explanatory, and to what extent it is merely coincident.

(ii) Criticisms of Jackson's Account

It does seem that as Jackson describes it the agent's derived desire before the onset of the craving was in the nature of a considered judgement, since it was arrived at in the light of all his relevant desires and beliefs. The passion or craving introduces a new element, but this may, at least sometimes, allowably tip the balance and change the effective desire. Jackson gives the example of thirst rationally causing the agent to want to drink because it provides some additional information. But he is concerned with cases where the effect of passion exceeds the effect of any extra information its occurrence provides. Where this happens the change will be irrational.

On the view of practical reason Jackson is operating with, irrationality must consist in the agent falling into error in either the area of probability or the area of desirability. In some way there is a failure to allow these factors adequate weight. But what could this amount to? It seems to me to suggest that the outcome of irrational failure could be seen as worse, in some independent terms, than the outcome which rationality would have provided. Any conception of benefit, though, which is independent of the agent's actual strongest desires sits uneasily with the basic premises of decision theory, and with the claim that weakness of will can be understood without any such conception.

Does Jackson's account entirely depend for its plausibility on some illegitimate borrowing of evaluative concepts? Perhaps a closer look at what occurs in the gap between information and final (decision-theoretic) value, where passion exerts 'undue' influence, will clarify the matter.

Decision theory sees the individual as maximizing subjective value. We may theorize that individuals not under the influence of any craving focus on what psychologists call 'terminal wealth states', and choose them over lesser states of satisfaction. So when not influenced by a craving the smoker prefers the greater benefits of abstaining over smoking and risking his health. The craving *frames* the options, in such a way that in its grip the individual focuses on the loss involved in giving up the intermediate state rather than on the gain in choosing the terminal state. Hogarth asserts that

the displeasure of a loss is evaluated differently from the pleasure of an objectively comparable gain . . . there is evidence that losses are weighted more heavily than gains. (Hogarth, 1981: 204)

So it might be that the craving provides a context in which the less desired object becomes more attractive without the benefit of any supporting change in beliefs. This could be seen as the Socratic position in modern dress. Individuals under the influence of passion suffer a kind of 'evaluation illusion' (Watson, 1977: 319), and opt for immediate pleasure over what was earlier preferred as offering the greater net benefit. Akrasia then turns out to be a form of instrumental irrationality: the agent fails to maximize subjective value.

This construal of Jackson does not seem to violate the theoretical constraints he has chosen, so perhaps he has succeeded in his aim. But we should note two things here. First, the Socratic position on weakness of will is a sceptical one, so if Jackson is to escape scepticism, as he wishes to, there must be some sense in which the agent's earlier assessment remains in force. Second, the account now seems little different from the position Charles detected in Davidson, where the agent was said to have lost sight of his important desires, except that in Jackson the important desires are distinguished by their temporal location rather than by their justification. We noted in relation to the earlier accounts that this kind of illusion was not central to akrasia. Jackson's modification is no improvement: it covers even fewer of the cases we recognize as genuine akrasia, and includes many that are clearly not.[7]

Jackson believes that an irrational change in effective desires, however filled out, is the key structural feature of weakness of will. As the example of the smoker demonstrates, irrational change in effective desires is indeed a key feature of instrumental irrationality, where this is seen as a failure to maximize *overall* desire satisfaction. But, as we will see in Chapter 5, there is something wrong with thinking that such instrumental irrationality gives the whole story of weakness of will. In particular, an irrational change in desires is neither necessary nor sufficient for weakness of will.

It has been argued by Christopher Cordner (1985) and by Bigelow, Dodds, and Pargetter (1990) that by spreading out the akratic conflict over time we lose it altogether. They claim that

---

[7] There is a second way in which a distortion of values may come about and which is in keeping with the spirit of Jackson's account. Passion could affect the agent's assessment of the probabilities. Before the craving to smoke hits, the agent may assess her chances of getting cancer if she smokes as very high. But under the influence of the craving she ignores the probabilities, focusing on statements such as 'It won't happen to me,' or 'My grandfather smoked and he lived to be eighty.' This will cover cases of self-deception and recklessness perhaps, but still does not extend to the central cases of clear-headed weakness.

if the conflict is a conflict of desires it is surely between desires that are held simultaneously, not between a past desire and a present desire. This is too strong; on any common-sense conception, Jackson's smoker is clearly weak-willed even if his desire for good health has temporarily deserted him, so that there is no conflict among synchronic desires. Weakness of will *can* involve a conflict between desires occurring at different times. However, Cordner and Bigelow *et al.* rightly point out that between the past strongest desire and the present strongest desire I may simply, and without the benefits of additional information, have changed my mind, and this change may have been accomplished without a trace of conflict, regret, or the sort of distortion that passion can induce. Preference reversal, for example, is a recognized phenomenon (Grossberg and Gutowski, 1987). I may have previously rated crayfish at 9 out of 10 and spaghetti bolognaise at only 5 out of 10, yet I take it that, when they are next offered on the same menu and I prefer spaghetti, I need not be displaying weakness of will, though my change in preference cannot be accounted for rationally—as a change in my beliefs.[8] Of course in such a situation I *might* fail to maximize subjective value by ordering as I do; I might not enjoy my meal as much as if I'd ordered crayfish. To the extent that I believe that crayfish will give me more in the way of pleasure it will be irrational, perhaps weak, to order spaghetti, but that is not the situation I envisage. I unreflectively wanted crayfish more than spaghetti last time, I unreflectively want spaghetti more than crayfish this time, and my previous desire-pattern need be no barrier to current enjoyment.[9]

Cordner (1985: 275–6) gives examples where more weighty conversions of value involve no new information. The man who

[8] Perhaps it could be accounted for in some other way. If my food preferences have changed this may be the result of some vitamin deficiency which I don't know about. Then my preference change is *non*-rational, but not I think *ir*rational.

[9] Jackson might say that my new desire for spaghetti provides some new information, in the way thirst provides new information, which *rationally* causes me to choose spaghetti. But then his position must be in danger of collapse. For what is it that distinguishes between the desires or bodily urges that provide the right kind of information and those which don't?

reads a familiar story in the Bible and is thereby converted to a new way of life need not have come across anything new at all that could rationally account for the change in him. Rather, Cordner argues, it is the case that old information has come to have a new significance. We do not think, however, that in acting on his new-found principles the convert is acting akratically.[10]

It is crucial to this counterexample that the agent's evaluative judgement changes as well as his strongest desire, so that when he acts it is in accord with his current judgement although opposed to his earlier judgement. In this case the effective desire is in line with the agent's evaluative judgement, and this is no mere coincidence. In the previous example I think we should say that I was not weak-willed when I ordered my meal, because, although my preferences changed, neither of them amounted to such a judgement, nor was there any other judgement or resolution which I contravened in ordering spaghetti.

It appears from this that the notion of evaluative judgement is not so easily detached from akrasia as Jackson has supposed. The requirement that there be an irrational change in desires can, however, be dispensed with, as it is incidental to the phenomenon. The last two examples have demonstrated that such a change in desires is not sufficient for the resultant action to count as weak. Bigelow, Dodds, and Pargetter show that it is also not necessary. They argue that a rational change in decision-theoretic value may result in akratic action. They give an example in which the extension of a deadline for marking papers results in an increase in the agent's desire to relax with a glass of wine. But this *rational* change in the strength of the desire leads to the breaking of a resolution to limit wine-drinking during Lent, and this (given certain provisos) looks straightforwardly weak-willed (Bigelow *et al.*, 1990: 43). Their example demonstrates that *irrational* change is not necessary to weakness of will. What it also suggests is that *change* itself is not necessary, for it was perhaps fortuitous in the above situation that the agent's decision-theoretically weak desire to

---

[10] Of course, his adoption of those principles might be reckless; but that, I maintain, is a different kind of failing.

keep a Lenten resolution was supported by the stronger desire to meet a deadline. Without it, the agent may have broken her resolution straight away. The problem in many cases of akrasia is not that desires change in strength but that they don't. Suppose the smoker's desires for a cigarette are just as intense after he changes his beliefs about the desirability of smoking as they were before. What makes him weak-willed now is that there has been a change in his evaluative judgements unmatched by a change in his desires.

Jackson is right in supposing that the akratic conflict involves more than our ordinary inability to satisfy competing desires. I also think he is correct in supposing that some feature of rationality is central to the structure of the conflict. However, I conclude that the role he gives to reason is too restrictive—weakness of will is not simply a failure of instrumental rationality and does not hinge on an irrational change in the agent's desires. Jackson's account misses the common definitive feature of akrasia, and so describes too little. Its initial credibility as a complete account derives from the use of examples which are independently plausible examples of weakness, and are so, it now seems, because of the place occupied in them by an evaluative judgement of the agent.

5. Hierarchical Accounts of Weakness of Will

The resources of decision theory have not yet been exhausted, however. Another decision-theoretic account of akrasia makes use of the notion of higher-order desires to reveal the structure of the conflict, and to explain temptation, weakness, and continence. This is, at least on a first reading, a much more plausible account than Jackson's, for it appears to be compatible with Davidson's common-sense idea that, when subject to weakness of will, we act while thinking that 'everything considered another action would be better' (Davidson, 1969: 112).

Richard Jeffrey points out that people form higher-order preferences. They are able to regard their desires in the same way as cats regard saucers of milk: 'as objects of desire or aversion which at least occasionally can be sought or avoided' (Jeffrey,

1974: 7). This is an ability that he and others regard as unique to, and whose possession is somehow constitutive of, persons. Thus we have our first-order desires, which are directly concerned with actions, and we may also have higher-order desires or preferences about those desires. But at any one time all our preferences have a single ranking in terms of strength, and when we act, we act on the highest ranking of our desires which we believe to represent an option. Jeffrey argues that choice reveals preference: the alternatives were either not preferred or not available.

In this distinction between first-order and second-order desires we have the seeds of a structural account and explanation of akrasia. Thus George M. Akrates may prefer smoking to abstaining without being weak-willed, but once we add in his higher-order preference that he prefer abstaining to smoking, Jeffrey's suggestion is that if he still smokes he is acting akratically.

Bigelow, Dodds, and Pargetter offer the most clearly delineated account of weakness of will in terms of a conflict between first-order and second-order desires. They take the phenomenon of weakness of will and its opposite, strength of will or continence, to occur only when a second-order desire is opposed by a relevant first-order desire. In such a situation, they say, we face *temptation*: 'To be tempted is to have a desire which you want *not* to be your strongest desire' (Bigelow *et al.*, 1990: 44).

If the second-order desire is stronger, in the decision-theoretic sense of being causally operative (i.e. if 'the action performed is the one which satisfies that desire': Bigelow *et al.*, 1990: 41), then the agent has shown strength of will. If the first-order desire is acted upon, the agent has been weak-willed. So weakness of will does not result from just any conflict or incompatibility amongst one's desires. It is only possible when we face temptation, which is defined as a conflict between paired desires—one a first-order desire, and the other a higher-order desire whose content must include that the first-order desire not be preferred in action.

An advantage of this view is that the relevant desires are held simultaneously, thus removing the temporal dimension of

Jackson's theory which rendered it vulnerable to counterexample. The authors argue that

Strength or weakness of will do seem to be present and exercised at the time of action; they do not seem to merely involve comparisons between the present and the past. (Bigelow *et al.*, 1990: 42)

Shifts in the relative strengths of the two desires may result from changes in circumstances and beliefs, but where both of the desires are still present to some degree, they must issue either in continent or incontinent action, or in no action at all.

This theory gives a simple and elegant account of conflict and temptation; it has the virtue of giving a symmetrical treatment of weakness and continence, and promises to fit all the cases which we would ordinarily call weak-willed, including those which Jackson's theory did seem to encompass. An irrational weakening in a higher-order desire, say for example the desire not to give in to one's desire for chocolate, can, as Jackson's theory suggests, result in weak-willed action, because the weakened desire may come to be overridden by a stronger first-order desire. The Bigelow, Dodds, and Pargetter theory also manages to exclude the examples which were a problem for Jackson. Conversions do not result in weak-willed action, say the authors, because they usually leave no trace of former higher-order desires. There is thus no conflict and no temptation. The distinction can also explain why I was not weak-willed in ordering spaghetti in preference to crayfish. For these were merely competing first-order desires. I was not in a situation of temptation and therefore could not display either strength or weakness of will.

Cravings, being immediately concerned with the objects of action, do seem to contribute directly to the strength of first-order desires, but only indirectly to that of second-order desires. They should, therefore, be accorded the high-profile role in causing weak-willed action that Jackson focused on. But not all occasions where second-order desires are overridden by first-order desires will involve cravings or felt desires. The theory of Bigelow *et al.* is able to encompass Davidson's main example of incontinence, in which the agent wearily gets up to brush his teeth in spite of his judgement that, all things considered, it would be better for him to stay in bed. Their theory cannot comprehend the irrationality that Davidson attributes to such actions; but perhaps this is not essential to locating and understanding the conflict. Perhaps we can and should replace the notion of better judgement with a reference to higher-order desires when discussing the weak-willed conflict.

6. *Objections to Hierarchical Accounts*

We have seen that mere incompatibility of first-order desires does not constitute temptation on the Bigelow, Dodds, and Pargetter theory, and thus cannot result in acts of strength or weakness of will. But do conflicts of the type set down by the theory *necessarily* result in the agent exhibiting strength or weakness strictly according to whether she acts on her first- or second-order desires?

I will argue that these structural conflicts do not occur only in cases of weakness of will—they cannot distinguish between weakness and compulsion for example[11]—and that there are opportunities for displaying continence or weakness in their absence. No further stipulations about the kind of second-order desires that are required for a conflict involving the will can make the account fit the phenomena.

Let us look at the account more closely. Suppose I am given to generous impulses. I have first-order desires to give the contents of my purse to door-knock appeals, street collections, and the like, but I rather wish I did not give in to those generous impulses. I have in fact a second-order desire that I should ignore my first-order desire and spend the money on myself. According to Bigelow, Dodds, and Pargetter the matter is straightforward: I am weak if I give the money and strong if I don't, regardless of which action would be considered morally better. The question of whether an act is or is not weak-willed is factual, not evaluative.

If we grant this then we may need to temper our tendency to approve of strength of will and disapprove of weakness. But

---

[11] Harry Frankfurt (1971) uses just this structure to explain compulsion.

there are two aspects of the claim. One is merely a matter of description: from an external point of view, when we ask whether an act is weak-willed we are not asking if we approve of it or not. But does this mean that the second part of the claim is true, that weakness of will does not essentially involve the agent's acting against some evaluation of her own? The authors appear to think so. They write:

A conflict between first and second order desires constitutes tempta-tion, whether the second order desire arises from moral beliefs of one sort, or of another, or from no moral beliefs at all. (Bigelow *et al.*, 1990: 47)

In support of their claims that *moral* values have no special role to play in akrasia, they have us consider a man who con-tinently does something he believes is seriously wrong. In this case the writers are probably correct in their diagnosis of the status of the action, but because they do not distinguish between moral valuing in a narrow sense and evaluation in a wider sense, they would have us conclude that evaluation is only contingently associated with akratic conflict. In fact, their own example does not support this conclusion.[12]

In the example the agent clearly acts in the light of a rea-son; he is not overcome by desire. He holds as a moral belief that everybody ought, just once, to do something seriously wrong. They should find out what it is like to do so. (One can speculate on the justifications for such a belief; perhaps he thinks the experience will teach humility.) While the individual wrong action that is chosen is in no sense justified, he judges that his doing *something* wrong *is* justified. So the 'ought' here is a normative ought. It does not arise from the agent's having a desire for the wrong action at any level (although, of course,

---

[12] Jackson also offers an example which he claims shows that we can act incontinently while doing what we judge best. This is the raped Catholic who is unable to carry out her resolve to have an abortion. Part of the problem with this example is that 'best' is ambiguous between 'morally best' and 'all-things-considered best'. But it is contentious for Jackson to award the title of best judgement to the woman's moral beliefs rather than to her consid-ered resolve. The example does not succeed in separating better judgement from akratic conflict. A similar point has been made by Cordner (1985: 280 n.).

he may). The agent acts not simply to fulfil a desire to perform that particular wrong action, but for the sake of some
other, larger purpose he has, and this will need to be mentioned
in any justification of his action. To the extent that we can understand this example at all, it does not show the irrelevance of
evaluation. Rather, the agent's evaluations are central to the
diagnosis of his action as a case of strength of will.[13]

Bigelow, Dodds, and Pargetter explicitly discard moral
valuing from their account but implicitly rely on other forms
of evaluation to lend credence to the role they give to higher-
order desires. This is no innocuous slip. The basic premises of
decision theory leave little room for evaluation *qua* evaluation
to play a structural role in the akratic conflict. In showing that
one's *moral* beliefs or allegiances are not always involved on
the 'right' side of the conflict (since they may themselves constitute the temptation to be overcome), Bigelow *et al.* believe
they have done enough to establish their point.[14] Certainly they
could follow a like pattern to establish that a variety of other
normative beliefs and ideals are each detachable from the core
conflict. What I maintain they cannot show is that it is possible to be weak-willed without acting against an evaluative
judgement of some kind, presumably of the all-things-considered
kind, which will sometimes properly overrule specific moral
considerations.

This need not, however, be a problem for the account. It will
not be if it can be established that second-order desires are
by nature evaluative. There is some suggestion to this effect
in the claims by Jeffrey, by Harry Frankfurt, and by Bigelow,
Dodds, and Pargetter that in forming second-order desires we
constitute and express our personhood. Frankfurt states that
'The capacity for reflective self evaluation . . . is manifested in
the formation of second order desires' (Frankfurt, 1971: 7);
Bigelow, Dodds, and Pargetter argue that strength of will is

---

[13] Alan Crooke has pointed out to me that the example resembles the case
of certain Buddhists who, lest they become over-attached to the attainment
of perfection, consider it 'best' to eat a little meat on one day of the year,
in order to compromise their vegetarianism.

[14] Frank Jackson's example of the raped Catholic is a case in point here.
Her moral qualms are the temptation, and she is weak in acting on them.

tied to higher-order desires because '*the will* is to be identified in some way . . . with higher order desires, with self control and with integrity' (1990: 48).

However, this suggestion is unconvincing on two counts. It is not consistent with the Bigelow *et al.* claim that the source of the second-order desire is irrelevant and it is not borne out by examples. Consider: I dislike strawberries, and when I am offered them I always refuse; but I have a second-order desire to like strawberries. Now, this desire need not have any source that I am aware of; I might simply have woken up with it one morning. Suppose that part of its content is that I not act on my dislike of strawberries, and further that I have no other relevant higher-order desires. It seems then that I am weak-willed when I refuse helpings of strawberries.

But this is somewhat counter-intuitive. In this case, not only has my second-order desire not *moved* me to action, we feel that it has not provided me with a *reason* to act, either. It has not provided me with any consideration in favour of eating something I dislike. My desire to like strawberries is perhaps a mere whim, but it fits into a broad conception of desire, and meets the conditions laid down for second-order desires that can be involved in temptation. And it could become stronger: it could become my motivating desire. I might eat strawberries despite not liking the taste, but I should not think myself strong-willed if I did so, any more than I think the anorexia nervosa sufferer strong for acting on her second-order desire not to act on any first-order desires for food. In the latter case the boot would seem to be on the other foot. She surely displays strength if she resists her irrational and destructive second-order desire.

It might be argued that if I claim that I *do* have an irrational second-order desire, then I don't act on it because I must have an even higher-order desire not to be moved by it, and *this* is the level at which my desires constitute evaluations. On this theory the irrationality of my desire must be located in the fact that an even higher-order desire opposes it.

But with which level of desires do we identify evaluation and the will? If we are not to ascend an endless hierarchy of desires, we must make a stipulation specifying the level at which personhood and the will reside. But as Gary Watson (1982*a*: 108) has pointed out, any such stipulation will be completely arbitrary. At whatever level we terminate the hierarchy of desires, we may still be left with desires like the ones described. We cannot deny the possibility: the anorexic, for example, *is* moved by her second-order desire and, as far as I can tell, need have no higher-order desires in the matter. Are we to call her rational and strong-willed? Am I to be considered weak and irrational for not eating strawberries? If the reductionist account of value offered by these higher-order theorists dictates these conclusions we may find ourselves embracing the alternatives no matter what the conceptual difficulties.[15]

It seems that characterizing the conflict as one between desires at different levels in a hierarchy is, in the end, little better than Jackson's attempt at defining akrasia through the temporal location of desires, or the similar Socratic move to explain it through the relative proximity of pleasures. It simply misses the mark. While higher-order desires may have some role to play in a full explanation of strength and

---

[15] Peter Singer has suggested to me that the examples I give don't work. First, in the strawberries case he suggests that the desire is not really higher-order: it could be redescribed as first-order. If this is a damaging criticism it is more damaging to the Bigelow, Dodds, and Pargetter account than to mine. For it would apply to a great many higher-order desires, including many that we would think could be involved in temptation. The plausibility and explanatory power of the account would be much reduced. Singer also thinks that my desire must have a source that would rationalize it. Certainly we could alter the example so that it did, say by adding in a belief that strawberries were necessary to maintain health, and thus make it a desire that I could be weak-willed with regard to—but why necessarily? I just deny that all desires or even all higher-order desires can be rationalized in this way.

Secondly, Singer finds no difficulty in calling the anorexic strong-willed, for he says it is just a case of a desire issuing from false beliefs. We do not, of course, insist that a person must be acting on the basis of true beliefs in order to display strength of will, but I think that for Singer to characterize the anorexic's beliefs as merely mistaken is to shrink the point. Her beliefs are massively deluded, and are so because she forms them in the grip of illness. We could accept the Bigelow, Dodds, and Pargetter line that the source of her desire is irrelevant, and call her strong-willed, but surely only at the expense of any link between strength of will and rationality. My example indicates that higher-order theorists must give up the 'honorific' associations which they claim hold between strength of will and integrity, rationality, personhood, etc. Theirs is a possible position, but not a very appealing one.

weakness of will, they cannot bear the weight placed on them by the account of Bigelow *et al.* Like the Socratic account and the Davidsonian account, it fails to distinguish between weakness and compulsion or to point the way to any credible account of self-control.[16] Self-control will allegedly be called for whenever a second-order desire is opposed by a first-order desire, and any action that results from the triumph of a second-order desire will amount to a case of self-control. Setting aside the doubts already raised about this apparently arbitrary stipulation, just how is self-control to be exercised? How might we *ensure* that it is our second-order desires that are satisfied? For all that has been said, it looks as though getting our first-order desires into line with our second-order desires will be purely a matter of chance; but self-control is supposed to involve more than luck. Quite generally, it is difficult to see how our practices of praising or blaming agents for exercising or failing to exercise self-control could be rationally sustained on this picture.

There is one last suggestion, however, which might rescue hierarchical accounts. Harry Frankfurt, in his discussion of freedom of the will, modifies the nature of the higher-order desires involved in the conflicts common to episodes of akrasia and compulsion when he says that, through the formation of a second-order volition,[17] the agent identifies himself with one of his conflicting first-order desires, he 'makes one of them more truly his own and in doing so he withdraws himself from the other' (Frankfurt, 1971: 13). The act of identification terminates the hierarchy and establishes the desires with regard to which we may be weak-willed or compulsive. Not all higher-order desires will be involved.

This is a promising advance. It disposes of the problems posed for less discriminating accounts by desires such as my desire

---

[16] Unlike the Socratic accounts, however (and here I include Jackson and, on some interpretations, Davidson), this one does not tend to assimilate weakness and recklessness. Judgement does not play a part in the structure of the akratic conflict, so there can be no cognitive failure. Recklessness would, for these authors, presumably involve some culpable error in means–end beliefs.

[17] A second-order volition is the desire that a particular first-order desire should be one's effective desire or will.

to like strawberries—though maybe not of those posed by the
anorexia sufferer's desires, since it seems likely that she might
identify with the desire to be thin. As well, the second-order
volitions might properly be given honorific associations because, as described, they appear to be connected with the
agent's autonomy. However, the act of identification is not equivalent to the formation of a higher-order desire, and Frankfurt
does not adequately characterize the difference or explain why
it could only occur at the higher levels. It appears that in claiming decisive identification as the important move Frankfurt is
offering a norm of action: 'Act only on those desires with which
you can identify,' perhaps. But then there seems to be no reason to tie the notion of identification to higher-order desires.

Bigelow, Dodds, and Pargetter discuss an example of a
career woman in the 1950s who thoroughly enjoys her work
and finds it most fulfilling, but who feels guilty about it. She
is nagged by second-order desires; and at this level she desires
most to be the sort of woman who wants to be a homemaker.
According to them the woman is weak-willed in pursuing her
career, unless she has an even higher-order desire to overcome
her conditioning (Bigelow *et al.* 1990: 48–9). But here it is plain
that the woman does not *identify* with her second-order
desires—these are just an uncomfortable echo of her conditioning. In spite of her conflict it is more plausible to see her
as identifying directly with her desires at the first-order level,
and there is no apparent reason why this must be endorsed by
a higher-order desire, or any further act of identification. So
Frankfurt should say that in acting on her first-order desires
the woman is not weak-willed.

But of course it *is* possible that the woman is still weak-willed,
for it is questionable whether identification does play the role
Frankfurt wishes it to play. Identification and evaluation may
come apart: it is possible that such a woman sincerely (though
perhaps mistakenly) believes that she should be home caring
full-time for husband and children, while nevertheless identifying herself with her work-related ambitions. Indeed, the fact
that she is not the sort of woman she believes she ought to be
may be a source of great regret to her. If Frankfurt wishes to

rule out this kind of split he will need to elaborate on the notion of identification.

7. Conclusion

As it stands Frankfurt's refinement cannot rescue higher-order accounts. It steers us back to the same problem that we looked to decision theory to help us avoid: the gap we noted between evaluation and desire. The difficulty of arriving at an adequate description of akrasia without explicit recourse to *some* concept of evaluation and judgement reinforces the view that these are not reducible to desires. To say this is not to rule out a *role* for desires in the formation of judgement; in the next chapter I will look at the proper place of desire and emotion in the process of deliberation. It is just to note that desires of whatever level are *not* judgements.

We are forced to retreat to a suitably normative notion of better judgement if we are to cover all the instances of behaviour that we want to call weak-willed and to exclude those we don't. But now the nature and ground of those judgements must be analysed with some care, and the internal connection between our judgements of value and our motivations for action must be argued for, not merely assumed. We must establish a link between them: the link that holds when we are continent and gives way when we are weak. The explanatory shortfall remains. It must be dealt with if we are to reach a full understanding of our most common failings.

4

Wanting and Valuing

I begin this chapter by examining an approach, rooted in the
Platonic view of human psychology, which distinguishes between valuing and mere desiring, in a way which both admits
the possibility of agents being moved to act contrary to their
clearly held judgements of value and purports to provide an
explanation of the grip which such practical evaluation ordinarily has on motivation. This approach, and in particular
Gary Watson's exposition of it, has much merit. Nevertheless,
in large part, it turns out to assume rather than explain the
link between valuing, desiring, and action, and such explanation as it does give tends once again to force the assimilation
of weakness to compulsion, and is silent as to the nature and
exercise of self-control. A closer analysis of valuing is needed
if we wish to understand both the distinction and the connection
between valuing and desiring in a way which will ground an
account of the moral-psychological phenomena.

My thesis has been that evaluation cannot be understood
in isolation from the notion of justification. Engaging in the
evaluative enterprise is engaging in a search for reasons. Practical evaluations are, in effect, the agent's conclusions about
the disposition of the reasons available to her.[1] In explicating
the *distinction* between valuing and desiring I focus, therefore,
on deliberation itself. The inadequacy of Humean accounts of
weakness of will has lent support to the view that there is an
irreducibly normative, desire-independent element to practical
reason and so to the view that the sources of considerations

---

[1] As I will go on to argue in my discussion of recklessness (see Ch. 6),
those conclusions may or may not be justified. To give evaluation a ration-
alistic cast is not to deny that there are many less than perfectly rational
evaluators.

that can have deliberative force go beyond those given by the agent's actual desires or interests. But this view now needs explicit defence. I claim, first, that the broad advantage Humean accounts of practical reason might be thought to possess is largely illusory and, second, that the Humean restriction on the scope of deliberation is simply arbitrary. The door is thus open for desire-independent reasons to play a role in evaluation. I then consider an account of practical reflection which makes the notion of justification central and suggest that this will require the substantively rational agent to be responsive to a broad range of considerations, including moral considerations, in reaching sound evaluative conclusions. In the latter part of this chapter I look at how response-dispositional theories of value make the *connection* between these evaluative judgements and desire. In the light of some objections to these accounts I suggest a Kantian modification to underwrite the defeasible link we have been looking for between normative judgement and desire. This solution points to the rational centrality of the capacity for self-control. It thus promises to illuminate the common-sense distinctions between recklessness, weakness, and compulsion, and to support the moral weight which has traditionally been placed on them.

1. Plato, Aristotle, and Watson: The Parts of the Soul

> Let us note that in every one of us there are two guiding principles which lead us whither they will; one is the natural desire of pleasure, the other is an acquired opinion which aspires after the best; and these two are sometimes in harmony and then again at war, and sometimes the one, sometimes the other conquers.
>
> (Plato, *Phaedrus*, 237e)

For Plato and Aristotle the soul was divided into distinct elements, the rational and the appetitive, each of which was seen to be a source of motivation. While Aristotle believed that the appetitive element could be influenced or persuaded (rather than simply dominated) by reason, he, like Plato, saw that the two could also conflict:

the rational principle of the continent man and of the incontinent, and the part of their soul that has such a principle . . . urges them aright and towards the best objects; but there is found in them also another natural element beside the rational principle which fights against and resists that principle. (*NE* 1102^{b}7)

Any such conflict between reason and appetite is distinct from a merely adventitious competition between desires, say between the desire to sleep and the desire to eat. It is not just that the desires engendered by reason and appetite respectively turn out not to be co-satisfiable on a particular occasion; on the Platonic view the object of desires founded in reason is fundamentally different from those of desires having their source in appetite. According to Watson, Plato saw the desires of reason as desires for 'the Good' (1982*a*: 98).[2] Such desires arise from or perhaps *are* evaluations. Desires having their source in appetite or even in enculturation arise independently of such judgements of worth, and are themselves subject to assessment by reason. A desire that is evaluated negatively by reason is therefore fundamentally in conflict with a desire founded in or evaluated positively by reason.

Let us consider how to interpret the Platonic idea of desires founded in reason. McDowell's account of virtuous motivation, which was discussed in Chapter 2, suggests that for every virtuous action there is a unitary perceptual state which is, in and of itself, motivating. Watson is not perfectly clear on this point, as we will see, but he appears to allow that thinking that something is good is conceptually, if not actually, distinct from desiring it; it is appropriate, he says, 'to speak of wants that are (or perhaps arise from) evaluations as belonging to, or originating in, the rational (that is, *judging*) part of the soul' (1982*a*: 99). Like Aristotle he appears to hold that reason is an original *spring* of action. If there is any order of appearance, judging something as good precedes and generates the desire for that good, so we will examine Watson's discussion of the distinction between wanting and valuing with this in mind.

The Platonic view of human psychology, as interpreted by Watson, points the way to an understanding of the akratic

[2] My discussion at this point largely follows Watson.

conflict very different from that which can be achieved on a Humean account of reason and motivation. The role of reason, according to Hume, is not to evaluate desires but to serve them. Reason tells us how to maximize the satisfaction of our desires; it has nothing non-instrumental to say on the question of which desires we should have. There is but one measure of our desires, and that is in terms of causal efficacy. What we most want is whatever we are most moved to try to get. On the Platonic conception of human psychology, however, there is another measure of our desires. Watson argues that 'the phrase "what one most wants" may mean either "the object of the strongest desire" or "what one most *values*" ' (1982*a*: 100). One may rank one's desires in terms of strength or in terms of worth, and it seems clear that we will be susceptible to akrasia whenever the two rankings are not in harmony.

Here we have contrasting orderings of the kind Davidson and Charles needed to support their analyses of akrasia, but which were not available to them from within the Humean framework. And this contrast echoes the distinction already drawn between normative reasons and motivating reasons. For, as Watson says, the possibility of ranking one's desires in this second way has the anti-Humean implication that a person may desire to do something without having, or even regarding herself as having, any reason to do that thing. Watson argues, via some powerful examples, that a person may in no way value what is nevertheless strongly desired. He says that it is just false that a mother who desires to drown her screaming baby in the bathwater values her baby's death or thinks she has *any* reason, no matter how small, to satisfy her desire. Now, of course if the mother were to act on her desire we would be able to offer a basic *explanation* of her action, in terms of the desire and her associated means–end beliefs. But on Watson's view this is not to concede that the mother acted with a reason, only that she acted intentionally. The mere presence of a desire does not by itself give us a reason to satisfy it. On the contrary: it might sometimes give us reason to eliminate it.

The role of practical reason, according to the Platonic view espoused by Watson, is essentially evaluative. Watson suggests

that a person's *values* 'Is that set of considerations which he
—in a cool and non-self-deceptive moment—articulates as
definitive of the good, fulfilling, and defensible life'; a person's
valuational system 'is that set of considerations which, when
combined with his factual beliefs (and probability estimates),
yields judgements of the form: the thing for me to do in these
circumstances, all things considered, is *a*' (1982*a*: 105). Now,
judgements of this form are clearly intended to be practical as
well as evaluative. But what grip do they have on the agent's
motivational system? How do these judgements become the very
considerations which move the agent to action? There are two
obvious ways in which reason may make the connection with
action on Watson's version of the Platonic view of psychology;
but each presents problems that are by now familiar.

2. *The Nature of the Connection between Reason and Desire*

(i) *A Necessary Connection*

The Platonic view, shared by Aristotle and Watson, sees reason (the valuational system) as a source of motivation in its
own right. So when the desires arising in this way lead to action
there is an obvious, direct connection between judgement and
action. The connection is not thought to be so tight as to exclude
the very possibility of akrasia; neither Watson nor Aristotle
suggests that the desires of reason are all-powerful. Nevertheless there are difficulties with this view, some of which have
already been canvassed in relation to McDowell's views.

Watson allows, as McDowell does not, the possibility that
we may explicitly disavow the object of our desires, or that our
desire for some object may far exceed the value that we place
upon the object. But he finds difficulty in admitting the re-
verse possibility—that we may not desire at all what we value
—and it is at least unclear in Watson how we could desire
something more weakly than we value it.[3] Yet this is no more

---

[3] Watson says, in the context of a claim that to value is also to want, that
'If, in appropriate circumstances, one were never inclined to action by some

improbable a situation than those he describes. Michael Stocker (1979) argues that the good does not of necessity attract, and that evaluation and motivation do not stand in the simple and direct relation supposed by Plato, Aristotle, and their followers. He claims that the relation is a complex one which may, on occasions, fail altogether. Lack of an appropriate desire to perform a valued action is commonplace, for, as Stocker observes,

Through spiritual or physical tiredness, through accidie, through weakness of body, through illness, through general apathy, through despair, through inability to concentrate, through a feeling of use-lessness or futility, and so on, one may feel less and less motivated to seek what is good. One's lessened desire need not signal, much less be the product of, the fact that, or one's belief that, there is less good to be obtained or produced . . . Indeed, a frequent added defect of being in such 'depressions' is that one sees all the good to be won or saved and one lacks the will, interest, desire, or strength. (1979: 744)

These are not cases where one's desire for what one sees as good is simply overridden by a stronger desire on the other side. In such depressions one's desire for the good may be blocked altogether though one's judgement remains intact. The situations Stocker describes are surely as familiar and believable as the examples Watson gives of agents desiring what they do not value. And they indicate that, while the dual system of ranking desires is needed to underpin an analysis of weakness of will and related failures of practical reason, it is necessary to give up the Platonic notion that reason also provides an *unfailing* spring of motivation. This view not only fails to account for the kinds of situations outlined by Stocker, it also blurs the important distinction Watson wishes to make between wanting and valuing, and lures him into inconsistency.

We have, according to the Platonic theory, two separate sources of motivation and two ways of ranking desire. When

alleged evaluation, the claim that it was indeed one's evaluation would be disconfirmed' (1982a: 106). The key word here is 'never'. It suggests that one may at least sometimes fail to be inclined to action by a genuine evaluation, and this sits oddly with Watson's main claim.

we evaluate our actual or anticipated desires, we are looking at the extent to which such desires are worth fulfilling, and we rank them accordingly. As Watson makes clear, we may judge some of our desires to be not worth fulfilling at all, regardless of their felt intensity or causal strength; such desires get a negative ranking. The Humean ordering in terms of the relative strength of the desires does not relate to felt intensity, but only to the propensity of the desires to get acted upon. Sexual desires or desires for a glass of wine or a day off may be phenomenologically much more salient to us than the desire to complete a dreary report or to clean the house, but if it comes to the crunch and we choose to write the report or scrub the bathroom in preference to sensual indulgence, we reveal that those desires are stronger at this moment. Our strongest desires are just those that defeat competing desires. Our weakest desires are those which get defeated by other desires.

If we focus just on the desires which have their source in appetite or enculturation, there is no difficulty in holding that the two rankings may be at odds with one another. A desire which we judge to be well worth fulfilling may be defeated by desires which are causally stronger; a desire that is negatively evaluated may prove to be efficacious. The contrast is illuminating. But as soon as we suppose that reason is directly productive of desire the waters get muddied.

What account should we give of the desires produced by reason? Watson does not say, but McDowell clearly thinks such desires, or concerns, will be appropriate to their object and this position seems consistent with Watson's Platonic psychology. If we are to act virtuously at all, we must act out of the appropriate concern, say, out of friendship or benevolence. This suggests that the desire produced, or drawn into operation, by reason must be a *direct* desire for the approved end.

Now if this is the way evaluative judgement works we have a problem. It appears on this account that *every* evaluative judgement, even those directed at independently arising desires, produces a corresponding direct desire for the end approved of by judgement, and these desires, though which have their source in evaluation, must be desires of some particular causal strength or other. I think we must assume that, according to this picture, the causal strength of such desires would be in harmony with the evaluative weight of the judgement that initiates the desire. After all, what explanation could be given for the occurrence of a desire whose strength was at variance with the very evaluation that engendered it? A variation in strength would indicate that the desire was in some respect independent of the evaluation, and this is just what the Platonic view denies with regard to such desires. It is at this point that Watson's view begins to look unclear.

He thinks that the distinction he defends between desiring and valuing 'depends upon there being independent sources of motivation' (Watson, 1982a: 100), and maintains that to value something is to want it, and that 'to attribute a want for something to someone is to say he is disposed to try and get it' (105). But in an earlier paper (Watson, 1977), he acknowledges that a desire may not march in step with its parent evaluative judgement. He supposes that 'when one acts weakly, one wants *to some degree* to do what one judges best' (my emphasis), and surprisingly goes on to assert that this does not entail any 'commitment to a general internalist view that a person necessarily wants what he or she judges best' (fn. 13). This idea, that some evaluations give rise to appropriate desires while others do not, is not explained, and does not sit well with the version of Platonism that Watson endorses.

If we concede that the Platonic view implies a harmony or consistency in ranking between evaluation and the causal strength of the desires which have their source in evaluation, what will be the outcome for the explanation of akrasia and associated phenomena? As long as it is allowed that there are *other* desires, which are not founded in reason, it initially looks as though we have the material to explain failures of practical reason without disturbing the Platonic assumption that to value something is necessarily to desire it. We simply invoke the metaphor of the battlefield. When reason and passion, both bearers of motivational force, are at war, 'sometimes the one, sometimes the other conquers'. Of course it is doubtful that this metaphor will extend to distinguishing between weakness and compulsion, or enable us to give an analysis of self-control. But there is a more fundamental problem that undermines the picture of the akratic conflict as a battle which reason may lose. I do not think that we will be able to acknowledge the phenomenon of weakness while the Platonic assumption remains in place.

If evaluation *necessarily* produces a desire of an appropriate strength, then whenever we evaluate pre-existing and independently arising desires, further *rational* desires will be engendered regarding them and their objects. If we negatively evaluate some desire, that is, if we judge that such a desire ought not to be acted upon, then *ex hypothesi* we will acquire a desire, commensurate in strength with the weight we attach to the judgement, not to act on the original desire. An all-things-considered judgement, the judgement which we act against in weakness of will, carries the most deliberative force. The considerations which support it outweigh all the considerations there are for acting in other ways. A commensurately strong desire ought similarly to be strong enough to block or outweigh any desires which the agent might have to act in other ways. Otherwise, what does it mean to say that the desire is in harmony with the evaluation? The notion is somewhat obscure, but it could be that the appropriate strength for such a desire is whatever strength is necessary to vanquish its competitors. If this is right, *and* there is a necessary link between reason and desire, the metaphorical battle is one which reason cannot lose. Both weakness and compulsion disappear from the moral map and we are left with a view indistinguishable from that of McDowell. If, on the other hand, we allow that some independently arising desires may be strong enough to defeat a desire which is engendered by and in perfect harmony with reason then those desires must count as compulsive.[4] Either way, there will be no more room for weakness of will on the Platonic conception of human psychology than on the Humean conception.

---

[4] For example: suppose you judge that, all things considered, you should give up smoking, but you have an intense desire to smoke which could be overridden only by an even more intense hatred of smoking. Surely your judgement does not entail that you develop an intense, even irrational, hatred of smoking. Such a level of hatred would not be in harmony with your judgement. Yet anything less will be ineffective against the desire to smoke.

Watson's undeveloped version of the Platonic view of reason as an original and separate spring of motivation obstructs the explanation of the phenomena of weakness and compulsion that his distinction between wanting and valuing was supposed to make possible. Fortunately, the idea that to value something is necessarily to desire it can be given up without disturbing this fundamental distinction. Watson's account leaves open other ways of construing the link between reason and motivation. The challenge is to find a sufficiently secure link.

(ii) A Contingent Connection

At one point Watson says that the difference between valuing and mere wanting has to do 'with the agent's attitude to the various things he is disposed to try to get' (1982a: 105). This is intuitively correct, but it needs careful explication if we are to get the kind of connection we are looking for between valuing and desiring. We have already seen that this attitude is not to be cashed out in terms of higher-order desires, nor is it necessarily productive of any *direct* desire for the valued action or goal. But if the attitude of valuing is distinct from that of desiring, the only obvious way of making a connection between them is too tenuous for our purposes.

Since reason will positively evaluate many of those desires that arise independently of it, when such positively evaluated desires get acted upon, the resultant actions may be said to be in accordance with reason or judgement. Does this accord amount to influence? It is not altogether clear from Watson's account how judgement affects the level or strength of independent desires. He thinks that agents can eliminate some negatively evaluated desires, say by the use of tranquillizers, or cultivate certain desirable passions. But though, given his Platonic conception of human psychology, he thinks that the evaluation system has a considerable grip on motivation, Watson does not express any clear view on whether judgement *qua* judgement is the kind of thing that will typically moderate the appetites rather than simply comment on them.

If it is not, however, it will be inaccurate to speak of judgement as having a grip on motivation in the happy circumstance where they select the same action. This is the mere fortuitous concurrence of judgement and desire which McDowell rightly rejected as failing to provide a sufficient account of virtuous action. Such a chance connection is likewise incapable of founding a sufficient account of weakness and compulsion, since it is unable to distinguish between them. For that we would need to have an account of self-control; and if reason cannot regularly influence desire by some means, there is nothing for self-control to *be*.

Aristotle, alone among those who endorse a Platonic psychology, argues explicitly that the appetitive, desiring element of the soul shares in the rational principle to some extent.[5] Though the desiring element does not perform the tasks of reason, it may listen to reason and take account of reason. Aristotle says that in the continent man it obeys reason; in the temperate man it is more obedient still, speaking with the same voice as the rational principle: 'That the irrational element is in some sense persuaded by a rational principle is indicated also by the giving of advice and by all reproof and exhortation' (*NE* 1102^{b}30). Thus the relation between the two parts of the self is analogous, in Aristotle, to the relation he describes between men and women or men and slaves. A slave 'participates in reason so far as to recognise it but not to possess it' (*Politics* 1254^{b}21). Slaves need and benefit from direction because they cannot formulate for themselves a rational principle on which to act. Similarly our desires are seen by Aristotle as the sorts of things that can, to a considerable extent, be shaped, directed, and modified by the rational part of the self.[6] While Aristotle's views on slaves and women no longer command support, his claim about the tractability of desires under the influence of reason remains compelling, even to some Humeans. Let's turn to some recent analyses of valuing which promise to develop and elucidate this common-sense idea.

[5] Watson (1982^a: 102–5) provides a persuasive account of how we may come to value what we in fact desire, which could be developed in a way compatible with the Aristotelian account.

[6] Where desires are immune or resistant to such organization and modification, as in weakness of will and compulsion, this does threaten a breakdown of rational agency and a divided self. I will suggest below that in these circumstances we must adopt a strategic approach to counter such desires.

These analyses concentrate first on the role of deliberation in accessing and establishing what is of value, and second on the impact that our judgements of value ordinarily have on motivation. They converge in a number of important respects. They each take it, explicitly or implicitly, that we cannot in principle separate the concept of something's being valuable from our capacity, at the limit of information and reflection, to recognize it as valuable and desire it accordingly. Thus they are all *response-dispositional* accounts of value. And they suggest that our desires may be considered more or less rational, and so more or less in line with what is valuable, according to how they survive or respond to certain rational processes. The desires we should have are the desires we would end up with after a thorough laundering by reason. James Rachels (1991), for example, argues for substantial modifications to the crude subjectivism which asserts that moral judgements merely serve to express or report the speaker's feelings of approbation or disapprobation. While he accepts that there is a conceptual connection between moral judgement and emotion, he does not think that untutored feelings are sufficient to constitute a moral judgement, for he believes that '*any* kind of value judgement . . . must be supported by good reasons . . . One *must* have reasons or else one is not making a moral judgement at all' (Rachels, 1991: 438). On this view, which we may apply to evaluation in general, such judgements are not merely visceral *responses* which dispose an agent to act in a particular way; they are essentially cognitive *conclusions*, which must be supportable by some appeal to broader considerations. I'll come back to the nature of such considerations shortly. But first let us see how Rachels thinks that these judgements are connected to desire.

(iii) Valuing as rationally privileged desires

Rachels offers a unified account which preserves both the connections between reason and evaluative judgement and the connections between evaluation and desire (or emotion). In effect he suggests that valuing *is* desiring, but that the desires concerned are privileged: they are those of our desires that have been shaped or produced by a process of thinking things through. He argues that if someone has thought things through 'in a thoroughly intelligent and impartial manner with their feelings being shaped by this process [then] their feelings would be as much in harmony with reason as is possible' (1991: 439). The attitudes or sentiments (of approval or disapproval) that are thus produced or sustained are properly called evaluative attitudes. Rachels takes it for granted that a process of thinking through the nature and consequences of some action or policy will typically affect the way a person feels. This is an empirical assumption, but one, after all, for which there is plenty of anecdotal evidence, at least among philosophers.[7] And as there is no suggestion that this process is the only factor shaping our feelings or desires, or that it necessarily has such an impact, I think it may stand.

This way of putting the matter appears to overcome a problem we saw earlier. It is not merely fortuitous that a *reasonable* person has the desires she has, since her feelings and desires have been exposed to reason, and have been formed and modified in the light of reason and information. However, the view that we may identify valuing itself with desiring (albeit desiring shaped by exposure to reason) cannot be sustained: it would suggest that our values are less stable than we might have thought, fading in and out of existence as we find ourselves in a more or less reasonable state. In the light of Watson's examples, as well as those suggested by Stocker, this seems unduly restrictive. Consider the mother who wants to drown her screaming baby in the bathwater. It is, Rachels would agree, false that the mother values drowning her baby, since we know that this is not a desire that would be sustained by careful reflection. However, in her distressed state, perhaps there are no desires present that would on Rachels' account constitute her valuing her baby's survival. In that state her ordinary desires to protect her baby and so forth may have deserted her. Does it follow that she does not, when in that state, value the baby's survival?

---

[7] See for example Frank Jackson's account of how he came to desire not to smoke more than he desired to smoke (Jackson, 1984: 13).

This would be an unfortunate conclusion and one which would be inconsistent with Rachels' views on the role of deliberation in evaluation. Rachels appears to hold that when we evaluate we are trying to figure out what it is that reason supports. Since the conclusions we reach here must be *cognitive* conclusions, they are surely capable of surviving variations in our conative states. It is the mother's beliefs about what she has most reason to do and to desire in the circumstances that are crucial in identifying her values, and of course she may know perfectly well that she would not desire to drown the baby if only she weren't so tired, and she may judge that being tired is not a reason for drowning the baby. Reason is on the side of taking all due care of the baby, and she knows it.

The problem faced by this agent, in common with agents suffering from illness, depression, or grief, or who are in the grip of anger or temptation, is not that her values have deserted her, as we would have to conclude from a strict reading of Rachels, but that the ordinary connection between judging something valuable and desiring it has been interrupted, making those values difficult to live up to.[8] In her state, she is at least susceptible to weakness of will, and she may even be under a compulsion to harm the baby. If she refrains from harming the baby through an exercise of self-control, it is surely not because of any identification of her judgement that she should not with her present desires. We cannot hope to gain an understanding of the problems of akrasia and compulsion, or of the operation of self-control, by assuming that valuing and rationally laundered desires are one and the same thing. Even this restricted identification of valuing with desiring is too strong, and would raise problems, already canvassed in relation to Watson's argument, regarding the causal strength of such desires.

Nevertheless Rachels' emphasis on the role played in evaluative judgement by the considerations we take as reason-giving points us in the direction of a more adequate account

---

[8] Of course a person's values may desert her at times. Under the influence of a desire we may take as reasons considerations which would not normally weigh with us, and so make judgements that we would not endorse in a cool moment.

of the connection between such judgements and action. Evaluative judgements are, plausibly, judgements about our reasons for action. Michael Woods has claimed that 'the concept of a reason for an action stands at the point of intersection . . . between the theory of the explanation of actions and the theory of their justification' (1972: 189). This intersection is where we must focus our attention. Reasons explain actions by motivating them. But, as we noted in Chapter 3, they must motivate actions and so explain them in the guise of reasons. All practical reasons make their initial link with action via the agent's acceptance and recognition of them *as reasons* of one kind or another. In the remainder of this chapter I explore what this means for both Humean and non-Humean conceptions of practical reason. When we examine the structure of deliberation we will find a formal rational connection between our avowedly evaluative judgements and the desires formed or modified in the light of those judgements which parallels that found between our ordinary means–end judgments and the desires formed in the light of them. This rational connection does, so I argue, permit a rich account of self-control, of weakness, and of compulsion that resonates with and illuminates the common-sense picture.

3. Reasons and Rational Agents

(i) The interdependence of reasons and evaluations

In their response-dispositional accounts of value Mark Johnston (1989) and Michael Smith (1992) take the view that there is some irreducibly normative input into our evaluations. Our evaluations are not mere desires, nor can they be perceptual or quasi-perceptual representations that elicit our responses in the unmediated way McDowell suggests. At best such allegedly powerful perceptions present us with defeasible reasons to value their objects, reasons which can themselves be evaluated and perhaps found wanting. It would be, as Johnston points out, incredible if 'all relevant reason giving properly terminates in appeal to such perceptual promptings'

(1989: 143). Smith argues that, though in deliberation we may appeal to several kinds of considerations including standards of morality, etiquette, and the law, as well as those already mentioned, the justifications these provide must in the end be weighed against each other, and the standards we appeal to at this point are just the standards of rationality. We ask what we have most reason to do or to value. At this point it becomes apparent, as Johnston observes, that 'the concepts of value and of substantive practical reasoning take in each other's washing' (1989: 162). Johnston's theory of value makes the interdependence explicit.

In Johnston's view something is a value (or valuable) just in case substantive practical reason suggests that it is; and something is a substantive reason for or against valuing some outcome or event or action

iff we are disposed stably to take it to be so under conditions of increasing information and critical reflection. (1989: 162)

Since reasons are in principle accessible to us on this formulation, so, via such good reasons, is value. Note that this formulation does not rule out desire or appetite as a ground of value. We may, as Watson (1982*a*: 102–5) argues, come to value appetitively motivated activities such as dining and sex. It just says that any putative value must be able to survive some rational scrutiny. Giving and requiring reasons is thus central to evaluation; such reasons properly function to support and modify both our general evaluations and the particular practical judgements that take our more general evaluations as their starting point.

(ii) Desire and deliberation

Johnston's principle is quite formal. It proposes a procedure for discovering or identifying our reasons but it does not attempt to answer the substantive question about what kinds of considerations the rational agent must take into account in working out what she has most reason to value or to do. This too is to emerge from the process. Smith suggests that law, etiquette, and morality may each supply us with relevant considerations but *how* they do so is a matter of long-standing controversy. For Humeans they do so instrumentally as they connect up with our contingent desires and projects, for Hobbesians and for latter-day economic rationalists they do so instrumentally as they connect up with our presumed self-interest, for Kantians of various shades they also do so categorically as they connect up with the dignity of persons as such. On the first two conceptions, then, our reasons for action will turn out to be relative to our individual ends; on the latter conception, at least some of our reasons for action will be shared.[9]

These different ways of thinking about reasons for action support and are supported by different pictures of what it is to be fully rational. That is, what one is prepared to count as a reason frequently depends on the ideal of rational action to which one subscribes. Thus those philosophers, such as Philippa Foot, who argue that our reasons for action arise from desire or self-interest find puzzling the insistence that moral considerations provide independent reasons for action. Foot's diagnosis is that we are confusing 'the moral judgement, which undoubtedly stands for any man, and the judgement about reasons which does not'.[10] For Foot the two are clearly distinct. So in 'Morality as a System of Hypothetical Imperatives' she argues that attempts to show that it is somehow irrational to ignore the dictates of morality must fail:

The fact is that the man who rejects morality because he sees no reason to obey its rules can be convicted of villainy but not of inconsistency. Nor will his action necessarily be irrational. Irrational actions are those in which a man in some way defeats his own purposes, doing what is calculated to be disadvantageous or to frustrate his ends. Immorality does not necessarily involve any such thing. (1978*a*: 161–2)

---

[9] This division corresponds to Kant's classification of imperatives in the *Groundwork* (414–17).

[10] But what is a moral judgement if it is not a judgement about what there is reason to do? That Foot here seems to be thinking of moral judgements as purely conventional is indicated by her comparison between morality and etiquette. A moral judgement will then be equivalent to a report of the conventions.

Foot's view is consistent with a tendency in moral and political philosophy to draw a distinction between the rational and the reasonable. Supporters of the distinction accept a particular account of reasons for action and then note that moral considerations do not of themselves provide such reasons. The term 'rational' gets reserved for those who display sophisticated means–end reasoning in the service of their personal projects (which may include moral projects) and perhaps also of their long-term self-interest. According to this view the fully rational agent is not, for example, required to take even the most serious interests of others into account except as they impinge upon her projects or interests. To do so is a form of supererogation; she has no *reason* to do so, though, mysteriously enough, she will be a more reasonable person if she does.[11] I do not accept this. The bulk of the argument in this book has been directed to establishing a rather different distinction: the distinction between valuing and desiring, between justification and mere explanation. We shall see that this is a distinction which Humeans cannot (and do not) altogether reject. But once allowed, such a distinction admits the possibility of moral (and other) considerations providing reasons for action directly and not merely as they pass through the filter of contingent desire. To be sure, the connection of such reasons to desire and action needs to be explained but this is not a problem exclusive to those who hold a Kantian or a broadly pluralist view on the sources of reasons for action.

The restricted Humean and prudential accounts of reasons and rationality are, presumably, motivated by the thought that reasons must be capable of explaining action and that moral considerations of themselves lack an obvious connection to motivation that considerations arising from desire or self-interest are thought to possess. But the connection of the reasons

[11] John Deigh, on the other hand, argues that moral judgements are not detachable from reasons: 'The judgement that one ought to do a certain action implies that one's circumstances require or merit the action, and therefore it implies that certain facts about those circumstances are reasons for doing it. The judgement, in other words, is not an intelligible thought independently of there being reasons behind it. One cannot coherently think, I ought to do such and such, though there is no reason for my doing it' (1995: 753).

arising from these considerations to motivation and action is not secure either. In 'Reasons for Actions and Desires', Foot gives this example of a prudential reason which does not, she thinks, depend for its existence upon the agent's present desires:

> consider the case of a man who knows he will be hungry tomorrow unless he goes shopping today. We will suppose that circumstances are normal; he has no reason for wanting to be hungry tomorrow and his house is not on fire. He has a prudential reason for visiting the shops. (1978*b*: 148–9)

Does this reason arise because he now has a desire not to be hungry tomorrow? Foot thinks not: 'It is not on such grounds that we can speak of a desire, and if reason depended on such things there would be few reasons indeed' (1978*b*: 148–9). Here Foot follows Nagel (1970) (and McDowell too) in arguing that while it is appropriate to attribute some such desire to the agent if he acts upon the prudential reason, the desire is somehow consequent upon the recognition of the reason. It does not create the reason.[12] Now as we noted in discussion of McDowell and Watson, the emergence of an appropriate desire in response to the recognition of a reason is not guaranteed. It is perfectly possible that I can believe I will be hungry tomorrow if I don't go shopping today, believe that this gives me a prudential reason to go shopping today, believe that of all the actions available to me this is the one I have most reason to perform, and yet fail altogether to desire to go shopping. Perhaps the link could be made more secure by equipping me with a constitutive desire for my own future welfare.[13] Some such desire is often assumed by economists

[12] In the light of this, Foot's insistence that moral considerations cannot provide reasons for action in the absence of desire seems arbitrary.

[13] This kind of move is rejected by Christine Korsgaard as an unconvincing device to reconcile what she sees as an incoherent pair of commitments: the view that all practical reasons are instrumental and the principle of prudence. 'The standard move is to treat the possibility that someone might desire something inconsistent with her overall good as if it were an uninteresting little piece of theoretical untidiness like the possibility that she might miscalculate or make a mistake' (1997: 231). I have already rejected this kind of explanation of weakness of will. Korsgaard diagnoses the source of the economist's error as lying in the assumption that the objects of desire are commensurable.

and political scientists. But even if we allow this move, which echoes the doubtful Socratic assumption that we necessarily desire pleasure above all else, the connection with motivation and action may still fail.

Though it is a truism that, other things being equal, we have reason to adopt the means to our ends, it is certainly possible to fail to desire the means. I want to finish my paper but I don't want to stay up all night writing; I want to be healthy more than I want immediate pleasure but this does not translate into a desire to refrain from eating chocolate. These means–end reasons, to stay up and write or to refuse offers of chocolate, are not fully independent of desire, since the ends they serve are founded upon the agent's actual desires; nevertheless they persist in the absence of any direct desire for the means. The connection between these reasons and motivation is not a necessary connection. It is best described as a contingent *rational* connection. It is a constitutive feature of rational agency that one is moved by the consideration that a certain action is the recognized means to one's chosen end; a failure to be so moved, is, other things being equal, a rational failure. Indeed, a general failure to desire and act in accordance with the means–end principle is a failure of agency itself. Thus normative reason-claims come in at the ground floor in any discussion of practical rationality.

The fundamental normativity of practical reason is acknowledged by some Humeans.[14] James Dreier (1997), for example, argues that if someone does not accept the means–end principle, and so sees no reason to adopt the acknowledged means to their ends, this deficiency cannot be remedied by furnishing them with another desire, for in so far as this gives them another end it will be subject to the same deficiency.[15] An agent is not motivated simply by the belief–desire pair cited in a

[14] It is also of course recognized by Kantians. Kant says: 'Who wills the end, wills (so far as reason has decisive influence on his actions) also the means which are indispensably necessary and in his power' (*Groundwork*, 417).

[15] Dreier considers the desire to comply with the means–end principle itself. It is clear that this would not fill the motivational gap between the desire for an end and a related means–end belief, because in each case there is some action that will constitute the means to *this* new end and by hypothesis the agent will not be moved by that recognition.

means–end explanation of her action, she is motivated by the reason it provides; that is, she must be capable of recognizing that the *fact* that a particular action is the means to her end gives her a *reason* to perform that action.[16]

Dreier argues that though the particular reasons it generates are all hypothetical, the means–end principle itself is a categorical imperative: 'Its demands must be met by you, in so far as you are rational, no matter what desires you happen to have' (1997: 96). I agree. The crucial question then is whether there is anything more to practical rationality than being governed, narrowly, by the means–end principle. Is there anything above (or below) the ground floor? Dreier is sceptical. He, like Foot, thinks that we will be unable to find any reasons to abide by morality that do not depend upon our contingent wants. But his reason for thinking this is suspect. He says:

the reason there is a problem about the justification of morality is that there are (possible?) beings who can recognize reasons, who act on reasons, who are not moved by moral considerations. A justification would show them what reason they have. So long as a person is M/E [means–end] rational, there are reasons she can act on, that can motivate her, reasons that she accepts as reasons. If we cannot provide her with a reason to abide by moral rules, then we cannot justify morality. (1997: 98)

But this is already to assume that the means–end principle constitutes the whole of practical rationality rather than an essential condition of it. The plain fact that you cannot

[16] Christine Korsgaard makes the same point in 'The Normativity of Instrumental Reason'. She says, 'neither the joint causal efficacy of the belief and the desire, nor the existence of an appropriate conceptual connection between them, nor the bare conjunction of these two facts, enables us to judge that a person acts rationally. For the person to act rationally, she must be motivated by her own *recognition* of the appropriate conceptual connection between the belief and the desire' (1997: 221). This is the bare minimum for rational agency. Alfred Mele has pointed out to me that toddlers can satisfy the conditions for intentional action but do not have the conceptual sophistication to recognize their beliefs and desires as reason-giving. This may be true, but to the extent that toddlers may be amenable to having means–end considerations pointed out to them, or the capacity to grasp a means–end connection and act in the light of it, they do have a primitive conception of reasons. To the extent that they are not so amenable they are not yet rational agents.

succeed in getting a being who is only means–end rational to accept a non-instrumental justification of a moral demand does not, of itself, tell us anything interesting about the reach of practical rationality or the rational status of moral considerations. The Kantian will just say that the individual who fails to be impressed by such considerations is less than fully rational. Unless there is something else to be said we are at a stalemate. Is there a way through? As a first step let us look more closely at the constraints on the content and process of deliberation suggested by the Humean view of the role of reason. Are these constraints warranted?

It is important to acknowledge here just how sophisticated means–end reasoning can get. The sub-Humean model of practical reasoning sketched by Bernard Williams in his 'Internal and External Reasons' (1981c) recognizes the complex skills required to balance our various desires and projects and so focuses to some extent on ends as well as means.[17] Through deliberation our ends may be modified and new desires formed. Considerations of convenience of means, coherence of ends, imaginative acquaintance with the likely consequences of some proposed action, and the acquisition of information may all have a role to play in revealing what the agent has reason to do and so we display more complete rationality when these considerations take their place in deliberation and inform our evaluative judgements. But, according to Williams, all these processes of deliberation are answerable to the agent's subjective motivational set, where this is understood broadly to include 'dispositions of evaluation, patterns of emotional reaction, personal loyalties, and various projects, as they may abstractly be called, embodying commitments of the agent' (1981c: 105). This is the place from which practical reason starts and to which it must return. While desires may change as a result of deliberation, for a reason statement to be true of an agent it must bear the right relation to *that* agent's desires. Thus it may be true of one agent, but not of another in precisely similar circumstances, that she has a reason to protect her

---

[17] Williams's view has been widely discussed. See, among others, Cohon (1986), Korsgaard (1986), Smith (1987, 1994: ch. 5), Velleman (1996).

savings or to keep her promise or to refrain from drowning her baby in the bathwater. This answerability of reasons for action to desire makes reasons profoundly relative: we can see why, on this account, moral and prudential considerations only provide reasons for us when we view them through the prism of desire. Moral considerations, like any other concrete considerations, do not provide reasons independently of desire; that is why we need not be irrational in failing to take account of them.

But note how, as the account of deliberation becomes more sophisticated, it loses much of its distinctively Humean character. Williams denies that his conception of what it is to have a reason is concerned only with explanation; it is also connected with the agent's rationality. He acknowledges that an agent may be ignorant of their reasons, either through ignorance of certain facts or through ignorance of some element of their motivational set. All that is required for the truth of a third-person reason claim is that the reason we ascribe to the agent is also what she could come to ascribe to herself upon deliberation. So even on this sub-Humean story the potential of a reason to explain action may be quite remote. The right relation necessary to establish a reason claim exists independently of the *agent's* now accepting that she has any reason to act. Williams, in fact, relies on a conception of what is involved in ideal deliberation in working out what we have reason to do, just as Johnston and Smith do in their response-dispositional accounts. He allows imaginative acquaintance into his conception but appears to rule out the idea that other people's interests have an independent deliberative claim on fully rational agents. For the Humean, other people's interests are to be taken as reason-giving only in so far as they make a connection with our subjective motivational set.[18] However, once the crucial dis-

[18] Depending on how one fills out the notion of imaginative acquaintance this may do much of the work the defender of moral reasons wants. Does the rational agent have to think about how it would be for others if *x* came about or only how it would be for herself? If she does think about how it would be for others, what weight must she give to the realization that it would, for example, be very unjust if *x* came about? It is here that the essentially interpersonal nature of justification plays a crucial role in the defence of a broad view of reasons for action, as I argue below. Smith (1994: 158 ff.) argues

tinction between what I am motivated to do and what I take myself (or would take myself), upon reflection, to have reason to do is admitted, as it must be even on a Humean account, this restriction on the scope of deliberation looks arbitrary.

While means–end considerations may be a focus of much deliberation, practical reflection cannot constitutively be restricted by our antecedent desires for particular ends. First, the contents of our motivational set are not always transparent to us, so we may not even know when something constitutes a relevant consideration in Humean terms. If so, it will be hard to limit ourselves to such considerations. Second, even when we are aware of our desires we cannot automatically treat them as reason-giving, since, ahead of reflection, it may be radically uncertain what, if anything, they give us reason to do. As Williams acknowledges, the deliberative process may subtract elements from the motivational set, elements which may have succeeded in motivating us had we not deliberated. In the light of these considerations I suggest that the only plausible reading of the story Williams tells about deliberation is one which sees our desires as providing part of the data which we survey critically in deciding what to do.[19] But if we are able to treat our own desires as data—that is, as *evidence* for what we might have reason to do, rather than as the reasons from which we must choose—then it ought to be possible to see the desires of others as evidence for what we have reason to do.[20]

---

that the most important way in which deliberation creates and destroys desires is through finding out whether our desires are 'systematically justifiable', that is, whether they could form part of a more unified and coherent desire set. While there are reasons for thinking that such coherence is desirable, justification, in my view, requires more than this.

[19] I thank John Campbell for this thought.

[20] Korsgaard (1996) claims that we do in fact treat each other's desires as reason-giving. See the next sub-section ('Reasons and Responsibility'). Scanlon also appears to offer a somewhat similar account of the relation between desires and deliberation in ch. 1 of *What We Owe to Each Other* (1998), though I am not sure I have understood his argument fully. He claims that desires almost never provide reasons for action in the way described by the standard model, though some reasons for action, say eating coffee ice-cream, will have subjective conditions. It is not enough merely to have the desire or to find one's attention directed by thoughts of the taste of coffee ice-cream; to have a reason to eat some, one must take these considerations as reason-giving. He says, 'such states are not, as desires are supposed to be,

If our own existing desires, *as data*, set the boundaries of deliberation, the Humean owes us an explanation of why this is so. Ordinarily we think that 'What do *I* want?' is only one of the questions we might consider when deliberating about what to do. 'What do others want?' may be another. In deliberation we make certain assumptions and a central one is that *qua* deliberators we are free to take into account any considerations that may be brought to our attention.[21] As such, I suggest that the conclusions of practical reflection are not inescapably the product of existing desires and ends and may conflict with these. If this is so, it is difficult to see a principled way of ruling out the possibility of the moral or prudential considerations attended to in deliberation providing reasons for action, independently of what we antecedently desire. Certainly such considerations may fail to move us to action. But there can be no special problem for an account of practical reason here that is

original sources of reasons. Rather, they are instances of an agent's identifying some other considerations as reasons, and they derive their reason-giving force from a combination of these reasons and the agent's decision to take them as grounds of action' (45). But there I think we part company. Scanlon thinks motivation lies entirely in taking certain considerations as reasons; he appears to share McDowell's cognitivist view of motivation. Nothing further is ever needed to explain 'how a rational creature can be led to act' (35). He therefore makes no distinction between explanatory and justificatory reasons (though perhaps reasons that have subjective conditions may map onto those I have been calling explanatory reasons). It seems to me that here he runs into difficulty, for he also claims that one's judgement of the reason-giving force of some consideration may be held constant and yet have different effects on action in different circumstances, even where these different circumstances do not cause one to change one's assessment of the reasons (34, 35). His description of those circumstances suggests that something other than the force of the reasons is capable of motivating or of varying motivation and he does not, I think, successfully exclude the possibility that desire plays this role. For example, he says that at a party the reasons given by the pleasures of drinking and conviviality to have more than two drinks may have a stronger effect on me than before the party (though the reason-giving force has not changed) and stronger than the effect of the reason I still take to have most force. My worries here are similar to my worries about Watson's Platonic account (see above). But perhaps I have misunderstood Scanlon.

[21] For an argument to this effect see Pettit and Smith (1996). See also Velleman (1989: ch. 5, on epistemic freedom). Of course it might be stipulated that the invisible hand of desire always constrains deliberation, so that our deliberative conclusions are just further evidence of the prior state of our desires.

not also faced in the case where, though we desire our end, we fail to desire the means to that end. In both kinds of case we fail to desire to do what we may well believe we have most reason to do. In an important respect we lose control of our actions and, as we shall see later, the process of retaining or regaining that control is similar in both kinds of case.

I take it that, since it is possible for the agent herself to accept that she has reason to perform a particular action in the absence of any direct desire to perform that action, it is possible that moral considerations founded in the interests of others could provide reasons for action in the absence of desire. This does not, of course, establish the claim that moral considerations *do* provide reasons for action, and so does not establish that we are more substantively rational when we pay attention to those considerations and at fault when we disregard them. What would establish such a claim? I do not have a knockdown argument on this issue and to attempt to do justice to the extensive debate on this matter would take me too far from my central project of explaining both the failures and successes of practical reason. Here I will restrict myself to a sketch of two related considerations which I believe support the adoption of a broad rather than a narrow view of what it is to be fully rational. The accounts of self-control, moral failures, and moral responsibility in subsequent chapters will, if successful, provide the main support for the adoption of this broad view by showing how it allows us to make sense of our practices and our experiences.

(iii) Reasons and Responsibility

Peter Strawson has drawn our attention to what he calls the participant reactive attitudes, natural human reactions to the good- or ill-will or indifference of others towards us, as displayed in *their* attitudes and actions (1982: 53). In adopting such attitudes of gratitude or resentment towards others, in holding them responsible for what they do, we accept them as fit for ordinary adult human relationships. Indeed a withdrawal from the participant stance is often a consequence of seeing someone as incapacitated in some way for such relationships. Strawson

argues that a general move from the participant to the objective stance, an abandonment of ordinary interpersonal attitudes,
is practically inconceivable. Our commitment to the participant
stance, and so to viewing ourselves and others as answerable
for what we do, is, he thinks, part of the general framework
of human life, not something that can come up for review as
particular cases can come up for review within this general
framework (1982: 55). Inconceivable as an abandonment of the
participant stance may be, however, this is, by itself, an inad-
equate explanation of the practices Strawson describes and does
not close off the possibility of there being something outside
of our practices which they reflect. I shall argue that only the
existence of a shared underlying anti-Humean view of reasons
and persons can serve to explain both the general practice
of holding each other responsible, and the principled, highly
discriminating exceptions to it. Only the truth of the anti-
Humean view can justify those practices.

If, as Kantians insist, moral requirements are requirements
of reason, discoverable by rational reflection, then they apply
to all rational agents and we appear to be on solid ground in
calling to account those agents who disregard them. If someone's actions are thus unjustified it does seem fair to blame
them. But if moral requirements are not requirements of reason then it does *not* seem fair to sanction people for failing to
comply with those requirements. If what one has reason to do
is fully determined by one's own particular set of motives, aims,
and interests then it will be a contingent matter whether or not
one ever has reason to do as *morality* requires. Undoubtedly
some people will have such reasons but others won't. Now if
this were our view of reasons it is clear that in holding these
others to account for their transgressions we would be demanding that they do what we ourselves recognize they have
no reason to do. Blaming them begins to look like coercion,
rather like disciplining one's cat or dog. If the Humean or
Hobbesian accounts of reasons were right and complete then
we should move to an economy-of-threats interpretation of our
practice of holding each other responsible. Blaming others can
be useful from our point of view since it provides transgres-

sors with a reason they might not otherwise have to comply with a moral code. But to interpret our practices this way is to misinterpret them. In particular, such an interpretation cannot explain resentment as a response to perceived mistreatment. What explains resentment is the belief that the perpetrator has ignored or discounted reasons supplied by the *victim's* interests, reasons that should have weighed with her.

Now the Humean may attempt to escape this argument by pointing out that moral sentiments based on a certain broad sympathy for others are distributed very widely in the population. So it is likely that most people will find, in their own motivational set, non-self-interested reasons to join the moral community and act as morality demands. And this provides the appropriate kind of support for our practices. But this response does not escape my argument, for it mislocates what we take to be the source of the moral reason and so the source of our resentment over callous and indifferent behaviour. Ordinarily we think that it is the victim's plight, not the perpetrator's sympathies (or lack of them), that supplies the reason to forbear or assist. Christine Korsgaard notes that

the reasons of others have something like the same standing with us as our own desires and impulses. We do not seem to need a reason to take the reasons of others into account. We seem to need a reason not to. Certainly we do things because others want us to, ask us to, tell us to, all the time. We give each other the time and directions, open doors and step aside, warn each other of imminent perils large and small. We respond with the alacrity of obedient soldiers to telephones and doorbells and cries for help. You could say that it is because we want to be co-operative, but that is like saying you understand my words because you want to be co-operative. (1996: 141)

Korsgaard's point is that we think and act as though the interests of others provide reasons directly, not derivatively. My claim here is that the *coherence* of our practices of holding each other responsible depends crucially upon this supposition. But some further argument is needed to underpin the *legitimacy* of our practices. Moral requirements must be shown to be a species of reasons for action that are available and applicable to all of us: not in virtue, simply, of our individual aims and interests and allegiances, but in virtue, first, of our shared rational capacities for critical reflection and, second, of our capacities for action in accordance with the outcome of such reflection even when it conflicts with our individual desires and interests.

(iv) The conversational stance and the norms of deliberation

If moral requirements are requirements of reason how do we uncover them? I have already suggested that there are certain norms which govern practical reflection and that these norms do not constrain us to entertain only those actions, principles, and policies that would in some way serve or complement our existing desires and aims. A spelling-out of these norms suggests that rational agents *will*, however, be constrained by the interests of affected others, that is, by moral considerations, in both their deliberations and their practical conclusions.

In an extension of Strawson's insight Philip Pettit and Michael Smith argue that both theoretical and practical reflection are modelled on interpersonal conversation. Within the conversational stance people

> listen to one another . . . they invest one another's responses with potential importance. They are prepared often to change their own minds in the light of what they hear from others and, if they are not, then they usually feel obliged to make clear why they are not and why indeed the others should alter their views instead. (1996: 430)

The idea here is that reason is not wholly self-contained or self-referential. Reasoning is something we must often do together.[22] Both practical and theoretical evaluations can be

---

[22] Pettit and Smith may resist this interpretation of their account. In his 'A Theory of Freedom and Responsibility' (1997) Smith makes it clear that when we engage in conversation with another we make the assumption that the other has the capacity to recognize and respond to the appropriate norms. And he argues, with respect to theoretical conversations, that the capacity we imagine him to have is entirely *his*. Our role in raising the gap in his beliefs with him in conversation is not essential (1997: 297). I agree that the capacity to recognize and respond to both theoretical and practical norms is a capacity that the agent has and can exercise in solitary reflection. But this is compatible with thinking that his conclusions are subject to conversational challenge from other rational agents and with thinking that conversations are the arena where our deliberative capacities are developed, supported, and

conversationally interrogated and there are norms governing such conversations, whether they are interpersonal or intra-personal. These norms turn out to set the conditions of agents being able to have a conversation at all. In so far as we do converse about what is 'right or wrong, good or bad, rational or irrational, sensible or stupid' (436), Pettit and Smith argue that we must presuppose that we are engaged in 'a common world-directed enterprise of sifting out fact from fiction . . . of trying to determine what, in the light of the facts, the agent is required to desire and do' (437). Further, we must presuppose that any conversational interlocutor has the capacity to recognize and respond to the demands of the norms govern-ing evaluations; that is, they must be disposed to change their evaluations in the light of evidence and argument, and their desires in the light of their evaluations. It is apparent that we do not occupy the conversational stance for free. Within it we are bound to take each other seriously, in the ways described, on pain of forfeiting our own claims to be taken seriously. The conversational stance is thus partly constitutive of the parti-cipant stance.

Pettit and Smith make no substantive claims about the outcomes of such conversations. But, given the connection already argued for between reasons and evaluation, it is clear, at least, that the outcome of practical conversations will be conclusions about our reasons for action. Can we make any educated guesses about the kinds of practical reasons that will survive conversational challenge? I have argued that there is conceptual *room* for the discovery of non-relative desire-independent moral reasons but might it not be equally likely that we will converge, say, on rational egoism?

I think it doubtful that the justifications offered by the ego-ist could long survive the challenges and the demands of the conversational stance.[23] It seems to me that principles and actions

checked. This is what I mean when I say that reason is not self-contained. In so far as the agent is in the business of forming beliefs and making evalu-ations he is answerable to others in the same business. As I will later argue, *qua* agents we are all in this business, and so answerable.

[23] A society of rational egoists is, I think, barely possible. At best (or worst) they might form an elite group within society. There can be no *community*

which can be justified to, and with, affected others must take them and their legitimate and important interests into account. These are included among the facts, in the light of which we together determine what it is we are required to desire and do. Now to find out what the interests at stake are, and take them properly into account, we need to understand what kind of lives these others lead; we need, as a first step, to *listen* to them. As Amy Gutmann says, 'reasoning by ourselves, rarely points us towards the conflicting perspectives of other reasonable people. People themselves often must point us in their direction' (1993: 200). Listening is an essential condition of conversation.

of rational egoists, just because the ongoing existence and stability of any community depends upon a significant proportion of its members accepting non-self-interested reasons for action. As Annette Baier notes, 'It obviously *has* suited some in most societies well enough that others take on the responsibilities of care . . . leaving them free to perform their own less altruistic pursuits' (1994: 25). She goes on: 'Yet some must take an interest in the next generation's interests. Women's traditional work of caring for the less powerful, especially for the young, is obviously socially vital' (29). Communities contain, and are responsible to, the ill, the elderly, the disabled, and children. And while we may all have self-interested reasons for wanting mothers to take good care of their children (and doctors to be dedicated to the welfare of their patients and builders to eschew quick profits at the expense of public safety, etc.), since it is plausibly in each of our interests to live in a safe and stable society, it is not the case that these are the mother's (or the doctor's or the builder's) reasons, or that we would even think that self-interest should be *their* main, let alone their only, consideration. It is not the case that we think that their reasons for acting in ways which serve the interests of others are wholly contingent on their happening to have an appropriate desire. Given a degree of plasticity of human nature, however, ideals of rationality may be self-fulfilling. Susan Hurley argues thus: 'for persons the question arises: what kind of agents, among those possible, should there be and what kind of agent should I therefore be? Persons can see themselves as various possible kinds of agent, and as co-operating in various forms of collective agency with other individual agents; and persons can take steps toward realising certain of these possibilities as opposed to others' (1989: 157–8).

The kinds of considerations we accept as providing reasons for action may therefore depend on what kind of agent we take ourselves to be, and this will in turn be constrained by what we come to see as possible for us. If we adopt a bleak Hobbesian view of human nature our view on what constitutes a practical reason will be correspondingly narrow. Egoists would do well to take care that their views on rational agency are not widely shared, lest, as Michael Stocker warns (in a different context), 'the world is increasingly made such as to make these theories correct'. He continues aptly enough, 'We mistake the effect for the cause . . . wondering why our chosen goods are so hollow, bitter, and inhumane' (1976: 466).

A refusal to listen thus constitutes resignation from the conversational stance and resignation from the search for reasons.[24] It is, so I claim, a deliberative vice, a form of recklessness not a form of rationality.

What does the requirement that we listen to each other amount to? Listening well and reflecting well require, among other things, the use of the imagination. Here we find a place and importance for certain conative states, such as love and sympathy, in practical reflection, though it is not the place given them in Humean theory. In Plato's *Symposium* love is allied to reason; love is 'the mediator who spans the chasm' between gods and men: 'by him the universe is bound together' (202e). Plato suggests that it is through the intercession of love that we can attain wisdom. I suggest that love and sympathy aid the imagination as a reflective tool. They can act as intermediaries between self and others; they take us beyond both narrow self-concern and narrow experience and permit us some insight into the lives of others. Thus they have an important *epistemic* role to play in practical reflection. This should not be overstated. Uninformed or romantic imaginings may lead us seriously astray; the imagination must be constrained, as well as exercised, by the requirement that we listen to each other, and the insights obtained through sympathetic identification must be subject to rational scrutiny. Nevertheless substantive practical reasoning, seen as involving at least the hypothetical representation and justification of our judgements and actions to each other in conversation, will be handicapped without these

---

[24] Korsgaard appears to hold a very similar view. She says that for the standard moral argument, 'How would you like it if someone did that to you?', to fail, we would have to hear the other's words as 'mere noise'. And this is impossible when we use a common language. We would therefore need to interpret the other's words as meaning something different in their mouths. Her example here is worth quoting: 'She says, "My career is just as important to me as yours is to you, you know. I have ambitions too." He says, "It isn't the same thing for a woman.' What isn't the same? Does "career" mean something different to her? Does "ambition"? How about "important"? Or (let's get down to brass tacks) how about "I"? . . . She's trying to obligate him. He's trying to block it. So he tries to tell her, and he tries to tell himself, that she's just making noise' (1996: 144). This is in my terms a resignation from the conversational stance, which requires that we reason together.

tools. Though imagination, love, and sympathy cannot take the place of reflection and argument, they can facilitate and inform such reflection, leading us to evaluative conclusions we might otherwise struggle to reach.[25]

Under these conditions of reflection it seems unlikely that all of the considerations which are found to have deliberative force will be purely prudential or will bear the kind of relation to our own antecedent concerns that the Humean supposes. My bet is that some of the reasons we discover within the conversational stance will look very much like core commonsense moral reasons. If so, contra Foot, villainy *will* be against reason and the moral agent displays more complete rationality than her self-interested cousins.

In this section I have argued that an examination (albeit brief) of the norms and processes of practical reflection provides no support for the view that the reasons uncovered by such reflection will inevitably be founded in the agent's desires or self-interest. Though desire and emotion often play an important role in reflection, there is no necessary connection between the operation of desire and our particular conclusions about what we have reason to do. These conclusions are cognitive states; the reasons we find in deliberation continue to have a claim on us even when love fails and sympathy takes a holiday. The job of the rational agent is one of balancing

---

[25] In the *Symposium* the love of men and women for their children and for each other prepares them for the love of beauty, temperance, and justice. Diotima, the wise woman, outlines the lover's progress thus: 'the true order of going, or being led by another, to the things of love, is to begin from the beauties of the earth and mount upwards for the sake of that other beauty, using these as steps only, and from one going on to two, and from two to all fair bodily forms, and from fair bodily forms to fair practices, and from fair practices to fair sciences, until from fair sciences he arrives at the science of which I have spoken, the science which has no other object than absolute beauty, and at last knows that which is beautiful by itself alone' (211b). Later she elaborates. True beauty is 'pure and clear and unalloyed, not infected with the pollutions of the flesh and all the colour and vanities of mortal life' (211e).

While I agree that love of other persons may lead us to more universal evaluative conclusions, such as the recognition of the value of justice and liberty, I do not agree that love of other persons is a mere stepping-stone to the good. It constitutes, at least in part, the good for us, as indeed may many other components of 'the colour and vanities of mortal life'.

plural and sometimes incommensurable claims on action, of deciding where the weight of the reasons lies, and then of acting in accordance with her evaluative conclusions.[26] It is to this last problem that we now return.

4. Rational Action

What kind of account of the connection between evaluation and motivation does this view of reasons and rational agents allow? Is there a connection which will make sense of both the usual successes and the common failures of practical reason? According to the analysis given above, we find out which action it would be most valuable for us to perform by deliberating on our reasons for and against doing what we do. But believing or judging that an action is the most valuable of those available to us, even if this is interpreted in terms of what we have most (normative) reason to do, still seems somewhat remote from actually desiring (and desiring most) to perform it. Given the truism that, among the actions we believe are available to us, we always try to do what we most want to do if we do anything intentionally at all, how is it that our actions are generally responsive to our values as well as to our desires? How, in other words, do we reconcile the somewhat Kantian view of reasons and evaluation just argued for with a standard Humean account of the explanation of action?[27]

The general claim of this section is this: in so far as we are rational we will be motivated to act in accordance with our evaluative judgements. This too is a truism given the argument that these judgements are, at bottom, judgements about what we have reason to do. The connection here, as in the instrumental case discussed earlier, is one of contingent rationality.

[26] Rawls argues that 'it is a feature of human sociability that we are by ourselves but parts of what we might be. We must look to others to attain the excellences that we must leave aside, or lack altogether' (1972: 529). This is a pluralist view, which allows that there are very many pursuits and ways of life which we do not choose for ourselves, but which are nevertheless justifiable, and indeed it is a loss to human society if no one chooses them.

[27] It has been Michael Smith's ongoing project to do just this and I owe a clear debt to him, as will be apparent in my discussion.

However, given that the preceding discussion has sought to establish the desire-independent content of many of our evaluative judgements, I need to do more than just assert the truism that there *is* a rational connection. I need to show *how* the connection is made between such judgements and motivation. In the remainder of this chapter I outline the theoretical framework which seems most promising and consider some apparent shortcomings. In the following chapter on self-control I show how the connection is effected under conditions of temptation.

(i) The response-dispositional account of the link between evaluation and action

The reconciliation we are looking for can, I think, largely be effected by an appropriate version of a response-dispositional account of value. Remember that the response-dispositionalist makes two claims. The first is that we cannot separate the concept of something's being valuable from our capacity, at the limit of information and reflection, to recognize it as valuable and desire it accordingly. The second is that the concepts of value and substantive practical reason are interdependent, such that some consideration is a substantive reason for valuing an action or outcome if and only if we are disposed to take it to be so under conditions of increasing information and rational reflection. I have argued, with respect to the second claim, that we may take some consideration to give us a reason for valuing some action, and so for judging that it ought to be performed, independently of our antecedent or current desires for such an action or outcome. When we take the two claims together, however, we can see that the theory contains the connection we are looking for. For the first has the implication that to regard something as valuable is, in part, to be disposed, in appropriate circumstances, to desire it. How does this work?

Mark Johnston suggests that 'valuable' and 'desireworthy' are near-synonyms, and that therefore judging something valuable is pretty much judging it desireworthy. Given this near-synonymity, he finds it 'readily intelligible' how judging some action to be desireworthy might lead to desiring (Johnston, 1989: 161). But, as Michael Smith has noted, to think that an action is valuable is to think it worth doing, and this is not the same as thinking it worth desiring. Smith prefers to explicate the connection between valuing and desiring through an analysis of the concept of desirability. To judge an action valuable is certainly to judge that it is desirable that it be performed; and he thinks that, given that such judgements are governed by the norms of rationality (as asserted by the interdependence claim), it is a platitude to say that 'what it is desirable that we do . . . is what we would desire to do if we were rational' (Smith, 1992: 345–6).

If we spell out this idea in terms consistent with Johnston's dispositional theory of value we get this formulation:

> An action is desirable in certain circumstances if and only if, under conditions of increasing information and rational reflection, we would come stably to desire that, in the event of our finding ourselves in those circumstances, we perform that action.

According to this analysis, then, objective desirability is to be identified with facts about the desires we ourselves would have after reflecting on our actual circumstances under ideal conditions for such reflection. Subjectively then, the belief that some action x is worth doing (valuable) in circumstances c is equivalent to the belief that it is desirable that I do x in circumstances c, which is equivalent to the belief that I would desire that I do x in c if I were (more) rational. And this is indeed Smith's view.

However, the link between judgements of desirability and motivation, where the measure of what is objectively desirable is given by what my fully rational self would want, still seems tenuous. On the one hand it might be objected that our fully rational selves are too different from us for the link to be plausible. On the other hand it might be pointed out that it is at least conceivable that an increase in information and reflection will not always deliver the promised harmony between evaluation and desire.

(ii) The remoteness objection

On the first point an objector might say: 'This notion of objective desirability is just a version of the ideal observer

theory. Here the ideal observer is conceived of as *my* ideally
rational self, but that self seems as remote from me in my imperfectly rational state as any other ideally rational self. Surely I
do not, in deliberating, explicitly take myself to be trying to
work out what my ideally rational self would do or desire. Why
should I pay any particular attention to what someone so different would want in my circumstances? Taken as a description of the deliberative process it surely misses the mark. An
agent who thought like that would be excessively and improb-
ably earnest. It also seems false as an account of the content
of the beliefs the agent comes to. Someone who believes that
there is reason to do *x*, so doing *x* is desirable, does not necessarily have the belief that doing *x* would be desired by her
if she were more, or even fully, rational: that is simply a different belief. Our desires, too, may be largely unaffected by information about the desires of our more rational selves, and it is
not immediately obvious that a failure to desire as we believe
our ideal selves would desire should count as weakness of will.
This way of analysing desirability would seem to have limited
power to explain how our actions can be responsive to our evaluative beliefs as well as to our desires.'

Smith's account, I think, will be immune to this first objection once we remind ourselves that for the most part our
rational selves are not very far removed from us—the practically relevant notion in deliberation is surely '*more* rational',
rather than 'ideally rational'[28]—and if we move in any case
to thinking of the notion of full or increased rationality as a
regulative principle which does indeed govern deliberation, but
which rarely needs to be invoked by the deliberator.[29] Considered not as a blow-by-blow account of deliberation or as
a description of the content of an evaluative judgement, but
simply as a regulative ideal, the principle Smith proposes has
considerable plausibility.

Since in deliberation we are often trying to work out which
of the available actions we have most reason to perform, our

---

[28] Agents may deliberate perfectly well without having a developed concept of ideal rationality.

[29] I am not suggesting it is the only principle governing deliberation. See
above on the norms governing the conversational stance.

practical judgements are appropriately constrained by our background knowledge and understanding of facts about the desires we would form under conditions of increased rationality. This is to say that, although we do not ordinarily ask directly what we would want ourselves to do in our circumstances if only we were more rational, if we came to believe that what we in fact want is seriously opposed to what we would want under conditions of increasing information and rational reflection, this would deflect our disposition to choose in accordance with our antecedent desires.[30] For here we begin to think that what we most desire to do is simply not worth doing.

Suppose, for example, I am drinking wine with friends. After two glasses of wine I am in the mood to keep drinking and though my friends are leaving I want to open another bottle. If I do, I will end up quite drunk and have a hangover tomorrow when I am due to give a presentation to a job selection panel. It is pretty clear here that what I want to do—drink a bottle of wine—is not what I would want if I were not already half-drunk. And I could know this. If challenged I may well agree that drinking more wine is not a good idea, though I still desire to do it.

This kind of split between one's present desires and the desires of our more rational selves is well illustrated in the case of the distressed mother who realizes that, but for her distress, she would not want to drown her baby. In such situations, in which our background assumption that we are fit deliberators is disturbed, I suggest we do become *directly* concerned with what we would want for ourselves if only we were more rational. The ideal which ordinarily regulates deliberation comes to the fore, and is here laid bare. It seems, then, that when we deliberate about what to do, we are indeed at least indirectly, and sometimes directly, concerned with what we would want ourselves

---

[30] I think that we make certain assumptions when we deliberate, and it is only when these assumptions are disturbed that we focus explicitly upon the question of what we *would* want under ideal conditions. Most times the question of what I would want is idle because I have no reason to think that I would desire differently, in my actual circumstances, even given more information and opportunity for reflection. We assume that we are fit deliberators and choosers except in certain defined circumstances.

to do as we are, now and in our actual situation, if only we were more rational or reasonable.

This qualification relating our judgements to our actual situation is important. It secures the practical relevance of our judgements of desirability. Sometimes if we were completely rational we would not be facing the choices that we do, and so it is argued that there is no more reason for us now to take any notice of what we would want under such different circumstances than there is reason for us to take notice of what some more remote ideal observer wants. In any event, it might be suggested, it is just not possible for us, in our less than fully rational state, to know what we would desire for ourselves if we were reflecting under ideal conditions. But these claims miss the mark against this version of the response-dispositional account. Most often we are able to predict confidently and accurately what we would want ourselves to do here and now, and to recognize the existing impediments to desiring in accordance with reason. The relevant difference between the distressed mother and her more rational self, for example, is minor and temporary. Her rational self is no stranger to her, it is not some remote ideal observer. It is the self she was a few minutes ago and will be again when the baby calms down. It is *her*self. Not only can she, while distressed and angry, know perfectly well how this self would want her to act in her current circumstances, she sees those desires as rationally privileged and so as placing a requirement on what she does even in their absence.

This way of responding to the remoteness objection suggests that our judgements of desirability are much as Smith says. In coming to a judgement that some action is worth doing, or desirable, it is as if the agent had formed a belief about what she would desire under more ideal conditions. For ideally an agent's regulated evaluative beliefs *will* track facts about objective desirability: about what, from her own point of view, she would want herself to do after a process of deliberation and justification carried out under the conditions described above.

Now how does this reconstruction of deliberative judgement in terms of desirability show the sense in which an action can be the product of both our desires and our evaluative beliefs, and so ground an explanation of the phenomena we are interested in? We have seen how such a judgement can be practically relevant: how can it be practically *effective*? It is necessary to consider this question, albeit briefly, before we move to the second objection.

According to Smith's response-dispositional account rationality requires evaluation and motivation to be in equilibrium, since to value something is to form a belief about what you have reason to do which is regulated by background considerations about what you would actually desire that you do in your current circumstances if you were more reasonable. It seems to follow, then, that rationality requires not just that your *strongest* desire be in accord with your all-things-considered judgements of desirability, but that your other desires too should align themselves with your different, and sometimes conflicting, judgements of *pro tanto* desirability.[31] It is at this point that the contrastive ranking of desires in terms of evaluative weights and causal strengths suggested by Watson comes into its own. On the one hand we may rank actions or outcomes from most desirable to most undesirable. On the other hand we may rank actions or outcomes from most desired to most aversive. In creatures like us, for whom valuing and desiring may come apart, and whose capacity to take proper account of all the factors that would count as reasons for us under ideal conditions is often limited, there will be no exact correspondence in the ordering of items on the two scales.[32]

---

[31] From my earlier discussion of McDowell's views, we know that in many actual situations there are a number of different and perhaps conflicting things that we might value or desire. This plurality of values and desires is not in itself any indication of irrationality, since it is implausible to suppose that, in the world as it is, we would come to believe that just one action was justified, or just one outcome was desirable, in each and every situation. Even at the ideal limit, I believe that I would desire both to fulfil my work obligations and to watch my child's performance; and there may be other things I would desire as well. So getting my work done and watching my child perform are both *pro tanto* desirable. See Susan Hurley (1985–6: 23–50) for a discussion of *pro tanto* reasons.

[32] This in itself is not a bad thing. I have suggested elsewhere (Kennett 1993) that, given our epistemic limitations, *some* division between evaluation and motivation is healthy. Those of us whose concerns are not homogeneous, and who do experience occasional conflict and mismatches between value and desire, are more likely to review our evaluative beliefs and have a sense of our own fallibility than those who don't. We will thus be more substantially reasonable human beings than those who don't.

For us, evaluation and motivation may diverge in two distinct ways: a desire for an action or outcome may be *stronger* or *weaker* than the value we assign to such an action or outcome in deliberation.

This will depend on how the strength of the desire for the action or outcome, relative to the strength of the agent's other desires, compares to her assessment of the degree of desirability of that action or outcome, relative to the degree of desirability she assigns to other outcomes. At the limit, it is possible that an agent might strongly desire to perform some action she judges wholly undesirable, or alternatively she might fail altogether to desire in accordance with some of her judgements of desirability, even to the point where she is actively averse to some action she judges desirable. This is often the case with phobias, for example, the fear of flying. Though I may judge it desirable to fly in some circumstances, I am strongly averse to doing so. In such circumstances we are in clear danger of failing to act in accordance with our judgements of desirability.

For the most part, however, though there will be no exact correspondence between the two scales, the *relevant* differences (that is, the differences relevant to our actual circumstances of choice and action) between us and our more rational selves will be small. The evaluative weight we give to some judgement of desirability will be matched by the causal strength of the associated desire, and not by accident, since we are, in the main, rational. Thus the explicit realization that under more ideal conditions we would desire to perform a different action may often be enough to produce the mandated shift in desire and action. One can quite easily imagine the harassed mother being chastened by the thought that harming the baby is not what she would want herself to do if only she were not so tired, and straight away being moved to put the baby out of harm's way. Here as elsewhere our desires do, ordinarily, wax and wane in the light of our evaluative judgements.

Circumstances are not always ordinary however. I will defer to the next chapter specific consideration of those familiar situations where our present desires do not yield so readily to considerations of what our more rational selves would want. The second objection considered here presents a more fundamental challenge to the response-dispositional account.

(iii) Scepticism about Smith's analysis of desirability

Interpreting my evaluative beliefs as, in part, regulated by beliefs about what I myself would desire for my current circumstances, if I were more rational, might appear to secure the practical relevance and psychological plausibility of the response-dispositional account. However there is a range of cases which suggest that the account fails. They suggest that even at the limit of information and rational reflection there may be conflicts between my evaluative judgements and my desires. There are hard cases where reason, as thus far interpreted, appears to run out. Consider the following example of the rational paedophile.

Suppose some individual, as a result of childhood sexual abuse, becomes sexually fixated on children. This individual later comes to reflect on the harm done to him in his own childhood and judges that despite his desires he should not make sexual approaches to children; he should not have sex with them. Does such an individual *believe* that if he were only more rational he would not desire to have sex with children? Is it the case that if he *were* more rational he would no longer desire sex with children? Maybe not! For this individual is, let us say, fully informed, has thought clearly about the issue and has subjected it, at least hypothetically, to the views of those affected. His evaluative conclusions are appropriately supported by the reasons available to him. Yet he is still sexually attracted to children. What distinction can we make between him and his more rational self that would preserve the relevant similarities while bringing the desires of his more rational self into line with his judgement? I think we may be forced to conclude that there is none. There is certainly no deliberative failure that we can repair.[33] Sometimes we are fully informed, sensitive, and reasoning correctly. Even then our desires do not always fall meekly into line with our evaluative conclusions; sexual desires are surely notorious in this regard.

The plausibility of my defence of the response-dispositional account appears to rely on the supposition that the obstacles

[33] This is not to say that there is nothing he can or should do about the state of his desires, just that his having them is, in the circumstances, not the result of a rational failing.

to desiring in accordance with reason are minor or temporary. But suppose the obstacles are embedded in the agent's psychology, as in the above case. Then, either the agent's more rational self is too remote from him to have any practical relevance—he becomes the ideal observer, since he does not share in the agent's constitutive bad luck—or the more rational self is likely to suffer the same mismatch between his judgements and his actual desires as the agent himself. If the second interpretation is right it suggests that the account of desirability is wrong. I can believe something is worth doing or desirable without having any disposition to believe that it would be desired by me even under more ideal conditions. How then do my evaluative beliefs connect with action?

(iv) A Kantian turn

Though I accept that this kind of situation occurs I do not believe that it need trouble us. Smith (1994: 150) acknowledges the possibility of a split between what it is desirable that we *do* and what it is desirable that we *desire* we do. (Some desires may be self-defeating, for example.) The practically relevant desire is the desire that one act in a particular way given one's circumstances, which in this case includes the unlucky sexual fixation.[34] Our paedophile's more rational self (while still experiencing recalcitrant sexual desires) will nevertheless desire that he act in accordance with his evaluative conclusions

[34] Let me be clear that the rational paedophile's psychology is not to be envied. The deep disharmony between his judgement and his sexual desires is a reflection of the damage inflicted on him. Other things being equal it is surely better to have, in Smith's words, a more 'coherent and unified desiderative profile and evaluative outlook' (1994: 159). I agree with Smith that this kind of unity may be a mark of a 'systematically justified and so rationally preferable set of desires' (ibid.), though sometimes it is not. (See my discussion of recklessness in Ch. 6.) We may imagine that the rational paedophile would (rationally) prefer such a coherent psychology. That is, he may have acquired, through deliberation, a general underived desire for a systematically justified set of desires and now sees his sexual desires as (in part) interfering with the achievement of this goal. In the case of less entrenched wayward desires, such as the sudden desire to drown one's baby, this more general disposition to coherence may cause one to lose the desire in question once one sees it as unjustifiable. But this will not be sufficient in hard cases. The rational paedophile may be working towards losing the disvalued desire through counselling and so forth. In the meantime he must do the best he can to exercise control over it.

and it is this which underwrites our judgements of desirability in hard cases. This desire differs fundamentally from our direct and specific desires for particular ends, even when they are direct and specific desires for ends approved of or suggested by reason. It does not arise unmediated from a perception of the good as McDowell and Plato would have it. Nor is it the merely contingent desire, postulated by externalists, to do whatever we believe is morally right. Rather, it arises from a disposition we have, *qua* rational agent, to act in accordance with our reasons as we understand them. It is clear that this, at least, is not a disposition which rational agents might have or lack (as they might have or lack a taste for sardines or the opera), since it is the very disposition which constitutes them as rational agents. That rational agency depends upon such a disposition is, I think, tacitly consented to by most Humeans as well as Kantians. The categorical requirement to take the means to our end acknowledged by Dreier gets its warrant from this more general requirement that we act in accordance with our reasons.[35]

---

[35] For moral externalists the absence of motivation to act in accordance with one's moral judgement in no way impugns the agent's rationality. The desire to act in accordance with such judgements is a contingent one. Smith (1994: 71–6) argues that externalist characterizations of moral motivation are unconvincing. We are to imagine an agent whose moral judgements have no direct impact on her motivations. Moral motivations will all be derivative from a moral judgement that I ought to do *x*, plus my self-consciously (and contingent) moral motive. But Smith claims that good people care reliably and non-derivatively for what they value; for family and friends, justice, honesty, and the like. He claims the externalist picture is of a moral fetishism. In some ways the rational disposition I have postulated occupies the role externalists give to the moral motive and so might be thought to fall under the scope of Smith's criticisms. But I think this would be misplaced. First, the rational disposition is partly constitutive of rational agency, so the connection is an internal one and failure of the connection *is* a rational failure. Second, it does not conflict with the further and distinct rational goal of a unified and coherent evaluative and desire set (see previous note). Nothing I have said would license the neglect of such a goal, though I would subject it to certain qualifications: some of these were suggested in my discussion of McDowell and others will emerge in my discussion of recklessness. But it is important to realize that it is a goal, not a reality, for most actual agents, who still have the practical problem of matching their actions to their evaluations in the absence of such perfect coherence. Smith's rational internalism and his arguments against externalism have received much discussion. See, for example, Miller (1996), Brink (1997), Copp (1997), Lillehammer (1997), Sayre-McCord (1997), Lenman (1999).

To the extent that this rational disposition is goal-directed the goal is broad indeed—it is, David Velleman suggests, the constitutive goal of action, 'the aim in virtue of which behaviour becomes action . . . autonomy itself' (1997: 49).[36] Agents act for reasons. The Kantian notion of autonomy is not one of unrestrained action but of action in accordance with, or determined by, reason. It thus contrasts with behaviour determined by mere inclination. In 'The Voice of Conscience' Velleman interprets Kant's view thus:

> by informing us of the absence of reasons for doing things, conscience rules out the possibility of our doing them for reasons, and, with it, the possibility of our doing them autonomously—or indeed the possibility of *our* doing them, since we are truly the agents of the things we do only when we do them for reasons. . . . the recognition that we would do something only non-autonomously deters us from doing that thing . . . The deterrent force of this recognition derives from our reverence for the idea of ourselves as rational and autonomous beings. (1999: 75)

So it is the disposition to autonomy, so described, which those of us who, even at the limit of rational reflection, experience a mismatch between our evaluations and our particular desires, must rely on to effect the connection between judgement and action. While inclination cannot always be commanded, either in ourselves as we are or, as the case of the rational paedophile reminds us, in our more rational but still identifiable selves, the disposition to act in accordance with our reasons is, with utter reliability, possessed by our more rational selves and to the extent that we are rational it cannot fail us altogether.[37]

---

[36] See also Velleman (1996), where he argues that desire-based reasons derive their rational influence from engaging our disposition to autonomy. And he acknowledges that considerations which are not based on desire may similarly possess the capacity to engage that disposition. Velleman here characterizes autonomy as the inclination towards conscious control, towards behaving 'in, and out of, a knowledge of what you're doing' (1996: 725). Kant's view appears stricter. One is only truly autonomous when one acts in accordance with reason (which will include acting in and out of knowledge). I accept the Kantian version though I adopt (in Ch. 5) the term 'orthonomy' for Kant's conception of autonomy.

[37] As Kant says, 'For love out of inclination cannot be commanded; but kindness done from duty—although no inclination impels us, and even though

5. *Conclusion: Towards an Account of Self-control*

In this chapter I have been concerned to set out both the distinction and the connection between valuing and desiring and so to expose the structure of the common situation in which self-control is called for. The account of deliberation, evaluation, and motivation developed here took as its starting point the Platonic distinction between valuing and mere desiring pointed out by Watson. In further characterizing this distinction and in identifying and responding to the problems in Watson's account of the connection between evaluation and motivation we have taken a distinctly Kantian turn. The analysis of deliberation, evaluation, and desirability arrived at permits us to see where our failures lie, and it appears that they lie just where common sense said they did. Recklessness is (roughly) a failure to take proper account of our reasons in arriving at a judgement of value; and this is clearly irrational when we analyse value in terms of what reason supports. Weakness and compulsion involve a failure to desire and act in accordance with our judgements of desirability, and this too is seen to be clearly irrational when we analyse desirability in terms of what we would desire that we do if we were (more) rational.

This account does more, however, than reveal the structure of our moral failings; it points the way to how we may avoid or repair them: it provides the theoretical ground for an account of self-control in action. It indicates that even when evaluation and motivation diverge, with the *desire* for x and the assessed *desirability* of x occupying different positions on the respective orderings, we may still have the capacity to act in accordance with our all-things-considered judgements of value. The exercise of that capacity is underwritten by our core rational disposition to act in accordance with reason and is central to the maintenance of rational agency. This disposition

natural and unconquerable disinclination stands in our way—is *practical*, and not *pathological* love, residing in the will and not in the propension of feeling, in principles of action and not of melting compassion; and it is this practical love alone which can be an object of command' (*Groundwork*, 399).

gives reasons their normative force and ensures that our justificatory reasons are not (wholly) hostage to our contingent desires. Continence in the face of countervailing inclinations is thus very far from being a stain on reason and virtue; it is rather, as Kant thought, a measure of our commitment to the rule of reason.

We are now in a position to explore more thoroughly the nature of self-control and the ways in which it may be exercised.

5

A Taxonomy of Agent-control

I have been arguing for the common-sense view that evaluative judgement and desire can diverge, and that the capacity for self-control is the capacity to bring one's actions into line with one's judgements of value when there is such a divergence between judgement and desire. And so it is. This is full-blooded self-control, and it is of central moral importance. It is this kind of self-control—self-control in the service of one's values—which is the focus of folk theory and which I am primarily concerned to make room for and explain: what it is, how and when it can be exercised, its virtues and its proper limits. However, agents apparently exercise forms of self-control in domains which need not connect with their beliefs (if indeed they have any) about what, all things considered, they have most reason to do. In doing so they at times adopt strategies resembling those which would help to bring it about that they act according to their values. This means that sometimes there is no simple answer to the question whether an agent has or has not exercised self-control.

I suggest that there is a hierarchy of control which agents may exercise over their actions, the early stages of which match up with the various stories about control which emerge from a reading of Davidson, of Socrates, and of Jackson. Each successive level in the hierarchy marks an increase in the capacity for rational agency. However, we exercise control for different purposes at each level and these purposes have the potential to conflict with each other. It is therefore necessary to begin any full discussion of self-control by carefully distinguishing the kind of self-control we have so far been talking about from the other respects in which agents may be said to have, or to lack, control over their actions.

1. Self-control, External Control, and Intentional Agency

All sorts of factors can bring about a divergence between our actions and our values. So far we have focused exclusively on one internal factor: the causal strength of the agent's desire for the outcome deemed desirable, relative to the causal strength of the agent's other desires. But there are other internal impediments to action in accordance with values, and there are also external impediments which may equally interfere with the successful completion of an action.

Sometimes we fail to do what we judge most desirable because, though we may want most to do what we judge most desirable, our desires are not causally strong enough. They are defeated by other psychological factors, such as shyness or nerves. I want to ask Arnie out to dinner but shyness overcomes me as I look in his eyes, and to my horror I cannot get the words out properly. I blush and stammer something entirely incoherent. On the high-diving board, about to make the dive that may earn me Olympic selection, I am gripped by nerves. I cannot bring off the dive; instead I flop ignominiously into the water. In such cases I have just as much need to exert control over myself, if I am to act in accordance with my values, as I do when the impediment is the state of my desires.

Note, though, that it is not structurally necessary to the cases I have just described that I judge it all-things-considered *desirable* that I perform the action in question. I need not think that the action I try to perform is the one I have most reason to perform. My desire to ask Arnie out, for example, may be completely at odds with my judgement that I should do no such thing, given that I am married to someone else. Olympic selection may be something I just happen to want. I may not be in the habit of making judgements about the worth or otherwise of the objects of my desire. Yet in these cases, just as in the cases as they were initially described, it seems that I might be able to overcome the effects of shyness and nerves, and get myself to ask Arnie out, or to complete the dive. And if I do, it is surely appropriate to say that I have exercised self-control. Doesn't this show, contrary to the conclusions of the preceding chapter, that it is in general a mistake to think that the agent's evaluations play an essential *structural* role in situations where self-control is called for?

Alfred Mele has labelled the exercise of control to perform actions which an agent judges she ought not to perform *errant self-control* (Mele, 1990). He uses the example of a youth who wants to be part of the gang and so wants to join in a house-breaking, although he judges, all things considered, that he should not. The youth is so nervous, however, that he has to steel himself to go through with the chosen course of action. Has he exercised self-control or not? It does seem paradoxical that if he had been overcome by nerves, which in itself looks like a clear case of losing control of one's actions, he would not have performed an action contrary to his judgements of value. As it is, he has apparently exercised control in performing an action which might normally be construed as showing weakness of will. For this reason Mele terms it errant self-control.

Mele's label is misleading, however. It suggests that self-control as we initially defined it has simply taken a wrong turn, or been diverted to a bad end. This clearly does not fit the cases where judgements of value are not at stake. In fact we will misunderstand what is going on in all of these cases, including those where nerves interfere with the performance of a *valued* activity, if we attempt to accommodate them in the structure outlined in the preceding chapter. For they are neither a version nor an inversion of the standard situation in which self-control is called for. What they show us is that there are other kinds of situations in which we may be called upon to exercise control, and other forms of control we may exercise in acting. In particular there is a parallel to be drawn here between control over one's actions and control over the world.

Sometimes our actions misfire. Someone bumps me when I am trying to write my name, the wind blows unexpectedly when I am trying to hit the target, the dollar drops just as I am trying to make a fortune by buying foreign currency. What I end up doing is not what I intended to do. In such cases it is true to say that what we need is not more control over ourselves, but more control over the world. However, these cases are of a piece with the cases of my failing to ask Arnie out, or muffing the dive due to nerves. There too I lose control of what I am doing, and, though the cause is internal rather than external (so that it might be said that in these cases, unlike the others, I lacked *self*-control), one story can be told about them all: in each case I do not act intentionally.

To say this is just to say, following Davidson, that what I do when I scribble illegibly on the page, fire the arrow above the target, stammer incoherently, or bellyflop into the water is not rationalized by my desires and my means–end beliefs. My actions are not brought about 'in the right way' by those desires and means–end beliefs. They do not constitute a primary-reason explanation for what in fact happened. What is at fault here is not my desires, but my means–end beliefs. For, though they may be otherwise reasonable (in that, for example, moving my hand in a certain way ordinarily results in my writing my name), they are mistaken in the particular circumstances I face. They do not take account of possible interference from external and internal factors. I end up with a false belief about which movements will result in the completion of the desired action, or else with a falsely optimistic belief about my current ability to make those movements. And so, armed as I am with false beliefs, I lose control of what I am doing.

The diagnosis of what has gone wrong in these cases allows us to construct a distinctly Davidsonian (and narrowly Humean) account of self-control which is entirely consistent with, and indeed falls out of, an account of what it is to have control over the world generally. When we exercise control over the world we act so as to *change* the world to fit better with our desires as we understand them (Smith, 1987). We close a gap between the way the world is and the way we want it to be. I want the world to be a place where I have asked Arnie out, gained Olympic selection, written my name, and hit the target: what must I do?

If I am to be successful in changing the world, I will need a set of true beliefs about how the world is and how any actions of mine will affect it. In choosing my course of action I must take into account any difficulties I am likely to face in executing the action, and adjust my plans accordingly. So if I foresee that the wind will blow as I am aiming for the target, I may time my shot for when it drops, or I may make allowances for the wind when taking aim. Equally, if I foresee the effect upon me of staring straight into Arnie's blue eyes while trying to ask him out, I may decide to phone him instead, in the true belief that this is how best to give effect to my intention to ask him out. *One* aspect of exercising control over the world so as to make it the way I want and intend it to be is, therefore, exercising control over myself. I must sometimes overcome or sidestep the internal impediments to successful intentional action.

Self-control, according to this Davidsonian picture, is simply a refined capacity for intentional agency, in circumstances where the potential interference with such agency comes from within the agent's own physiological or psychological make-up, rather than from without. Does this refined capacity for intentional agency exhaust our capacity for self-control? If it does, it follows that an agent who acts intentionally cannot *in that very action* manifest a lack of self-control. It is only when intentional agency fails that we could say that the agent lacked self-control.

I do not mind acknowledging that those individual actions which overcome the threats posed to successful action by nerves or embarrassment display at least narrow self-control. Some of them may indeed go further, since sometimes the demand for this kind of control flows from a normative requirement, accepted by the agent, that she act in a particular way; and in these cases the resultant action does seem to count as displaying full self-control. But sometimes intentional self-control is exercised to bring about actions that are in direct opposition to such requirements; at other times it is exercised without any regard being paid to such requirements.

Now, it would be too much to call the successful intentional agent self-controlled merely in virtue of the fact that she acts intentionally. Such an agent, though proficient at manipulating the world, and overcoming any bodily faintness or rebellion that blocks the way to action, may be imprudent, impulsive, reckless, and unprincipled. Any such person would be thought of as being substantially out of control. There is a normative aspect to our use of the term 'self-control' which is not captured in this narrow Davidsonian picture. A refined capacity for intentional agency may be an element in full-blooded self-control; obviously the capacity for intentional agency is a prerequisite for *any* exercise of control, and so may rightly be thought of as constituting the first level in a hierarchy of agent-control of actions. But far from exhausting the notion, this capacity is conceptually peripheral to our normatively loaded notions of self-control. Mere intentional self-control is just a special case of control over the world, and as such it may be exercised by a hopeless heroin addict as efficiently as by a model of temperance, provided they each have appropriate, true means–end beliefs to tell them how to act, and act effectively in the ways that they intend.

2. *Self-control and Instrumental Rationality*

There is a richer Humean story which may be told about self-control which is more subtle, and harder to distinguish from full self-control, than is intentional self-control. Like full self-control it can require a considerable degree of self-knowledge and clarity of perception. Interestingly, this is a story which is consistent with the Socratic analysis of weakness of will given by Jackson. What we will call *instrumental* self-control constitutes the second level of the rational hierarchy.

Here is a fairly common situation: David is driving home; he is hungry, so he stops at a row of shops to pick up a take-away. There are two options: he can get fried chicken and chips from the chicken shop, or he can get mixed vegetables and rice from the Chinese restaurant. David knows from past experience that he would regret buying the chicken. Though he desires the taste of chicken, he does not desire the greasiness that goes with it and the feelings of nausea this tends to induce in him. He knows that he would both sate his appetite and get more in the way of overall enjoyment from eating the rice and vegetables, which are also very tasty.[1] If he now

---

[1] I am supposing here that health is not a deep consideration. No harm will come of David choosing chicken, apart from transient feelings of nausea. It is just that he will get less pleasure or desire satisfaction overall from eating it.

thought carefully about his options and how they would serve his existing desires he would end up wanting the Chinese food more.

However, with the smell of fried chicken in his nostrils, David does not think carefully about how best to serve his desires, taken together, and so does not end up deriving from those existing desires a strong enough desire for the rice and vegetables. He just goes ahead and chooses the fried chicken and, predictably, regrets it after the first few mouthfuls, when the grease overtakes the taste. Now, David does not buy the chicken unintentionally. His buying the chicken is rationalized by certain of his desires and means–end beliefs, and is caused in the right way by them; so he is not lacking in intentional self-control. Nevertheless it seems right to say that David displays a certain lack of control in buying the chicken, since he does not act in the way that best serves his desires given his beliefs.

How do we analyse David's failure? Let's return to Socrates. Remember that in the *Protagoras* Socrates claimed that pleasure is the only good, and that we are innately disposed to choose the path which we believe leads to the greatest pleasure. Choosing the course which will lead to the lesser pleasure over the course which will lead to greater pleasure is to be explained by the relative proximity of the pleasures. The nearer, lesser good seems the greater good; the agent suffers from an evaluation illusion. In the psychological literature self-control is seen similarly—as a now-versus-later issue. We have to choose between alternatives which arrive at different times. Agents show self-control when they prefer larger rewards in the future to smaller rewards in the present (Rachlins, 1974) and act accordingly.[2]

This looks to be the right general approach to take in explaining David's choice; but we can refine it further by looking to Jackson, who argues that our desires are conditioned by our beliefs. How much we want something will usually be tempered by our assessment of the circumstances in which we

[2] Rachlins also discusses techniques and strategies for achieving self-control similar to some of those I outline in this chapter. See also Mele (1990, 1992) for a discussion of techniques of self-control.

believe that thing is likely to come about. Desires are complex. Given the likelihood that the circumstances in which David eats fried chicken are circumstances in which he comes to feel queasy, David's desire to eat fried chicken is usually counter-balanced by his desire to avoid queasiness, leaving only a small, net positive disposition to eat chicken. However, in circumstances where these two desires come apart, and the probable greasiness of the chicken is not nearly so salient as its smell and its projected tastiness, the simple desire for fried chicken is able to swamp the desire for the alternative of rice and vegetables. David's hunger, combined with the smell of the chicken, provides a context in which the overall less-desired option becomes more occurrently attractive, without there being any change in his underlying belief- and desire-states. The result is significantly less desire satisfaction for David than he might have had. In Humean terms he fails, in his role as an instrumentally rational agent, to maximize subjective (decision-theoretic) value.

What is common to all cases of instrumental irrationality is that the agent fails to derive instrumental or extrinsic desires of appropriate strength from her strongest intrinsic desires. As Williams's sub-Humean account of reasons and deliberation should imply, opportunities for instrumental irrationality are abundant. The explanation of such irrationality is most often, as Socrates suggested, a kind of ignorance. We have seen that agents may be ignorant of the existence or content of some desires, ignorant of the consequences of acting on some de-sires, or ignorant of which actions are required by their desires. Desires that are not phenomenologically salient may be crowded out by those that are, or they may simply be forgot-ten under the press of circumstances. For example, my desire to relax this evening with a copy of *Pride and Prejudice* and a glass of wine, though stronger than my desire for the altern-ative of a glass of water and repeats of *Seinfeld*, won't lead me to stop at the bottle shop and the library on my way home if at that time I am wholly preoccupied with the traffic and with thoughts of the class I have just given. I end up less satisfied with my evening's activities than I might have been had I remem-bered the relevant desires at the appropriate time.

How can such practical failures be remedied? How could David have remained in control when assailed by the aroma of fried chicken? A detailed discussion of the techniques of self-control must wait until later in this chapter. It appears, though, that instrumental self-control is largely a matter of keeping one's attention focused on the relevant facts.

In this case, had David reminded himself of the unpleasant consequences of eating the chicken, and of any other desires which would remain unsatisfied by his choosing chicken over vegetables, he may well have derived a stronger instrumental desire for the vegetables than for the chicken. For he would thereby have better satisfied his existing desires to eat something tasty and not to feel nauseous. And of course David *could* have focused on the relevant facts: they were not inaccessible to him. His ignorance was of the kind which Aristotle thought was the key to understanding weakness of will: he had the knowledge but did not use it.

The instrumentally self-controlled person, then, is the person who is disposed to think carefully about her actual desires, and about which action would best serve those desires *overall*, in circumstances where those desires are in danger of being forgotten or where a lesser immediate satisfaction beckons bright. In common with many cases of intentional control the instrumentally self-controlled agent is aiming to maximize satisfaction, given the way the world actually is. Once again this kind of self-control need not be connected to the agent's values or to her judgements of desirability. A deep desire for revenge may be best satisfied by a long-term strategy to bring about another's downfall. An agent with such a desire may need to exercise considerable control over her impulses to harm the other here and now, by reminding herself of the disadvantages of precipitous action. She knows that the revenge will be sweeter and more complete if she waits. In this respect she is in control; but in another, more important respect she is not.

The agent who is merely instrumentally self-controlled knows her desires well; she keeps them in view and serves them efficiently. In this respect she is a model of rationality, and beyond criticism by Humean standards. But of course we have seen that there is more to rationality than this: our strongest desires may be completely at odds with our rationally privileged, all-things-considered judgements of desirability. To be controlled by the desire for revenge when you do not *value* revenge is to be a model neither of rationality nor of control. In such cases we will be reluctant to dignify action that is directed solely towards satisfying our strongest desires with the label 'self-control'. The key to this reluctance is that the normative element is on the wrong side of the equation, and obviously so.

It seems that we are happy to count both intentional control and instrumental control as genuine self-control when the actions which display such control are considered in isolation from the agent's values, or when the outcome is that she acts according to her values, or when the outcome is that she acts in ways which do not violate her values. We are less happy to recognize an action as exhibiting self-control at all when such control leads to action which is clearly in direct opposition to that recommended by the agent's judgements of value, for here she does what she may believe she has *no* reason to do. In these cases we tend to say that the agent lacks self-control, despite the fact that she may have displayed a high degree of intentional or instrumental control over her actions, and despite the fact that these other forms of control are sometimes appropriately labelled self-control.

The different forms of control which an agent may exercise over her actions will often be at odds with each other since, for example, acting in accordance with a judgement of desirability may require the circumvention or suppression of the agent's antecedently strongest desire, rather than its satisfaction. In exercising self-control in the service of her values, an agent may fail to behave in an instrumentally rational manner. Or in overcoming some obstacle to intentional action the agent may do what she thinks is all-things-considered undesirable. In these mixed cases there will be no univocal answer to the question, 'Did the agent lose control?' We will have to specify what kind of control we are interested in.

If we think about the various forms of control as forming a hierarchy or pyramid of agent-control, with intentional control at the base, sophisticated instrumental control at the second level, and evaluative self-control at the third level, we will have some grasp of how to go about answering such a question. First we will want to know what kind (or kinds) of control was called for, and second, how the control was exercised. The call for third-tier control—that is, the call to exercise control to bring one's actions into line with one's evaluations —also encompasses those failures at the intentional or instrumental level which in the circumstances threaten the agent's capacity to act according to her values. This makes it proper to describe some cases where failures at the first two levels are overcome as cases of third-tier self-control. What is common to the different kinds of control are certain strategies, techniques, or habits of thought, which in individual cases constitute the exercise of control. These will be discussed in detail below. What is specific to self-control at the third level is that it derives from and expresses the agent's commitment to the rule of reason.

3. Autonomy, Orthonomy, and Self-control

In the last chapter I introduced the Kantian notion of the autonomous agent as the agent who is under the rule of reason and is thus to be distinguished from the individual who is ruled by mere inclination. Kant thought that moral considerations just were rational considerations, so an agent who rejected such considerations could not be fully autonomous. But as we have seen there are different kinds of reasons for action and an agent may be under the rule of one kind of reason, say reasons of self-interest, while rejecting the rational claims of morality. Kantian autonomy is, in any case, to be distinguished here from those notions of autonomy which have more to do with freedom of choice and action than with reason.

(i) Autonomy and self-rule

Gerald Dworkin points out that ' "autonomy" is used . . . sometimes as an equivalent of liberty . . . sometimes as equivalent to self-rule or sovereignty, sometimes as identical with freedom of the will' (1988: 6).[3] It is not my purpose to explore these and other variations in the use of the term in any detail here, though I shall have something to say in a later chapter on the implications of Frankfurtian accounts of freedom of the will. I take it that the idea of self-rule or individual sovereignty underlies our ordinary use of the term. Autonomy is usually seen as the capacity to plan, shape, and direct one's life. Through one's free, considered choices one makes one's life one's own. Autonomy thus makes possible dignity, integrity, and responsibility, though it may not guarantee them.

The basic liberal conception of autonomy shares with the Kantian conception a commitment to the moral sovereignty of the agent. This suggests that a Kantian conception of the intrinsic value of persons underlies liberalism.[4] However, the liberal view of autonomy as the freedom of each agent to form and follow her own conception of the good life can also fit quite comfortably with a sophisticated Humean account of desire and deliberation. According to a Humean account the self-directed agent is not rationally compelled to justify her conception of the good life to others or to take their interests into account. The boundaries of critical scrutiny are, as we have seen, given by her own desire-set.

Freedom and self-direction are also central to an existentialist notion of autonomy, but the existentialist sees freedom as unavoidable and moves from liberal conceptions of the good life as guiding our particular choices to the idea of radical, undetermined choice. Appeals to value or to inclination to guide deliberation and action are equally denials of our freedom and so are in bad faith: Sartre claims that we are not 'provided with

---

[3] Dworkin goes on to point out the wide variety of other ways in which the term is used. It is, he says, 'equated with dignity, integrity, individuality, independence, responsibility, and self-knowledge . . . with qualities of self-assertion, with critical reflection, with freedom from obligation, with absence of external causation, with knowledge of one's own interests. . . . About the only features held constant from one author to another are that autonomy is a feature of persons and that it is a desirable quality to have' (1988: 6). The term is thus useless for our purposes without careful specification of its application.

[4] John Rawls is the most prominent example of a Kantian liberal.

any values or commands that could legitimise our behaviour. Thus we have neither behind us, nor before us in a luminous realm of values, any means of justification or excuse' (Sartre, 1956: 295). He goes on: 'I can neither seek within myself for an authentic impulse to action, nor can I expect, from some ethic, formulae that will enable me to act' (297).

The autonomous existentialist agent acknowledges the fact of her freedom and abandons the false quest for rational justification. In plumping for one option rather than another she creates herself and is wholly responsible for that creation. Free action is the equivalent of a leap of faith, a transcendence of determinism.[5]

Where autonomy is conceived of as self-rule, in either of these ways, its achievement may be a matter solely of intentional or sophisticated instrumental control: the challenges of self-rule may be entirely divorced from broader considerations of desirability. On the Sartrean model, for example, I may need to steel myself to do as I intend but in my efforts to steel myself I cannot have recourse to my reasons for intending this, since there are none beyond the intending itself. The self-directed agent could reject the rule of reason (so far as this is possible while remaining an agent) or, like the Humean, have only a limited conception of the kinds of considerations that are reason-giving, accepting only those that arise from her own desires or interests. An agent may be autonomous in the sense of being self-directed without being autonomous in the Kantian sense. Since the term is applied very widely, I need to find a different term for agents who, in addition to possessing the capacity to plan and direct their lives in the sense allowed by Humeans, accept that at least some of their reasons for action arise independently of desire and persist in the absence of desire and who are capable of acting in accordance with their reasons as they perceive them.

---

[5] Sartre does argue that when we will our own freedom we must necessarily will the freedom of others. If this is right then some Kantian constraints on our particular choices seem to be implied. But the claim that our freedom depends upon the like freedom of others is not compelling when freedom is described in this way.

(ii) Orthonomy

Pettit and Smith (1993) use the term 'orthonomy'. They say that the orthonomous agent is one who is under the rule of the right. The rule of the right can be more or less narrowly conceived. Broad orthonomy is very close to the Kantian conception of autonomy.[6] According to the broad conception, an agent is orthonomous when not only are her desires and actions appropriately responsive to her *beliefs* about what is desirable, but also those very beliefs and desires accord with the facts about what is *truly* desirable: that is, with the facts about what she would stably desire that she do at the ideal limit of information, rational reflection, and dialogue with others. To the extent that we are rational—to the extent, that is, that our goal is to act in accordance with reason—we must want our judgements of desirability to reflect facts about what is truly desirable. The broadly orthonomous agent will thus be appropriately sensitive to evidence that her existing values may be mistaken, and will be resistant to unfounded and capricious value changes.

On a more narrow conception, an agent is orthonomous when her actions are desirable at least by her own lights: when she desires and acts in accordance with her beliefs about what she has most reason to do. Such an agent has orthonomy as her goal but may have false beliefs about what is truly desirable. In these terms self-control at the third level is simply a capacity for narrow orthonomy or, more accurately, strict orthonomy. Since concordance between evaluative beliefs and actual desires might sometimes be merely fortuitous, or have been brought about in the wrong way,[7] it will be useful to distinguish between these two conceptions. Mere narrow orthonomy involves no exercise of self-control, and an agent who is narrowly orthonomous need not be disposed to exercise self-control in situations where her judgements and desires come apart. The strictly orthonomous agent, however, does exercise self-control when tempted. Since this kind of control is

---

[6] Close, but Pettit and Smith may well reject, as I do, the Kantian claim that moral considerations are always rationally overriding.

[7] How this might happen is discussed in detail in the last two chapters.

exercised to bring the agent's actions into line with her view about what is, all things considered, desirable in the circumstances, it demonstrates a more complete capacity for rational agency than either intentional control or instrumental control, and thus earns its elevated position in the hierarchy.

At this point in the discussion, we will be concerned principally with strict orthonomy and with the mechanics of orthonomous self-control. A defence of these mechanics against a charge of paradox will follow, along with an examination of the proper limits of self-control, in the course of which the notion of broad orthonomy will be reintroduced.

4. How is Orthonomous Self-control Exercised?

First, a reminder of when orthonomous self-control is called for. The central case arises when there is a mismatch between an all-things-considered judgement of desirability on the one hand, and the agent's actual strongest desire on the other. Jane believes that under conditions more favourable to reason she would most strongly desire an action other than the one she in fact most strongly desires. Say, for example, she strongly desires to eat a cream cake, though for reasons of health she does not judge it desirable to do so. If she goes ahead and performs the action she deems less desirable, we say she has lost control.

However, losing control in this way is compatible with Jane retaining both intentional and instrumental control over her action. She does not eat the cream cake unintentionally and, though she judges that good health is more desirable than the pleasure to be got from eating cream cakes, she need have no *actual* desire for health to generate any instrumental reason to refrain.[8] I have already noted that some techniques or strategies of control are common between levels, and in my

---

[8] This kind of situation is discussed in Kennett and Smith (1996). Frog and Toad used to have an intrinsic desire for good health, a desire which was lost when they could not attend exercise classes for a while. Nevertheless they retain the belief that good health is more desirable than immediate pleasure.

discussion of these strategies it should be plain enough when this is the case. But, though we may occasionally bring it about that our actions match our values by an act of intentional self-control (as we may suppose I do when I eventually phone Arnie to ask him out, or by a process of instrumental rationality, as, for example, when David finds on reflection that overall his desires are best served by refraining from fried chicken), intentional and instrumental control remain conceptually distinct from orthonomous control. It is this third kind of control which best answers to the common-sense notion of self-control.

There are several ways self-control may be exercised, and some have been foreshadowed in my discussion of intentional control and instrumental control. But *how* we exercise self-control over an unruly desire will depend largely upon *when* we perceive the need for it.

(i) Diachronic Self-control

Suppose Jane knows in advance that come tea-time she will want most to eat a cream cake. In the event, she may *now* be able to act so as to ensure that when the time comes she does not eat a cream cake. There are two central ways in which self-control across time, or *diachronic self-control*, may be exercised.

First, Jane could perhaps do something to block the onset of the desire, such as attending a Weight Watchers meeting or taking an appetite-suppressing pill. Second, if there is no satisfactory way open to her to prevent the desire occurring, she might instead consider structuring her future circumstances so as to ensure that the desire cannot be acted upon, or at least to increase the likelihood that it will not be. So she might exercise self-control by leaving her money at home today so that she cannot go and buy a cake when the craving strikes; or she might raise the cost of satisfying the desire by, for example, undertaking some public action such as a bet.[9] By such means we very often can get our actions to conform to our values.

---

[9] See Jon Elster (1979) on self-binding, and Howard Rachlins (1974) on commitment, for further discussion of this strategy.

The diachronic forms of control have a place in most people's lives, since it is after all simple prudence to plan ahead for the smooth realization of those values and projects which we see as being of continuing importance to us, and such planning may be desirable even when we do not fear any future loss of self-control. Diachronic self-control is also relatively unproblematic for the agent, since the earlier circumstances of action, in which a strategy is put in place, differ significantly from the later circumstances, in which the agent's orthonomy is threatened. Suppose Jane's craving for cake only starts at around tea-time. Before then her desire to eat cake is much weaker than her desire to stick to a healthy diet, just as it should be, given her judgement that a healthy diet is most desirable. That is why her desire to eat cake doesn't defeat her attempt to leave her money at home, or her attempt to attend a Weight Watchers meeting. In giving an account of diachronic self-control, then, we do not have to confront the apparent paradox which Mele (1988) worries is inherent in the notion of self-control.

(ii) Synchronic Self-control

How is it, the question goes, that we can at one and the same time be vulnerable to a loss of control and yet exercise control? What motivates the exercise of self-control? If Jane does not eat the cream cake when tempted, this must surely be explained by a lack of opportunity, or by a greater desire to do something else at that time, i.e. the thing that in the circumstances constitutes self-control. Either way, it appears that Jane's vulnerability was always more apparent than real. She may *believe* she wants the cream cake most but what she *does* gives the lie to her belief. This is a problem for accounts of synchronic self-control; but I will argue that it is the paradox itself, not the exercise of control, which is more apparent than real.

First we should note that not all exercises of self-control involve actions. I will argue that self-control exercised at the time of vulnerability is primarily, and perhaps wholly, a cognitive matter. Sometimes self-control is simply a matter of having the right thoughts at the right time. Now, not all thoughts are actions. It would, I suggest, be overly lavish with desire attribution, as well as counter to common sense, to try to explain each and every thought by insisting that the thinker desired to think it. If the thoughts that in some circumstances constitute self-control are not actions, we are not forced into paradox in offering an account of synchronic self-control. Second, even when the success of an exercise of self-control involves action or depends upon the existence of suitable non-cognitive states in the background we do not need to assume that the desires involved in, or motivating, such an exercise are, individually at least, stronger than the desire over which the agent seeks to exercise control.

How, then, do we exercise synchronic self-control? Synchronic self-control is always in the first instance cognitive, because its exercise is a matter of differential focus of attention. When an agent realizes that her actual desires do not match her judgements of desirability, and that she is therefore in danger of losing control of what she does, there are three ways in which she may focus her attention so as to bring it about that she does as she believes she should. First, she may *restore* the focus of her attention. Second, she may *narrow or redirect* the focus of her attention. Third, she may *expand* the focus of her attention.

Jane has decided that, all things considered, it is most desirable to restrict her intake of fatty foods. Let's suppose that, though she takes all sorts of considerations to be relevant—health, appearance, and, given that she has told everyone that she is going on a diet, the esteem of others—the reason why Jane *actually* makes this judgement is because of considerations of health. Her family has a history of heart disease, and she has been advised that it would be prudent to lose weight. This fact about her judgement may be captured counterfactually as follows. Had sticking to her diet not promised to contribute to her appearance, or to esteem in the eyes of others, but only to improvement in her health, then Jane would still have thought it desirable to diet. But if health had required her to put on weight instead, though appearance and perhaps even the esteem of others (given the widespread idealization of slimness in our society) had still required her to diet, then Jane would have thought it most desirable to gain weight, rather than to diet.

Now, let's suppose that around tea-time the strength of Jane's desire to eat cake does not match the value she attaches to that activity; and that the reason for this mismatch is that her desire to eat cream cakes increases at tea-time, ending up stronger than it should be. As tea-time nears Jane finds herself thinking more and more of cream cakes: their delicious taste and texture, the creaminess, the smoothness, the sweetness of the crumbs and the sticky icing. These thoughts tend to crowd out thoughts of health, and her desire for cream cake intensifies. Here it is plain that Jane is vulnerable to a loss of control and, given her state, it is easy to imagine her going down to the cafeteria and buying a cake.

However, we can also imagine her not being led astray by her refractory desire, since Jane knows that her eating cream cakes is not all-things-considered desirable. If she restores the original focus of her attention, and thinks again about health and diet and the undesirability of eating cream cakes, Jane may yet succeed in acting orthonomously.

For example, Jane might refocus her attention on the desire to eat cream cakes, and remind herself of how irrational it is for her to desire to eat cream cakes so much when doing so is not correspondingly desirable. Very often, irrational desires will shrink in response to such reprimands. Fear, anger, jealousy, and the like are particularly susceptible to reprimand when they lack a proper object. We remind ourselves that this is just a film, or that it is only the breeze blowing in the trees and not a burglar, or that this widget is an inanimate object and not a sneering enemy. When they work, such reminders or reprimands bring about self-control.

In the same vein, Jane might refocus her attention onto her original reasons for coming to her evaluative conclusion. She can make those reasons more salient by considering them more extensively. She might remind herself of the importance of health, and of the contribution made by diet to health; she might imagine more vividly the discomfort of being overweight, the restrictions that ill-health would place on her activities, and the emotional burden on her family if she were to become ill.

If her desire for cream cakes wanes as it should in the face of her reflections, and her desire for health increases, she successfully exercises self-control. For many agents the effect of such reminders and rehearsal of their reasons *is* salutary. Perhaps they may serve to arouse or to quiet a pre-existing desire; equally they may engender new, rationally mandated desires. Either way, such reflections make it possible for the agent's values to resume centre stage, and for the appropriate desires to be more salient, so that desires are realigned with values.

However, though this technique is often successful, it would be a mistake to suppose that it always is. Sometimes we have desires that are insensitive to negative evaluation, or which fail to re-engage with our reasons after those reasons have resumed their proper place in our thoughts, and so we remain vulnerable to a loss of control. Fortunately, when returning the focus of our attention to our reasons is ineffective, or likely to be unsuccessful, other techniques of control are available.

Jane's problem is that her considered judgement, that health is more important than the pleasure to be got from eating cream cakes, does not in the circumstances engender a desire for health strong enough to overcome her excessive desire for cream cakes. Let's suppose further that restoring the focus of her attention to her reasons fails to redress the imbalance between her desires. Nevertheless we can imagine her regaining control. When the craving strikes, rather than continuing to think of cream cakes, she may simply narrow the focus of her attention so as to block out all such thoughts. Perhaps she thinks only of whatever it is that she happens to be doing, concentrating minutely on the movements of her fingers at the keyboard as she works, or the pounding of her feet on the pavement and the beating of her heart as she jogs her way to fitness. Alternatively, she may redirect her attention more radically: perhaps she does not consider her range of reasons for eating or not eating cream cakes, she just turns away from the whole subject and thinks of something else instead, say, a film she has seen recently, or the problems of a friend.

By such means Jane may occupy her mind until the craving passes, so remaining in control. This too is a widely recognized technique of self-control. Women giving birth have been taught to breathe in a certain way during contractions. This does not lessen the pain, but concentrating minutely on breathing techniques turns one's attention away from the pain, and so makes it more bearable. Similarly, runners may deal with stitch, breathlessness, and feelings of weakness that might incline them to give up by simply not thinking about them. They run mechanically, their minds on something else: spending imaginary lottery winnings, perhaps.

The methods of self-control so far outlined are distinctly cognitive. Jane's exercise of self-control seems to be largely a matter of her entertaining or excluding certain thoughts at the appropriate time. The *effectiveness* of having these thoughts may sometimes, to be sure, depend upon there being an appropriate non-cognitive state in the background; for example, a desire for health which is in danger of being overlooked when thoughts of cream cake are especially salient. Reminding ourselves of the existence of these desires is the very stuff of instrumental control, and this is sometimes the best and most obvious way of remaining orthonomous. Yet, though the desires are there in the background, thinking of them or not thinking of them is what is important here, and that is, of course, entirely cognitive. The thought need not itself be motivated by a further non-cognitive state. And in cases where we redirect our thoughts, or narrow the focus of our attention, it is not clear that any desires need to be postulated in the background. What we have is perhaps best described as a cognitive habit with certain triggering conditions; in the case of orthonomous self-control, this might simply amount to noticing that our judgements of value and our desires are out of alignment and so we are in danger of doing what we believe we have less or no reason to do.[10] Certainly the aim of teaching

[10] We can of course imagine agents employing these techniques for purposes other than self-control. Someone might try to evade uncomfortable feelings of guilt by counting stitches or watching a movie instead of reflecting on their actions. Jane might turn her thoughts away from what she is doing as she walks downstairs and stands in the queue to buy a cream cake. What

these techniques of self-control to agents is that they become automatic, and they can be very effective: we can easily imagine Jane getting into the habit of focusing on the movement of her fingers on the keyboard whenever the craving for cream cakes begins.

With this technique too, however, Jane may be unsuccessful, and the reason is perhaps obvious. Some recalcitrant desires are simply so salient that nothing will remove the associated thoughts from the agent's mind. Jane's desire for cream cakes may be such that she is literally unable to stop thinking about them come tea-time. If Jane is to exercise self-control under these circumstances, it may require more from her than a redirection of her attention. It may require a more active manipulation of her desires, and an explicitly foregrounded commitment to acting on her reasons as she sees them.

(iii) Expansion, Aggregation, and Commitment

Suppose Jane, having failed to remove thoughts of cream cakes from her mind, is queuing up to buy a cream cake at tea-time, and that behind her are two of her friends who will see what she buys. Now, we know that besides valuing health, Jane also values the esteem of her friends and, let us say, desires their esteem to a corresponding extent. In this situation, Jane's desire to be thought well of combined with her somewhat weak desire for health may be sufficient to deter her from buying the cream cake.

Note that Jane need not think that the esteem of her friends is any part of what makes it desirable to diet. She might think that what makes it desirable is simply the fact that dieting will contribute to health. But if her desire to be thought well of by her friends leads her, in a context in which her desire for health is too weak to move her all the way to action, to do what she

marks a use of these techniques as an exercise of orthonomous self-control is (i) that the trigger for the employment of them was the agent's realization that she was vulnerable to a loss of orthonomous control, that she is about to do what she believes, all things considered, she has less or no reason to do, and (ii) that she *justifies* her use of the techniques by reference to her all-things-considered judgement.

judges it independently desirable to do, then Jane will have reason to be glad that she desires the esteem of her friends.

It is of course fortuitous that Jane acted in the manner prescribed by her values on this occasion. It might have been extremely uncommon that anyone she knew was standing in the queue; sheer chance, then, that her desire to be thought well of was activated. Besides, though Jane does the right thing on this occasion, surely she does it for the wrong reasons. Remember that McDowell argues that for an action to count as manifesting a value, the concern articulated in the judgement of value must

exhaust the agent's reason for acting as he does. It would disqualify an action from counting as a manifestation of kindness if its agent needed some extraneous incentive to compliance with the requirement—say, the rewards of a good reputation. (1979: 332)

Jane's refraining from cream cakes on this occasion appears to have nothing to do with the value she attaches to health as such, so why call it an exercise of self-control in the service of her values?

Perhaps in the situation as described there is no exercise of self-control, but situations like this serve to remind us that very often we have more than one reason to do what we deem most desirable; and we may quite deliberately conscript our extra reasons in the service of self-control. McDowell's restriction on motivation seems unjustified. Michael Stocker for one argues that 'it is not within human reason to achieve goals without means, nor without means that are merely means' (Stocker, 1990: 62). According to Stocker the use of mere means is no bar, as such, to achieving the good, and this is just what I wish to argue with regard to the employment of our own motives as indirect means to our legitimate ends. If we focus on such additional reasons and desires as we have *because* we know that we will need an extra incentive to move us all the way to the valued action, this is an exercise of orthonomous self-control.

Here is how it works. Let us consider two cases where different values are at stake: Jane's case, and a friendship in which it is practically urgent that the agent act as a friend should, or her friend will suffer, and their very relationship will be undermined. Individual decisions made in the keeping of a diet are rarely this urgent, since (perhaps unfortunately) the rational agent knows that eating a cream cake *this time* is not going to make a noticeable difference to her weight or her health. However, to take the dieting case first, Jane may indeed look to the other reasons that she has for refusing cream cake. There is the good opinion of her friends, and her desire to be fashionably slim. It may occur to her that by denying herself the cream cake she could spend the money saved on her favourite charity or on a new book. Though perhaps none of these considerations taken alone would have sufficient motivational clout to move her to action, taken together they provide the incentive Jane needs. Her too weak desire for health is bolstered by these further unrelated desires, which her deliberations uncover or create, and so she does as she should.

Jane's exercise of self-control through expansion and aggregation of her motives is not wholly cognitive, since it depends both upon her finding additional reasons to act in the ways that she values, and on those reasons engaging desires of an appropriate or at least a sufficient strength. So it depends upon the presence of some appropriate non-cognitive states in the background. While this means that a successful exercise of self-control may be contingent upon the agent having an adequate range of interests, values, and desires, it is hardly fortuitous that she does. It will be a rare agent indeed who has no such resources to call upon in situations where she faces a loss of orthonomous control.[11] In such situations it is not only acceptable that she call upon these resources, it may even be required that she do so; that is, reason may strongly support her doing so.

Suppose, for example, that my friend urgently needs my help, and suppose further that, though I do indeed value my friend and judge that I ought to take immediate steps to help her, I simply fail to have the rush of warm concern and desire to help that usually motivates me on these occasions. There is a

---

[11] McDowell's moral agents may find themselves in this unfortunate position.

yawning gap between the deliberative weight I attach to helping her and the strength of my direct desire to do so. Perhaps
I am tired and stressed from a difficult day at work; I have a
headache and the only desire that is salient is the desire to lie
down in a dark room. Contemplating the good of friendship
in an attempt to restore my motivation to what it should be
is beyond me right now. Yet it is clear that I should help my
friend, and that not to do so in these circumstances would be
reprehensible in the extreme.

Now, of course my friend would prefer that I act out of
warm concern for her. I might prefer that too: I will be
understandably reluctant to own that I had to search around
for additional incentives or that I acted from a joyless sense
of obligation on this occasion. But friendship, like many other
values, can require certain actions from us no matter how we
feel. When we hold such a value, we take it to offer us reasons
for acting which are importantly distinct from our desires of
the moment. To make the connection with action, though, we
must work with the desires of the moment. So getting ourselves
to act may require us to search through the other reasons and
motives that we have, or can create, to find something, however irrelevant, to give motivational support to the valued action.
This is not, or not necessarily, an exercise of instrumental rationality, since it may not maximize satisfaction. If my judgement
concerning which action was required had been different, I might
have had to marshal a very different collection of desires. My
concern here is not in maximal satisfaction but in doing as I
judge I ought to do.

If we insist on motivational purity at such a point, we may
well find ourselves motivationally impotent.[12] Commitment to
a value brings with it a willingness to work on our motivation,
and to make explicit use of the motivational resources available to us. Our commitment to our friends will be wishy-washy
if it does not prepare us to scrape up other motives to get

---

[12] Kant also stresses motivational purity in his insistence that an action
with moral worth must be done from the motive of duty alone. Herman (1981)
allows that other, co-operating motives may be present but argues that the
motive of duty must be sufficient for the performance of the worthy action.
So I depart from both Kant and McDowell here.

ourselves over the line when the customary desires of friendship fail us, as fail they might in many quite ordinary circumstances. But just what does this talk of commitment amount to? What is it over and above the holding of the value itself, which in this case yields the belief or judgement that it is most desirable that I help my friend? What motivates my search for extra reasons, if it is not a desire to help my friend? And if it is this desire that motivates me, doesn't this show, contrary to the assumptions we have been making, that the desire to help my friend is not too weak—that it is indeed my strongest desire? We seem to have run headlong into paradox.

Here too I argue that the paradox is more apparent than real. What prompts my search, my scraping around for additional incentives, is not a simple first-order desire to help my friend. Its source is, of course, the disposition spoken of in the previous chapter: the constitutive concern we have *qua* rational agent to act on our reasons as we see them. It seems that, in so far as I am rational, I will desire to do whatever I judge it is most desirable to do, whether or not I succeed in directly desiring the action concerned for its own sake.

The role of this rational disposition, then, is to bring it about that the agent performs the action she judges she has most reason to perform. And as we have seen, there are usually several ways in which this may be achieved. Most of the time the desire to do whatever we believe we have most reason to do remains in the background, but it may be explicitly foregrounded to forestall what the agent believes is an imminent loss of self-control. When I realize that I just don't want to go rushing out into the night to be at my friend's side, *and* that rushing out is just what I believe I have most reason to do, the dissonance between the two invokes my constitutive concern that I act in accordance with my reasons.

It is doubtful that an explanation of the efficacy of the desire to do what I believe I have most reason to do needs to rest on a claim that it must at some point be the agent's single strongest desire. My desire to complete my work is not always stronger than my desire to watch television; nevertheless it is often strong enough to spoil the pleasure I would otherwise take in watching television. The desire to act in accordance with reason can be active while being weaker than some other desire. It can work in two ways. First, when foregrounded it may be sufficient, combined with my somewhat weak desire for the valued end, to get me over the line. Second, it can work through a snowball effect, collecting and aggregating the additional desires uncovered or stimulated by reflection until the agent's overall disposition to act in the way required by her values is stronger than any of her lone dispositions to act in other ways.[13]

The point might nevertheless be pressed that if I engage in a search for additional motives *instead of* performing the disvalued action I have not escaped paradox, for the desire to do *that* must be stronger than the desire, say, to eat cream cakes. I have already argued that not all thoughts are actions and those thoughts which constitute an exercise of self-control which are not actions evade paradox. But, given that *some* thoughts may be considered actions, motivated by the desire to act in accordance with reason, I need to say a bit more on how such actions can constitute synchronic self-control. Mele (1997) points out, and I have already acknowledged, that we can act on more than one desire at a time. Now the actions which constitute the loss of self-control, say buying and eating the cream cake, take time. There is nothing to stop Jane from trying to find any additional reasons she has for refraining from cream cakes at the very same time as, acting on her then-strongest desire for cream cake, she makes her way to the cafeteria. If, by the time she gets there, her desire to buy and eat a cream cake has been weakened or outweighed by further reflection and aggregation of opposing motives, so that she buys a piece of fruit instead of the cake, she has successfully exercised synchronic self-control.

---

[13] When I talk of aggregation here I am not suggesting that the agent forms a single complex desire, say to listen to music and eat chocolate while in the bath, or, to use an example of Alfred Mele's, to think of frogs' legs while eating cookies (Mele 1997: 120). These would be agglomerated desires, as Mele terms them, and it would indeed often be puzzling why anyone would form single desires with those particular contents. I am talking of desires the agent notices are conjointly satisfiable and suggesting that what is aggregated or totalled is not the desires themselves but the motivational push to follow a certain course or plan of action which promises to satisfy those several desires.

The actions which on occasion constitute self-control may also take time to be effective. Perhaps my desire for a quiet night is not immediately overridden by the combination of my weak desire to help my friend plus my constitutive desire to do what I judge I have most reason to do. Initially I remain slumped in my chair, but while sitting there I purposefully reflect on the additional reasons I have for leaving the house and travelling across town to her place. If I succeed in uncovering or creating sufficient aggregate motivation to visit my friend, and do so, I have exercised control over a desire which was present and strongest *at the very time* at which I undertook the exercise. This deserves to be called synchronic self-control.[14] There is no paradox in explaining the operation of self-control in this way.

How secure is the capacity for self-control so described? It might be argued that an agent may have a rogue second-order desire to act in opposition to her first-order judgements of value, and this may work in much the same snowballing fashion on first-order desires as the rational disposition I have described. Rogue desires may arise out of the blue at any level, and so we may be subject to weakness and loss of control at any level. However, the kind of commitment I have been talking about is systematically derived from an appreciation of our normative reasons *qua* reasons. So it should, in Frankfurt's words, ' "resound" throughout the potentially endless array of higher orders' (Frankfurt, 1971: 91).[15]

[14] This constitutes some revision of my views in Kennett and Smith (1997). I thought, initially, that actional self-control, as described by Mele (1997), was really a form of diachronic self-control, since, in the example given by Mele, Frog and Toad did continue to eat cookies until their thoughts of cookies as frogs' legs effectively reduced their desire for cookies. So they did lose control at the time. It now seems to me that the closer the proximity to action the harder it is to draw a clear line between synchronic and diachronic self-control. And not much may hang on it. In the two examples I have given the disvalued action (eating cream cakes) was not performed and the valued action (visiting the friend) was performed in spite of very present danger.

[15] There is however no connection between commitment and rationality in Frankfurt. Commitment is a matter of decisive identification with a first-order desire for Frankfurt, but the notion of decisive identification is left unanalysed, and could well amount to just plumping in Sartrean fashion for one alternative over the others.

Of course such commitment is not a matter of our happening to have second-order desires with which we then 'decisively identify', as one reading of Frankfurt seems to suggest; rather, reflective endorsement of some policy or action attracts our constitutive desire to do what we believe we have most reason to do. The iteration of this desire has some rational guarantee.[16] By comparison, other higher-order desires that might compete to determine our first-order dispositions look very much like loose cannons. They are unlikely to recur with any regularity, and so will themselves most often be susceptible to control from one level higher. The agent with a rational commitment to acting on her values is therefore not in much danger of being ambushed by wayward desire at some higher level. Her capacity for self-control is robust: she is for the most part strictly orthonomous. An agent without such a commitment needs a far greater degree of moral luck to remain even narrowly orthonomous.

5. *Broad Orthonomy and the Limits of Self-control*

Self-control is a good thing to have. It enables us to match our actions with our judgements on many occasions when the strength of our desires does not perfectly match our assessments of desirability. But it is not an unqualified good. An agent who has, in addition to her values, a rational commitment to acting on those values is not yet under the rule of the right, for those values might themselves be unreasonable. A more thoroughgoing commitment to the rule of reason is required to maintain broad orthonomy. But broadly orthonomous agents need not always display strict orthonomy: it is possible to be too self-controlled.

An agent who is broadly orthonomous certainly values *doing* whatever she believes it is desirable or valuable that she do, and this will often motivate the exercise of self-control. But

---

[16] Although the constitutive desire that I should do whatever I judge it is most desirable that I do is first-order, I can of course derive this second-order desire that I desire that I desire to do whatever it is, etc.

the orthonomous agent needs to be equally concerned about getting those beliefs right. This rationally mandated concern directs us to pay attention to those features of a situation that would play a justificatory role in any reason-giving exercise.

Now, it is apparent that our judgements of value will not always accord with the facts about what it is most valuable to do in the circumstances. We know that we may be mistaken in these matters as in anything else; and, as we have seen from a discussion of McDowell, feelings of certainty can be an unreliable guide to virtue. Broadly orthonomous agents will therefore display a degree of humility about their judgements of value. They will remain open to reflective revision in the light of various kinds of evidence that they may be mistaken. And one kind of evidence of evaluative error comes from our sympathies. Sometimes our apparently recalcitrant desires and affective responses to situations stand as indicators of what is really valuable, rather than as cues for the exercise of self-control. As such, they may rightly prompt us to re-examine our position and our evaluative conclusions.

This is the lesson to be learned from the examples given by Jonathan Bennett (1974). Both Heinrich Himmler and Huckleberry Finn experienced conflict between their judgements of value and their sympathies. Himmler saw his sympathies as providing no occasion to review his belief that it was necessary to purge Europe of its Jewish population, while Huck lacked access to the kinds of arguments that might, in his own eyes, have justified his unwillingness to return Jim to slavery. Yet in each case we think that it was their sympathies rather than their evaluative judgements which tracked the correct values —the values which could ideally be justified to others—and so we think that Himmler's rigid self-control, his capacity for strict orthonomy, was in the circumstances a bad thing, while Huck's lack of control was a good thing.

Now of course wayward motives are not always reliable indicators that our judgements are in error. Indeed, they are often properly countered by an exercise of self-control. It is not always immediately clear from the data provided by our sympathies, for example, whether we should revise or resist (Bennett,

1974: 133; McIntyre, 1990: 380–1).[17] Therefore, since the cues which signal the need for revision of values can be phenomenologically very close to those which signal the need to exercise self-control, an otherwise laudable openness to love and sympathy may render agents somewhat vulnerable to losses of control. In being the kind of people who are, in Bennett's words, sensitive to the prick of sympathy, we run the risk of not always resisting when we should. However, this is a price worth paying. Given that none of us is omniscient about value, our experiences of conflict, with the resultant uncertainty and occasional loss of control, earn their keep by making moral progress and moral discovery possible.

Consider, by contrast to an openness wrought of sympathy and humility, the character of the person who is over-concerned with exercising self-control. First, it is apparent that the person who takes the exercise of *diachronic* self-control to extremes, and structures her life and her character so as to avoid any situation where she will be vulnerable to a loss of control, closes off the possibility of evaluative discovery and revision. Such an agent is likely to lead a restricted and impoverished existence, devoid of spontaneity, short on surprises, and short on the kinds of contacts and experiences which might lead to reflection and revision. This may be intended on the part of the person who relies so heavily on the self-binding techniques discussed earlier; but it is hardly ideal, and might indeed amount to a reckless disregard of reason. Where this mode of self-control is embedded, it bespeaks either narrowness and rigidity of character, or an unhealthy timidity and lack of trust towards oneself and the future. While the strategies which constitute diachronic self-control are handy to have in a tight spot, too much self-binding reduces the chances of the agent attaining a broader orthonomy.

Second, it can be argued that *synchronic* self-control too can be taken to extremes, both in general and on particular occasions, to the detriment of the agent concerned. The earnest

---

[17] Bennett (1974: 124) points out that sometimes it is right to resist pressure from our sympathies, such as when we restrain a frightened child for a necessary inoculation. At other times such pressures should lead to revision.

person who exhaustively searches through her reasons on each and every occasion (no matter how trivial) that her judgements are vulnerable to a motivational deficiency also fails to realize important values in her life, for example spontaneity, and might readily be accused of excessive seriousness—of lacking a sense of proportion about the importance of her own activities. There is a desirable mean of self-control which such a person fails to realize.

Even when the matter at stake *is* serious and significant, however, and self-control seems emphatically called for, there are situations in which the exercise of such control would be inappropriate. Suppose for example that your all-things-considered judgement is that you should tell the truth, but by doing so you know you will disadvantage your friend, so you are reluctant to speak out. You are so reluctant, in fact, that you are not sure you will be able to do it—unless, that is, you focus on your vengeful dislike for another person who will also be damaged by your disclosures. If you don't call upon your dislike for this person, you may not be able to perform the action that you believe is required of you. Nevertheless, you ought to decline to be influenced by such motives. A person of good character will run the risk of losing control rather than call upon some positively dishonourable or disgraceful motive which would, even so, have given support to the action recommended by her deliberative judgement.[18]

It might be argued at this point that, if all of the above is granted, the *worth* of self-control, as the capacity for strict

---

[18] There are other occasions, too, where it would be better not to exercise self-control. Sometimes when the personal cost of exercising self-control is very high, it will be rational just to revise our judgements about what we should do. For example, it might be that I could exercise sufficient self-control to get myself on a plane, rather than a train, to go to a conference in Sydney; and given that I acknowledge my fear of flying to be without rational foundation, maybe that is what I should do. But it might not be worth the stress, or the sheer terror, that such an exercise would cause me. Given the costs involved, it is rational for me not to attempt self-control in this instance. I should rather revise my judgement and take the train instead. Naturally, the appropriateness of this decision depends on the purpose of my trip. If my mother is gravely ill, there is no case for me to revise my judgement; I am straightforwardly weak if I take the train when it is practically urgent that I fly.

orthonomy, is exceedingly limited. If broad orthonomy is what is important, perhaps we should give up being concerned about developing our capacities for self-control and focus solely on getting the right values in place. For surely the broadly orthonomous agent is neither especially vulnerable to a loss of self-control nor prone to exercise it inappropriately. Such agents are sensitive to and motivated by the reasons that there are. Self-control, it might be said, is precisely *not* an issue for agents under the rule of the right. But this seems to me to be mistaken. It is to revert to a McDowellian conception of moral motivation and its relation to virtue. The truth is that even people of good character and irreproachable values will at times need to exercise self-control in order to act in accordance with their reflective judgements of value.

There are two reasons for this. First, as we have noted, reflective agents revise their values when they find good reason to do so. But motivation often (and understandably) lags behind such value revision. Imagine that a member of Greenpeace comes to visit, and, in the course of a long and reasoned discussion, convinces you that the planet is in a precarious state, and that we must all do everything we can to lessen the deleterious impact of our activities on the environment. You hadn't thought much about it before, but now it is plain to you that it is desirable, for example, that you walk to the local shops and to work instead of taking the car. But you are in the habit of taking the car, so walking is bound to seem inconvenient at first. The strength of your desire to walk doesn't yet match your new judgement about the desirability of walking as a way of getting around; and there are some residual hankerings for a lifestyle which is dependent on the careless consumption of fossil fuels, which you now repudiate. In this kind of situation even conscientious agents, who normally find that their motivations march in step with their values, are vulnerable to a loss of self-control, and may need to make use of some strategy for self-control if they are to conform their actions to their revised judgement.

The second reason is that the *pro tanto* nature of justificatory reasons means that, in many situations, there will be several outcomes or actions that the agent has reason to desire, and it may be a close call between them.[19] A judgement is made, but the closeness of the competing desires may require a conscious exercise of self-control to ensure that it gets acted upon. If the agent is not sufficiently alert to her reasons, there is the risk that a particularly salient desire may lead to action outside of judgement. This is a risk that we *all* face, and that people of good character face up to. We all of us have a special responsibility to know ourselves: to know how our reasons and motives may vary over circumstances, to know what circumstances we are likely to face, and to know what strategies are available to overcome inevitable variations in, and discrepancies between, reason and desire. Orthonomous agents are deliberately alert to their range of reasons and to the motivational implications of these reasons. This very alertness is both an important aspect of self-control and, on occasion, a cue for value revision.

While there will be occasions, then, when the exercise of self-control comes at too high a price, it is not usually an inappropriate, or even an inferior, response to the recognition that a particular action is required by some value that we hold, since experiencing the need to exercise it is often the inevitable concomitant of a very proper sensitivity to plural concerns and values.

6. Conclusion

In this chapter I have been concerned, first, to mark out and distinguish between three levels of agent-control; second, to tackle practical questions about how and when self-control is to be exercised; and third, to deal with some normative questions about the virtues and proper limits of self-control. A range of questions remain, however. I have not yet considered the role the various forms of agent-control play in the allocation

---

[19] A pluralist conception of value, such as I have been supporting, must conceive of the possibility that in some, perhaps many, situations there will be no unique best action or outcome. As Susan Wolf points out, 'the pluralist believes that the plurality of morally significant values is not subject to a complete rational ordering' (1992: 785).

of moral responsibility, and I have barely touched upon the difference between an agent who lacks self-control altogether, and the agent who possesses the capacity for self-control but fails to exercise it. It is scepticism about this distinction that has led certain philosophers to assimilate weakness of will to compulsion. I believe, however, that the analysis given here promises to set the intuitive distinction between weakness and compulsion on firm ground; and a tripartite distinction between recklessness, weakness, and compulsion should make possible a fruitful account of the conditions of moral responsibility. To make these distinctions and apply them to questions about the responsibility of agents for their wrongful acts will be the task of the next two chapters.

6

Moral Failures and Moral Responsibility: Recklessness, Weakness, Compulsion

The common-sense distinctions between recklessness, weakness, and compulsion which were set out at the beginning of this book are historically contentious. Although some philosophers, notably Socrates and McDowell, themselves have difficulty accounting for compulsive behaviour, their focus has typically been on weakness of will. The tendency has been to assimilate weakness to either recklessness or compulsion.

So, for instance, the Socratic view is that weakness should be assimilated to recklessness. Taking it for granted that no one intentionally acts in a way which is contrary to their better judgement, these theorists argue that the weak agent, rather than lacking anything in the way of self-control, must really be suffering from some sort of evaluation illusion. Like the reckless agent, the weak agent takes insufficient care in coming to a practical judgement, and so falls into judging to be best the course of action which she usually judges to be worse. The difference, if there is one, can only be that the reckless agent, unlike the weak agent, may have no history of good judgement on the matter at stake to contrast with her present poor judgement.

On the other side there is the view, put most convincingly by Gary Watson (1977), that weakness should be assimilated to compulsion. Watson acknowledges that the weak agent need not be suffering from any illusion. She may clear-headedly judge the course of action she fails to pursue as better than the one she actually pursues. But, seeing no way in which someone who has the capacity for self-control could fail to exercise it, Watson goes on to argue that she must really lack self-control, and really be unable to do otherwise than she does. Watson thinks that, at the time of the relevant action at least, the weak agent, like the compulsive agent, lacks the capacity for self-control.

I believe that these attacks on the common-sense distinctions are mistaken. The earlier distinction between normative and motivating reasons, and the account of evaluation given in Chapter 4, show that it is possible to act intentionally contrary to our judgements of value, so ruling out the assimilation of weakness to recklessness. The account of self-control given in Chapter 5 makes it possible to defend the ordinary view that those who have the capacity for self-control do not always exercise it. The weak-willed person, unlike the compulsive, has, but fails to exercise, the capacity for self-control at the time of action, and this has clear implications for the allocation of moral responsibility to weak agents. Recklessness on the other hand is characterized by failures at the level of judgement, rather than by failures of control, though reckless agents may happen also to be dispositionally weak or compulsive. I shall argue that reckless agents are either culpably ignorant of good reasons, or else unduly self-centred and indifferent to good reasons.

In this chapter, then, I first explore the nature of recklessness, weakness, and compulsion and refine my account of the distinctions between them. It should become apparent that, though at the periphery weakness shades into recklessness or compulsion, the central cases of each kind of failing are distinct. My second task is to show how these distinctions underwrite a common-sense account of moral responsibility.

1. The Compulsive Agent

Gary Watson (1977) suggests that the mark of a compulsive desire is its capacity to motivate the agent contrary to her judgements of the worth of her actions. He worries however that, if this is a sufficient condition of compulsive motivation, then weakness of will is just a species of compulsion; for weak agents too are motivated by desires which run counter to their judgements of value. Watson goes on to suggest that the desires of the compulsively motivated agent are too strong, in the following sense: even if such an agent possessed ordinary skills of resistance, these would not be enough to counter the recalcitrant desire. But he thinks the same is not true of weak-willed agents, who are culpable precisely because they do not possess those ordinary capacities for resistance and control 'which we hold each other responsible for acquiring and maintaining' (Watson, 1977: 332).

Let's put aside Watson's account of weakness of will for the moment. His account of compulsion seems to me to be substantially correct, at least for the central cases, though underdescribed. I too want to argue that the distinguishing mark of a compulsive desire is its imperviousness to certain techniques of control. However, and this constitutes a slight correction of Watson's view, it is neither necessary nor sufficient that compulsive motivation be contrary to the agent's actual practical judgements, though that is usually how such desires are revealed as compulsive for the agent.

According to common sense, the agent who is compelled could not have done otherwise. She simply had no capacity for control over the actions in question. But what does this amount to? We have seen that there are various levels of control which agents may exercise over their actions, and that they may exercise that control either diachronically (that is, in advance of the situation in which they believe their control would be threatened), or synchronically (that is, at the moment of vulnerability). It is not required that an agent fail in all aspects of control before her actions are considered compulsive, however: some capacity for control is compatible with the ordinary notion of compulsion. In particular, such an agent may be perfectly instrumentally rational in pursuing a compulsively desired end. We need to be more precise about which kinds of lapses count as compulsion.

The loss of intentional control sometimes signals compulsion. People paralysed by fear or shyness may be literally unable to do anything that counts as intentional action when accosted by those sensations. Phobic behaviour, though not usually explicable in terms of the comparative strength of the agent's desires, should therefore count as compulsive. However, most compulsive behaviour is performed intentionally, in accordance with a desire of the agent concerned. These are the cases we will concentrate upon.

A drug addict may act both intentionally and efficiently in procuring and consuming the drug of her choice. And, given that it is possible to value one's own addiction, she may display narrow orthonomy in so acting. What she judges most desirable is also what she desires most to do. What makes it the case, then, that her desire to consume drugs is compulsive? This will depend on the truth of certain counterfactuals. If the agent had judged that drug-taking was not desirable, would her desire to take drugs have diminished in response? If not, was there any technique of self-control available that would have enabled her to resist her desire to take drugs?

If our answer to both these questions is negative, if it is apparent that there was no effective strategy of control available, or that its use would have been too difficult in the circumstances, then we may conclude that the agent was in fact compelled in her drug-taking activities. But it is essential that we consult the counterfactuals before making such a judgement. The mere fact that a desire is strong tells us little, as it is apparent that people may pursue ends which they desire very strongly without us feeling in the least inclined to judge their pursuit compulsive. The ordinary notion of a compulsive desire is of a desire whose strength is literally irresistible: that is, it is both disproportionately high relative to the agent's other desires, and largely, if not completely, independent of the agent's judgements of value, even if it does not always conflict with them.

Let us develop this notion of irresistibility a little more. The account of synchronic self-control given above allows us to make sense of an idea that some have found incoherent (e.g. Feinberg, 1970*b*: 282). First, the irresistible desire is usually so phenomenologically salient that the agent just cannot stop thinking about it. It may be such as to defy any strategy aimed at distraction and redirection of attention. So in this sense it forces itself upon the agent. Second, its causal strength must be largely or completely insensitive to such negative evaluation as the agent may make in the course of trying to exercise self-control. The stereotypical compulsive desires are impervious to reason. Third, even if the agent rationally values acting in accordance with her judgements of value, and so tries to marshal such other desires as she can find by thinking of additional reasons for acting in the way recommended by her values, these together will still not outweigh the desire in question. The gap in strength between the compulsive desire and the rest cannot be bridged by her at this time. The desire is thus impervious to exercises of control. It is quite literally overwhelming, and the agent acts out of compulsion.

An irresistible desire is not defined by its content. While the desire to consume drugs is the kind of desire commonly cited in discussions of compulsion, any desire may become compulsive. It is an open question, for example, whether Davidson's action in getting out of bed to brush his teeth, though he judges it would be better not to, is a case of weakness, as he imagines, or of compulsion (Davidson, 1969: 101–2). His desire to brush his teeth satisfies the first two criteria: he apparently cannot stop thinking about it, and it is impervious to reason. But we do not know enough about the agent's psychology in this case to judge whether the gap between the weight he attaches to his deliberative judgement and the strength of his desire could be bridged by other desires more in tune with his judgement. What we do know is that if a desire is compulsive, no attempt by the agent at synchronic self-control will be successful. We tend to rely on evidence provided by the agent's behaviour over time in coming to the judgement that his actions are compelled. If the agent persistently chooses some sincerely disvalued end, and is impervious to reason and distraction when the object of desire is available, we have good grounds for thinking that he does not exercise self-control, at least in part because he cannot.

However, an agent may still be able to exercise diachronic self-control to thwart a compulsive desire. My idea of a compulsive desire is of a desire that is irresistible when it is upon us: that is, impervious to attempts at synchronic self-control. But it need not be ever-present. As we have seen, an agent may take various steps to block the onset of a disvalued desire, or to make it difficult or impossible to act upon the desire. The alcoholic may put a time lock on the liquor cabinet and go to an AA meeting. Even an agent whose desires are compulsive may have some capacity for orthonomous action (that is, action in accordance with reason) with respect to such desires. These agents may therefore have to bear some responsibility for actions performed under the press of irresistible desire.

2. The Weak-willed Agent

Common sense assumes that the weak agent has, but fails to exercise, the capacity for self-control. This is the view I will defend. Though there is a spectrum of weak behaviour which, at one extreme, shades into compulsion, this assumption is central. When we chide someone for breaking her resolution to quit smoking, or indeed when we reproach ourselves for failing to get out of bed when the alarm goes off for that early morning swim, we assume that she and we could have done otherwise. Whatever the temptations of the warm bed or the cigarettes, we think that it was, at that time, open to us to take the course of action we most valued. Of course, we may be wrong in the particular assessment that we make, particularly in the case of other people's actions; but equally we may be right in it. I suggest that there is nothing fundamentally misconceived about making such assessments.

It is not, or not merely, as Gary Watson (1977: 333–4) proposes, that the weak give in to desires which they could have resisted had they possessed normal levels of self-control. As he points out, this is consistent with their being unable to resist at the time of action. On my account this does not make a sufficiently sharp distinction between weakness and compulsion, for it suggests that the desires involved were impervious to any attempt at self-control which, given the weak agents' underdeveloped capacities, they could actually have made. Though there are cases which are properly described in this way, they occur where weakness shades into compulsion. Indeed, such agents may be behaviourally indistinguishable from compulsive agents, but these are not the central cases of weakness. I claim that we do not usually blame the weak person for past failures to develop the capacities and strategies which would have enabled them now to resist their recalcitrant desires. This is the kind of blame more appropriately directed at some compulsively motivated agents. The ordinary view insists that we blame weak agents primarily for not exercising the capacities they possess at the time they are called for.

In providing some philosophical support for the ordinary view it may be helpful at this point to set out schematically the differences and similarities between continence, weakness, and compulsion. Sceptics about weakness of will typically place great weight on the similarities between weakness and compulsion, while glossing over the equally significant similarities between weakness and continence. No one, so far as I know, has suggested that weakness is really a species of continence, though McDowell is almost equally disparaging of both. Yet weakness and continence share characteristics which distinguish them both from compulsion. The truth is that weakness is intermediate between compulsion and continence. It has no unique defining characteristic. Rather there is a unique combination of statements which as a set applies only to weak-willed behaviour.

Take a situation, S, where an agent is tempted to take a cigarette. Let J be the judgement that she should not accept the cigarette. Assume she makes that judgement in S. Now, in situation S, the weak agent and the compulsive agent will both accept the cigarette, so contravening their evaluative judgement, while the continent agent will refuse. Let A be the action of smoking a cigarette. So far S looks like this:

Compulsive	Weak	Continent
J	J	J
A	A	$\sim A$

This is the comparison that so impresses the sceptics. Weakness and compulsion are so far indistinguishable.

But now that we have established the disposition of the facts, let us consider some relevant counterfactuals. For it is in this region that the gap opens between weakness and compulsion. Consider a counterfactual close to that suggested by Watson:

R. If the agent had exercised some reasonable strategy of self-control she would not have taken the cigarette.

Now, given that we have a central case of compulsion, the table for *S* should look like this:

Compulsive	Weak	Continent
J	*J*	*J*
A	*A*	*~A*
~R	*R*	*R*

Watson would agree that it is true of the weak agent, but not the compulsive agent, that she could have effectively resisted the desire for a cigarette via some technique of self-control, though he never discusses the mechanics of such resistance. But he uses 'could' in a much weaker sense than the ordinary sense in which we might understand the word. The weak agent could have conformed her action to her judgement if she had possessed certain skills which Watson thinks she does not in fact possess.

How is this claim to be established? In the actual world the antecedent of the conditional is true of the continent agent, whose desires, we are to suppose, are comparable in strength to the desires of the weak agent. The continent agent does exercise self-control and does not take a cigarette, thereby confirming the truth of *R*. But what about the agent we suspect of weakness? On Watson's account, we must inspect her desire for a cigarette to determine its objective resistibility according to community standards.

Now, while this appeal to community standards has a long and honourable history, reaching back to Aristotle (*NE* 1150^b7 ff.), I think it is, in the end, of doubtful use in making the distinction between weakness and compulsion. If we wholly detach the concept of resistibility from the individual agent's capacities to resist and attach it instead to community standards, we are limited to saying that the compulsive agent has irresistible desires which she is in fact unable to resist, whereas the weak agent has resistible desires which she is in fact unable to resist.

This is an open invitation to scepticism, which makes the difference between weakness and compulsion seem merely semantic. It is insensitive to the phenomenology of weakness, and unlikely to underwrite any significant moral distinctions. For, according to this account, neither agent could have done otherwise, and so it seems they should be blamed or excused together for their present failures to conform their actions to their values. Indeed, it is not even clear how they might be blamed for past failures to do what was necessary to avoid their current predicament. The problem is iterative, since if they previously could have performed some act of diachronic self-control, then on Watson's account they would have.

The devil here is Watson's assumption that those who have the capacity for self-control will exercise it. This is what forces the adoption of the external community standard. With this assumption in place, the possible world in which the weak-willed agent could resist the desire for a cigarette seems at least as far away as the world in which the compulsive agent could resist the desire for a cigarette. In each case, in order for the agent to refuse, she must be very different from the way she actually is. In the case of the compulsive person, she must have a different set of desires. In the case of the weak agent, she must possess skills and capacities which she does not possess in the actual world. The sense in which the weak agent could, while the compulsive could not, resist the desire for a cigarette is anaemic in the extreme. It is of little practical relevance. As it stands, then, R alone is not sufficient to establish a morally significant distinction between weakness and compulsion.

If we reject Watson's assumption, our main problem is to demonstrate that the weak-willed person does indeed have the capacity for self-control. For, given not just

R. If the agent had exercised some reasonable strategy of self-control she would not have taken the cigarette,

but

C. The agent could have exercised such a strategy,

we can then make a clear distinction between weakness and compulsion, provided also that we can give some teeth to the 'could' in *C*. I suggest that the completed table should look like this:

(1)

Compulsive	Weak	Continent
J	*J*	*J*
A	*A*	~*A*
~*R*	*R*	*R*
~*C*	*C*	*C*

As Watson rejects *C* in the case of the weak agent, for him the completed table will look like this:

(2)

Compulsive	Weak	Continent
J	*J*	*J*
A	*A*	~*A*
~*R*	*R*	*R*
~*C*	~*C*	*C*

I have been arguing that ~*C* negates the force of *R* in the case of the weak agent and tends to collapse the distinction that Watson suggests. But what arguments can be given to show that Table (1) offers the correct picture? How do we establish the claim that the weak-willed person, like the continent person but unlike the compulsive, could have performed the valued action by an exercise of self-control which itself was possible in the circumstances?

As we have seen, self-control in action is largely a matter of focusing our attention away from features of our situation that would incline us to act against our practical judgement, or redirecting it upon considerations which will either modify the recalcitrant desire or give extra motivational support to our judgement, to ensure its effectiveness in leading us to choose and perform the appropriate action. The agent who exercises self-control has the right thoughts at the right time. The suggestion is that the weak agent is one who could have had such thoughts and for whom such thoughts would have been successful.

But, even if we grant that such thoughts would have been effective in resisting the recalcitrant desire, how is it established that an agent could have had such thoughts in the first place? A determinist will say that, given the way I actually am when I snuggle down in bed rather than get up for a swim, given the way my desires stand, I could not have had any thoughts apart from those I actually had. So I could not have chosen and acted other than I did. If determinism is true then surely there can be no distinction between weakness and compulsion; so the distinction must depend upon the further assumption that determinism is false.

This objection suggests that there will be a deterministic explanation to be had for each and every thought we think. There are two ways of reading the determinist claim here. The first, scientific reading appeals to the laws of physics or neurophysiology to back up the claim that I could not have done other than I did. But it can be argued that this is not a level of explanation which is relevant to moral concerns and moral distinctions. Even if this reading of determinism is true, it would be extraordinary for me to excuse my own laziness on those grounds, and it would be equally odd for me to excuse you. Appealing to the state of the world at some time in the past, plus the operation of the laws of physics, to explain my neglect of some obligation *now* won't wash with those who are aggrieved by my behaviour, and for good reason. R. Jay Wallace points out that it cannot follow from the truth of determinism that no one has the capacity for self-control. The capacity for reflective self-control is a matter of broad psychological competence,

like the power to speak a given language, or to add and subtract large numbers, or to read and play music on the piano. It would be very strange to suppose that determinism per se would deprive people of psychological capacities of this sort—as if the confirmation of determinism would give us reason to conclude that Jane Austen lacked the competence to write in English or that Maria Callas had no capacity to sing. (Wallace, 1994: 182)

Our ascriptions of psychological capacities and competences, including the capacity for self-control, do not require or gain justification from the truth or falsity of some general proposition in physics or neurophysiology. A defence of our moral distinctions, which assume these capacities, and of our consequent practices of blaming or excusing, must therefore be conducted in folk-psychological terms of beliefs, desires, intentions, and actions. At this level the crucial determinist claim is just this: that of the actions I believe are available to me I will, if I do anything at all intentionally, perform the action which bids fair to satisfy my strongest desires. However, this may be a more promising way to attack the distinction since, if true, the claim will be true of both weak and compulsive actions, and so it appears to lend support to the sceptic about the lack of a distinction between them.

The support, though, is merely apparent. For, as suggested in the discussion of techniques of self-control, we can avoid acting on our single strongest desire if the aggregate strength of other, conjointly satisfiable desires outweighs it. How we aggregate our desires is largely up to us. It depends on how we think about them. And we can argue that, for the most part, thinking is not an action, and so falls outside the scope of this second reading of the determinist claim.[1]

If an exercise of self-control had to be motivated by the agent's strongest desires at the time, synchronic self-control would not be possible and we would be right to be sceptical about the distinction between weakness and compulsion. But no one suggests that we inevitably have the thoughts whose having bids fair to satisfy our strongest desires. Thoughts are typically not amenable to rationalization in the way that actions are. Indeed there is often no folk-psychological explanation at all for our having or failing to have certain thoughts. 'I didn't think of it' or 'I forgot' may be all there is to be said of our failures.[2] It is not obvious from this that I could not have had the appropriate thoughts. (I am not going to excuse myself on the grounds that I forgot that it was my turn to collect the children from school.) So it is not obvious that I could not have exercised self-control. However, this is not a complete

---

[1] Some thinking is actional, with the usual antecedents of action. Mental arithmetic is an example.

[2] Likewise there may be no such explanation for chance rememberings. For example, I may, out of the blue, find myself thinking of my daughter cutting her doll's hair when she was small.

response to the sceptic. It is still unclear what we mean when we say that I could have exercised self-control.

I suggest that the claim that I could have exercised self-control is best interpreted as the following modal claim:

> If there is a close possible world in which I do exercise self-control, then I display weakness of will if here and now I fail to do so.

There are various ways of making out this modal claim. I will explore two: the first suggested by David Velleman's account of epistemic freedom (Velleman, 1989) and the second a common-sense reading setting out the pragmatic criteria for deciding when self-control is possible. Neither of these accounts conflicts with determinism.

To take the psychological reading of the determinist claim first, it is not clear from the fact, if it is one, that my actions are determined by my strongest overall desires that I could never choose to act other than I in fact do. For, as David Velleman argues, our choices at least sometimes determine what it is that we are preponderantly motivated to do. Velleman thinks that intentions are really expectations about what we will do next. Once formed, such expectations attract our constitutive desire to know what it is that we are doing, and this may often be sufficient to alter the balance of our motives and make it the case that we are preponderantly motivated to do what we choose. While our behavioural predictions are subject to evidence, provided by our antecedent desires, about how we will act, Velleman thinks that they are not fully constrained by such evidence:

Our motives indicate which action we're going to perform next, and yet we aren't obliged, epistemically speaking, to predict the action they indicate. For they indicate which action we'll perform next only by virtue of indicating which action we'll intend, and if we predicted some alternative action to be our next, we would thereby intend it, thus making our alternative prediction come true. (Velleman, 1989: 148)

This will be true in many of the cases that we would want to categorize as weakness of will. We have latitude in what we may expect whenever such expectations 'would be sufficient to shift the motivational balance in favor of the action predicted' (159).

Velleman's account of freedom is supported by the phenomenology of weakness. When I later reflect upon myself as I was this morning, lying in bed, knowing that the best thing to do would be to get up and go for a swim, I may reproach myself for not having simply decided to get up. I make the presumption that this would have been enough to get me out of bed, usually on the basis of previous experience. My weakness was in not forming an intention which it was open to me to form: an intention which, in the world where I do form it, is enough to swing the motivational balance in favour of my getting up.[3]

Velleman thinks our wills are epistemically free. But this is perfectly consistent with the second reading of the determinist thesis—that our actions are causally determined, that we never act against the balance of our motives, given our beliefs. The account of self-control that I have given does not challenge such a thesis. It depends very much on the possibility of shifting alliances of desires, under the direction of reason, bridging the initial gap between evaluation and (direct) motivation.

Now, as for the second way of making out the modal claim, the initial scientific determinist objection quite fails to touch our ordinary concerns, or to disturb our differential ascriptions of weakness and compulsion. The truth of any proposition to the effect that a person could or could not have exercised some psychological capacity is determined in a largely pragmatic fashion by consulting the evidence provided by their actions over time. Had Jane Austen submitted a tedious, badly written manuscript following *Pride and Prejudice* or *Emma* her editor would have been entitled to mark it 'could do better'. We call someone weak, rather than compelled with respect to some action, when we believe that she could have exercised self-control; that is, when we believe that had she had certain thoughts, or formed certain intentions, she would have been

---

[3] What do I mean by saying that it was open to me to form some other intention? One way of thinking about this is to say that in the world where I form some other intention it is still recognizably *me* that forms it. In deliberating, then, the intentions which are open to me are the intentions which I can identify with across worlds. If we think about alternative intentions and actions in this way we should escape Frankfurt-style objections to 'could have done otherwise' conditions. This notion of cross-world identification is presented by Daniel Cohen (1999).

able to resist the desire which ran counter to her judgement. And we are entitled to believe that she could have had such thoughts, and formed such intentions, if she actually has done so on previous similar occasions of vulnerability.

If, for example, you have in the past overcome the temptation to take a proffered cigarette by thinking of your additional reasons for not taking one, so allowing all the associated desires to weigh against the desire to smoke, we take this as evidence that you could have done so this time. We think it is true that, had you done so, you would not have taken a cigarette. If you have, in effect, gritted your teeth and acted on your belief that you could say no, by simply forming the intention to say no, then you could have done so again, given that your beliefs have not changed. If you usually stick to your diet by reciting Hamlet's most famous soliloquy to yourself when the craving for chocolate starts, why did it not occur to you to do that on this occasion too? Unless you can point to some relevant difference, the judgement that you could have done so is well founded.[4]

What kind of difference is relevant to the distinction between weakness and compulsion? We are not talking here about differences which justify an alteration of the agent's original evaluative judgement. If I do not get out of bed for my morning swim today, it might be that I am tired from an unusually late night, or depressed or unwell. In these circumstances let us say I would be justified in concluding that a swim would do me no good. Rather than acting as a cue for the exercise of self-control, my feelings of reluctance this morning may signal the need for a review of my plans. The salient question here is not whether I could get out of bed if I tried, but whether I should try.

Our interest at the moment, however, is in those differences which do not support or effect a change of judgement

---

[4] We may also take someone's demonstrated capacity to exercise self-control in one domain, say with respect to diet or cigarettes, as a sign that they have the capacity to exercise control in other domains. The techniques of self-control are common between domains. However, the temptations of cigarettes and lying to save face, for example, are quite different and sometimes these differences will be relevant to our moral judgements.

on the part of the agent. A difference relevant to the distinction between weakness and compulsion must be one which alters the gap between judgement and desire from bridgeable to unbridgeable, or else affects the agent's ordinary capacity to adopt the strategies that would bridge that gap. When an agent is very tired or depressed, she may simply lack the capacity to focus on the considerations that usually get her to do the right thing. Or the desire to smoke may have grown much stronger and the opposing desires weaker, so that even focusing on those considerations no longer leads her to do the right thing. In these cases the similarity between past situations and the present one is superficial. In modal terms, the world in which she does the right thing is significantly different from the world in which she finds herself.

Now, it might be claimed that all situations where we fail to exercise self-control fall under the scope of this explanation. But the bare fact that this time you simply did not think of considerations which ordinarily move you is not a large difference. This is to repeat the original error of those who have found the similarities between weakness and compulsion mesmeric. What matters here is not the truth of determinism, but, I reiterate, the truth of certain counterfactuals, conjoined with the evidence provided by the agent's behaviour in relevantly similar situations. Suppose it is true, given the state of your motives, that if you had reminded yourself or had been reminded, perhaps by a friend, of your reasons not to smoke, you would not have accepted a cigarette. Suppose it is true that if you had counted to twenty the craving would have passed. Suppose it is true that if you had simply decided to say no, you would have said no. The truth of the claim that you could have adopted those strategies on this occasion (i.e. that you now possess the capacity for self-control) is, as I have said, established pragmatically: by reference to relevantly similar instances, both prior to and succeeding the occasion of failure, of such exercises of control. If it is true both that you could have adopted the strategies, and that they would have been successful in assuring that your action matched your practical judgement, these conjointly constitute a sufficient condition for calling your action weak, rather than compulsive.

3. *The Reckless Agent*

The reckless agent is not to be distinguished from the weak agent or the compulsive agent by virtue of a capacity, or lack of capacity, for self-control in action. In the first instance the reckless agent's failure is at the level of judgement. Unlike weak agents, stereotypical reckless agents do not experience conflict between their judgements of value and their actual desires (though I will shortly claim that one kind of reckless agent may sometimes experience such conflict). Either they do not bother making such judgements, adopting instead some other norm to govern their actions, or the judgements they do make, though manifestly unreasonable, are matched by their desires. Reckless agents are typically careless of considerations which ought to weigh with them.

So, for example, while the weak agent gives in to the desire for an extra drink, while holding on to the judgement that she ought not to have one because she will then not be fit to drive home safely, the reckless agent is unimpressed by such considerations. 'What the hell', she says, as she accepts the drink; 'that's no reason not to have a good time.' Or perhaps she dismisses the claim that her driving abilities will be impaired by alcohol. In the face of all the evidence to the contrary, she insists that *she* at least can drive better after a few drinks.

Now, it is fair to impute to such agents a belief that they could have chosen to do otherwise, and would have succeeded in doing otherwise had they so chosen. They do not think of themselves as compelled. While a compulsive agent may also judge badly, it is the invariable mark of the reckless agent, unlike the compulsive agent, that their judgements are manifestly unreasonable. They simply cannot be justified. We assume, then, that to get reckless agents to do the right thing—say, to refrain from taking another drink—it is first necessary to get them to judge that refraining is the right thing to do in circumstances of this sort. It is only then that the question of their capacities for self-control can arise.

It is an open question at this point whether or not such an agent would succeed in acting in accordance with a more reasonable judgement. No doubt there are mixed cases. However, whether or not all reckless judgers must also be dispositionally weak or compulsive is not the focus of the discussion at this point. There is more to be said about the reckless judgements themselves.

There are several kinds of failures which occur at the level of judgement, only some of which render agents liable to blame. There are non-culpable mistakes of fact, and innocent blunders in reasoning. But there are also failures which properly count as moral failures—where the agent's judgement issues from negligence, self-deception, arrogance, or excessive selfishness. While some of these moral failures might not consistently be recognized as recklessness, I think they do fall under its umbrella. Reckless judgements are not just wrong, but obviously wrong; and the rationalizations commonly engaged in by reckless agents do not alter the quality of their judgements, or their degree of culpability for the actions resulting from them.

4. The Varieties of Recklessness

(i) Undue Influence and Rationalizations

Sometimes our judgements of value are unduly and improperly influenced by our actual desires. In saying this I do not, of course, suggest that we should take no notice of our affective states in arriving at our evaluations. This *would* be unreasonable. For, as I have already argued, our desires and emotions may be valuable in themselves, or may stand as indicators of value. Emotions of love and compassion both enrich our lives and remind us of our responsibilities to others—of the need to take their situations into account. And even when some desire or emotion is evaluatively neutral, or is perhaps one which we evaluate negatively, we may still quite properly take it into account in reaching a particular practical judgement about what to do. There are limits, however, on the degree to which we should accommodate such desires.

If I dislike someone, and so desire not to be in their company, then, even if I acknowledge my dislike to be wholly irrational, I have at least a defeasible reason to decide not to invite that person to join my table for dinner. But this may not give me a warrant to exclude them, if by doing so I injure their feelings and deprive my other guests of a desired companion. Suppose, however, that though there is clear evidence that the person will indeed be hurt and my companions disappointed, I come to the opposite conclusion, and so judge that it would be best not to invite her. In permitting my desire not to be in this person's company to override, silence, or distort all other considerations, I surely show a reckless disregard of these considerations, and reach a judgement which is unfounded in the totality of reasons actually available to me.

How can this happen? We know that a desire may run counter to best judgement. But what is the mechanism by which such a desire takes over the reasoning process itself, bending our evaluative conclusions to match its demands? There is a body of evidence which suggests that such bending of our evaluations is endemic, and occurs in response to a perceived initial mismatch between our desires and our evaluative beliefs.[5] Leon Festinger proposes that

dissonance, that is, the existence of nonfitting relations among cognitions, is a motivating factor in its own right . . . cognitive dissonance can be seen as an antecedent condition which leads to activity oriented towards dissonance reduction just as hunger leads to activity oriented towards hunger reduction. (Festinger, 1964: 3)

Where an agent's desires or actions do not fit with her antecedently held values, she will be under some pressure to reduce the discomfort of dissonance by restoring consistency

---

[5] See for example Gilovich (1991), cited in Mele (1988: 353), who reports that 70% of high school seniors thought they were above average in leadership ability, and *all* students thought they were above average in their ability to get on with others. As Mele notes, motivation has clearly had a hand in producing conclusions which are so out of line with the facts. He argues that given that most people want it to be the case that they are above average, the cost of falsely believing that they are not above average is much higher than the cost of falsely believing they are above average: 'They would at least pay an immediate and significant hedonic price for acquiring the belief that they lack the property at issue . . . and their acquiring the false belief that they have this property would normally be quite harmless' (1988: 355). I argue that in cases of recklessness the false belief is not harmless.

between them. Instead of closing the gap between desire and judgement by an exercise of self-control, as the continent person does, the reckless person may close the gap by an unwarranted shift in judgement. Dissonance reduction here involves 're-evaluation of the alternatives in the direction of favoring the chosen and disfavoring the rejected alternative, or both' (Festinger, 1964: 30).

This will involve both repression of evidence adverse to the judgement to be formed and wishful thinking. So the partygoer, desiring another drink, forms the (wishful) belief that she, at least, drives better when drunk, and so judges that another drink is perfectly in order. The driver late for an appointment decides that the speed limits in the area are unreasonably low and so can be safely ignored. And the date-rapist judges, against the evidence of his date's resistance, that his state of sexual desire is or will be shared by her. Each of these judgements is unsupported by the reasons available to the agent. Each is desire-driven. In the course of rationalizing their judgements, these agents have cooked the books. The conclusion has dictated the evidence and arguments selected to support it, and opposing evidence is not sought, or is ignored, repressed, or explained away. If our evaluative beliefs, like our other beliefs, aim at correctness, then it is apparent that this particular way of forming and revising beliefs about our reasons for action and the worth of our actions is deeply flawed.

To what extent, though, is the agent to blame for the way in which desire impinges upon evaluative judgement? A determinist worry arises again at this point. Some writers appear to suggest that the processes by which agents reach such apparently irrational judgements are outside of conscious control. Writing about the subversion of rationality, Jon Elster claims that the sour grapes phenomenon, whereby the agent decides that something which is unavailable is, after all, undesirable, 'is a purely causal process of adaptation, taking place "behind the back" of the person concerned' (Elster, 1983: 117). Similarly, we are to assume that rationalization, which is what we are primarily interested in at this point, also takes place behind the back of the agent, since, as Elster concedes, 'in some cases adaptive preferences and adaptive perception (i.e. rationalisation) can hardly be distinguished from each other' (123). Evaluations made under pressure to reduce dissonance can involve both approaches or mechanisms. Elster argues that agents, by and large, adapt to the feasible set; and of course what it is feasible for us to choose is, Velleman would agree, largely determined by how our desires stand before our choice.

So it might be claimed that reckless agents cannot judge or evaluate otherwise than they do, given their desires. Their evaluations are merely the outcomes of what Mark Johnston calls mental tropisms: non-accidental, purpose-serving, sub-intentional mental processes (Johnston, 1988: 66). If Festinger is right that we have an inbuilt motive to reduce or avoid dissonance, perhaps we cannot avoid adjusting our evaluative beliefs to suit our circumstances. Narrow orthonomy may be a state of equilibrium toward which we human beings naturally tend. Perhaps values quite generally are shaped behind our backs, and rational process is always and only a veneer. If this is so, there can be no significant moral distinction to be drawn between the judgements of reckless agents and the judgements of temperate agents.

Perhaps not surprisingly, I think we have no reason to accept such an argument. For, first, a motive that is inbuilt is not thereby an overriding motive. Let's grant that we have some constitutive concerns, of the kind described by Festinger and Velleman, for self-understanding and internal coherence. But we have many other concerns, constitutive and acquired, which we may take account of in forming a judgement of value, several of which may compete with the undiluted concern for coherence between evaluative judgement and desire. And we are quite capable of recognizing that mere narrow orthonomy (that is, either a chance consonance between judgement and desire, or a desire-driven consonance) does not in any case adequately serve our desires for self-understanding and coherence. As a consideration in favour of changing one's mind about the reasons one has, it is very weak.

Second, changing one's judgement is only one possible response to the discomfort of dissonance. Working to alter the balance of one's desires is another response; putting up with it is yet another. The evidence seems to be that many people have the capacity to resist the pressures placed on judgement by a wayward desire, even if they cannot or do not resist the desire itself when it comes to choosing an action. Heroin addicts and smokers may come to value their activities, but we know that very often they do not. Though they lack orthonomy in action, they display it at the level of judgement. Both the weak person and the compulsive person can consistently and rationally value getting their particular evaluations right: that is, in accordance with the deliverances of substantive practical reason. The reckless person manifestly does not. It is this failure of iterativity—the silencing or improper realization of this rational concern—which underlies all forms of recklessness, and marks it out as a moral failure rather than as blind adaptation, or as mere cognitive dysfunction.

(ii) Culpable Ignorance, Culpable Arrogance

Persons who are broadly orthonomous learn an appropriate humility about their epistemic capacities and their evaluative beliefs. Since they rationally value getting correct beliefs about what they have reason to do, they realize they have reason to take care in forming and revising their practical judgements, so as to take proper account of all the factors which constitute substantive reasons for acting one way or another. Now, this carefulness may result in them suffering conflict and uncertainties, since, often enough, there are several courses of action which there is reason to choose and, often enough, it will be a close call between them. In many situations no one course of action will be clearly the best. Perhaps no one course of action will be the best, anyway.

I have argued that these experiences of doubt and conflict tend to result in a further openness to evidence and argument, including, of course, to evidence provided by sympathy, empathy, and emotion. Broadly orthonomous agents are those who come to realize that the world does not always co-operate with our moral enquiries by providing a single correct answer to the question 'What should I do?'; and that, sometimes at least, even where there is such a correct answer to an evaluative question, they may not have arrived at it. While they may be secure in many, even most, of their judgements, they are not arrogant or overconfident. They recognize the limits of their own epistemic capacities.

Reckless agents are not, it need hardly be said, like this. They do not take account of all the things which constitute substantive reasons for acting. Often they do not take account of any of them. But a reckless agent's failure to take account of her reasons in forming both her general evaluations and her particular practical judgements is not always to be accounted for in terms of the underhanded machinations of certain desires. Not all reckless agents are given to self-deception, rationalization, and wishful thinking. The ignorance of some agents is to be explained primarily by their lack of humility with regard to their epistemic capacities and their evaluative beliefs. Though they may claim to value truth, their commitment is only to the truth of the particular view they endorse; they simply do not entertain the proposition that this view could be mistaken. An overweening belief in their own infallibility justifies to them their dismissal of anything which might constitute counter-evidence to conclusions already reached, and entrenches their errors. So it is that they show a disregard for reason which counts as reckless.

Unreflective conservatism and knee-jerk radicalism are not usually thought of as species of recklessness (at least the former is not), but on this account they both are; and, I think, rightly so. For each side arrogantly assumes a monopoly on both truth and virtue, and this is at the core of their failure to take proper account of the reasons that are available to them. Like McDowell's virtuous agents, their focus is unduly narrow, their responses and judgements simplistic.

However, though it is apparent that their unreasonable judgements are not wholly disinterested, arrogant agents are in an important respect unlike the agent who makes an ad hoc judgement under the press of desire. Theirs is not mere narrow orthonomy: the equilibrium that rationalizers achieve by a shift in judgement. For the agents we are now considering, a variation in desires should provide no occasion for a shift in evaluative judgement. Indeed, many arrogant agents will be able to exercise considerable third-tier self-control in order to override any emergent recalcitrant desires, and to act in accordance with their reckless judgements.

So the committed revolutionary may need to quell her natural sympathies for her hostages during a hijacking. The religious traditionalist fights fatigue and goes off to address yet another meeting on the dangers of admitting women to the priesthood. Such agents do rationally value acting in accordance with their first-order evaluative judgements, and so they are disposed to exercise self-control whenever these judgements and their desires come apart. Arrogant agents may thus be strictly orthonomous. The connection between their judgements and their actions is not contingent upon their antecedently possessing a desire of appropriate strength to do the thing they judge ought to be done.

But they are still not broadly orthonomous, since they are not appropriately governed by the additional executive concern that their reasons for acting be good reasons. And, where an agent is not appropriately concerned about the nature of the reasons on which she chooses to act, her ignorance of good reasons can only be considered as culpable ignorance. In this crucial respect, then, arrogant agents and self-deceptive rationalizers are exactly alike.

(iii) Unrestrained Autonomy: the Outlaws

A third kind of recklessness, and one that is most central to both common-sense and legal conceptions of reckless action, is that of the thoroughgoing egoist. This is the variety of recklessness that is rooted in a fundamental indifference to the reasons provided by the legitimate claims and concerns of others.[6] These agents are not blinded, either by desire or by

---

[6] Susan Wolf has pointed out to me that some agents who are indifferent to the claims of others may be equally unmoved by the perception that some course of action is required by their own interests. They may, for example, be motivated by a deep self-loathing or by a religious or ecological commitment that takes no account of human interests at all. This is true but not an example of unrestrained autonomy. To the extent that such agents are to be regarded as reckless they may be considered arrogant. The agent whose indifference to both moral and prudential claims stems from self-hatred may not be reckless at all. She may, rather, be suffering a disorder similar to depression, which mitigates her responsibility, though here the effects are on her capacities for good judgement rather than on her capacities to act in accordance with those judgements. See the discussion of depression below.

ideology, as the self-deceptive agent and the arrogant agent are. Rather, their actions manifest indifference to, not (culpable) ignorance of, the reasons for refraining from actions that are provided by, for example, the likely bad consequences to others. So the self-centred builder may cut corners to increase profits, knowing all the while that this will endanger later occupants of the building. And the self-centred journalist cares not at all about the effects of her intrusions into private grief or trauma in the course of an exciting chase for headlines.

It would be a mistake to think of such agents as weak-willed. The cases I am thinking of are not examples of greed and self-interest overriding evaluative judgement. Rather, the problem is that these agents, unlike straightforwardly weak agents, are not governed by the deliberative norms revealed in the conversational stance (which, I have argued, must give the interests of others some non-instrumental standing) in reaching their practical judgements or actions. They are more narrowly concerned that the desires they act upon be the desires they want to act on: desires which will further the projects with which they identify. The norm by which they are governed is a norm of identification. It says something like this:

Act only on those desires with which you can identify.

Now, though the desires with which we identify need not be self-centred, it is typical in the case of reckless agents that they are. So I am supposing that the builder mentioned above identifies without qualification with his desire for money, the journalist with her project of gaining notoriety by getting a scoop. These reckless agents, then, unlike weak or compulsive agents, conform to Frankfurt's model of autonomy: they enjoy freedom of the will. Free agents are not slaves to their desires, as compulsive agents are, nor are they neutral with regard to conflicts among their desires, as wantons are (Frankfurt, 1971: 10–13). Instead they make some of their desires their own by decisive identification with them: they decide which of their first-order desires they wish to be motivated by. Freedom, for Frankfurt, consists in being moved by the desires you want to be moved by.

If this is all that freedom consists in, then it is readily apparent that a free agent need not be broadly or even narrowly orthonomous. Frankfurt suggests no broad rational constraints on the desires and projects with which agents may choose to identify. Of course, the agent possessing freedom of the will can display a high degree of instrumental rationality. And, given that the desires they identify with (i.e. the desires which serve their projects) may not always be their strongest occurrent desires, they may need a sophisticated capacity for self-control to secure their freedom. But there is no restriction on the content of the desires and projects which a free agent may adopt. These may range from the innocuous to the appalling.

For agents like this, then, there need be nothing under-handed or behind the back about the workings of desire and self-interest in their choice of projects and actions. These will be quite explicitly in the foreground, and the agent may consider at length what kinds of actions, what kind of life, would be most challenging, amusing, exciting, advantageous, or otherwise appealing to them. Some such agents may prove to be brave, resourceful, and clever. They may sail solo around the world, represent their country in Olympic events, undertake scientific research, or turn to crime. They are not dominated by occurrent desire as compulsive agents and wantons are, so many of them will be quite capable of deciding that certain desires will interfere with their more central projects, and of dealing with them accordingly. What is common to these agents is that the concerns and interests of others figure in their deliberations, if at all, only as an obstacle or an enhancement to the projects of the self-centred agent. They will not otherwise figure as independent reasons for or against any project that the agent has in mind.

Reckless agents of this third kind are thus like the wanton in one crucial respect: they are simply not in the business of finding, supplying, or responding to justificatory reasons. They do not falsely believe, as the ideologue might, that their commitments would survive the kinds of reflective, imaginative processes outlined in Chapter 4, and, under ideal conditions, gain reasoned acceptance from others. Such considerations are strictly irrelevant to them. The reckless egoist, like the arrogant agent and the self-deceived agent, does not display broad orthonomy, but her failings are even more severe; she is, either in a particular respect or altogether, beyond reason in its broad sense. Its constraints are to her like the rules of a game which she does not choose to play. She is an outlaw.

5. *Recklessness, Self-control, and Moral Responsibility*

So far, talk of moral responsibility has been interwoven with description and analysis of the various kinds of moral failure. Indeed, our very practices of praising, blaming, and excusing appear to motivate the distinctions we make between the various kinds of moral failures, and between those failures and innocent errors of judgement or action. It is now time to clarify the structure on which our attributions of responsibility hang.

The ordinary view recognizes that there are two dimensions along which moral culpability is to be assessed: judgement and self-control. Agents who fail in self-control are either weak or compelled; agents whose judgements are manifestly unreasonable may be reckless. I will consider the dimension of judgement first.

Agents who fail in either self-control or judgement may of course have a complete or partial excuse. In the dimension of judgement we recognize that some errors are innocent or excusable: youthfulness, intellectual impairment, tiredness, emotional pressures, serious deprivation or ill-treatment, and lack of information may each impair an agent's ability to judge well, and so reduce or remove the agent's responsibility for error. For example, children who innocently ape the racist judgements of their parents cannot be said to be reckless in their judgements, for they have no other salient source of information, and their experience leads them to believe that their parents are reliable providers of information. But other errors are not so innocent.

In this chapter I have distinguished three forms of recklessness. The reckless agent may be indifferent to or careless of reasons arising from the needs and concerns of others, a fact which will be reflected in their judgements and actions; or they may be given to self-deception and rationalization about their reasons; or they may be unduly arrogant and inflexible, and so inclined to ignore or dismiss the reasons available to them. Agents are commonly held responsible for actions which flow from their reckless judgements, since it is assumed that they had both the information and opportunity to form better judgements, and had shown themselves to be, in other relevant respects (or on relevantly similar occasions), competent deliberators. So we may suppose that the driver who is late understands the arguments in favour of obeying speed limits, the hijacker on other occasions has condemned terrorist action as illegitimate and unjust, and the journalist is well aware that she would not like her privacy invaded in the way she plans to invade the privacy of others. Indeed, it is constitutive of their recklessness that these agents form their judgements against the evidence without excuse. Consequently, their failures may be considered far more serious and complete than the failures of those who judge rightly but then succumb to temptation, since it is not just the reckless agent's actions but her very values which are bad. Her lack of concern, humility, and honesty constitute serious character flaws.

Thus the adulterer who gives in to temptation while judging that she ought not to betray her husband, and suffers subsequent pangs of regret, is perhaps easier to forgive than the one who does not see such a commitment as providing any reason to refrain. For we suppose that it is in general easier to judge well than it is to act well. There are fewer pitfalls; the agent who acts well must first judge well, and then deal with the practical problems posed by any shortfall in her desires.

It is interesting to note at this point that we are more likely to identify with the weak agent's failings than with the callousness, arrogance, and intellectual dishonesty of the reckless. For these are characteristics, like narcissism, which, when pronounced, are incompatible with full engagement. Peter Strawson argues that holding people responsible is something we can only do from within the participant stance: through standing, either actually or vicariously, in certain kinds of interpersonal relationships with them. It ought to follow from such a view that we are less inclined to hold agents responsible for reckless acts than for weak acts. Yet, in everyday cases at least, I think we quite correctly see reckless agents' failings as more severe, and in consequence we judge them more harshly.

By contrast the occasional loss of self-control is a familiar, perhaps inevitable, failing in creatures like ourselves. We have seen that we may strongly desire what we do not value, or we may fail to desire what we do value. In such circumstances we are at risk of failing to act in accordance with our values. For self-control to be possible, there needs to be some way to overcome the impediment to action in accordance with value which is posed by wayward desires. If some such strategy is open to us, we say we have the capacity to control what we do. If we exercise this capacity we are continent; if we have this capacity but don't exercise it we are considered weak-willed. But if there is nothing feasible we can do to get our actions on track with our values we are considered compelled. The traditional view of how self-control connects up with moral responsibility holds, broadly, that continent people are responsible for what they do, weak people are likewise responsible for what they do or fail to do, but people who act compulsively must be excused.

This requires some elaboration and some qualification. Moral responsibility comes in degrees. The ordinary view implicitly recognizes both degrees of difficulty in the exercise of self-control (and indeed of judgement), and a distinction between those who are capable of synchronic self-control and those who must instead rely on diachronic techniques of control. Factors which impinge on the ease with which the capacity for self-control can be exercised mitigate responsibility. Some of these are obstacles to good judgement as well: for example, tiredness, emotional pressures, and lack of information. So the difficulties in foreseeing, and thus being able to forestall, some one-off situation in which synchronic self-control will be beyond reach could lessen the responsibility that an agent bears for the action resulting from such a loss of self-control. Or it may be that, though one's reasons taken together will garner adequate motivational support for an evaluative judgement, this is not at all apparent, and may become so only after extensive reflection. Given that the agent has the ability to undertake reflection at this level, and that there are reasons to be found upon reflection, it is clear that the agent has the capacity for self-control. But the difficulty in exercising that capacity will sometimes be accepted as a mitigating factor when responsibility is allocated—though when the matter at stake is very important this may not be an excuse; we will say that the agent should have made the effort. There will be other epistemic and practical factors which on occasion constrain or impede the exercise of self-control, and so affect the level of responsibility which we bear for our actions. The availability of diachronic self-control, for example, can be affected by all sorts of external factors: social expectations, cultural constraints, levels of income, and so on.

Let's first consider, however, a case where there are no such mitigating factors. Take a person who must choose whether to protect herself from some minor embarrassment by lying, or to tell the truth and suffer the consequences, thereby protecting another from unfair loss of reputation. Now, suppose that this person will, if she reflects upon her reasons in the ways outlined in the preceding chapter, gain ample motivational support for her otherwise ineffective judgement that she should tell the truth. If she has shown herself to be a competent deliberator, able to reflect on her reasons, and yet she fails to do so, going along instead with a surface disposition to protect herself by lying, it seems that she should be held fully responsible for her failure, her particular motivational deficit notwithstanding.

Compare this robust allocation of blame with occasions on which the agent is held responsible for an outcome even though it is acknowledged that the agent did not have the capacity for self-control at that time. These are occasions where an earlier exercise of self-control, which itself was possible, would have resulted in the agent successfully conforming her actions to her evaluative judgement. So, for example, perhaps the alcoholic cannot help accepting a drink when offered one by her regular drinking companions. At this time she may lack the capacity for self-control altogether, since her desire for a drink is now so great that no set of considerations available to her would deliver up desires strong enough to defeat her desire for a drink. She is in fact compelled in accepting the drink. But suppose she could easily have foreseen that she would take a drink in this company, and have adjusted her arrangements accordingly. Perhaps she has done so on other occasions. There was a time, then, when she could have exercised self-control with respect to this situation, and so she is appropriately held responsible for not having done so. However, the blame for the mess she is now in must be directed at her past negligence rather than her present decisions. The person who confronts us now is to some extent a victim of her past. We come to view her as divided, and the responsibility we allocate to her is therefore partial and fragmented. She may be responsible for the state she is in, but no longer for the particular actions she performs. She is to be pitied as well as blamed.

Here we see a plausible instance of holding someone responsible while explicitly adopting an objective stance towards her. It is useless to remonstrate or otherwise morally engage with a person in this condition, but that does not get her off the moral hook. Responsibility for past failures is still responsibility, and carries clear implications regarding the agent's future obligations to exercise self-control, especially diachronic self-control. That her behaviour was once compelled is not a complete defence. Our ordinary allocations of moral responsibility are to be suspended altogether only in quite exceptional circumstances.

Such a circumstance exists in the case of someone who falls unexpectedly into a deep depression, and as a result fails to fulfil some important obligations. Since the state could not have been foreseen, there is nothing this person could reasonably have done to prevent its onset. And now that it is upon her, not only may there be no effective technique of synchronic control available to her, she may also be incapable of taking steps that would alleviate the depression in the future, or that would guard against the actions she might undertake while afflicted. Perhaps her judgement is affected by her depression, and she cannot see the point of doing anything. But equally she may be aware that seeing a doctor and taking antidepressants would help to overcome the depression, and she may realize that this is desirable. Nevertheless her misery, or perhaps her apathy, is so complete that it defeats even the poss-

ibility of asking for help. Clearly such a person is not responsible for her actions.

Now, this of course is an extraordinary circumstance.
Though it is certainly possible for apathy to be complete, it is
equally certain that few depressives are literally unable to do
anything to alleviate their state.[7] If even depressives can make
some headway in the exercise of self-control, it is apparent that
in the ordinary case the resources that can be drawn on are
extensive indeed. Wherever there is some room to manoeuvre,
there is an accrual of moral responsibility; and, as the earlier
discussion of self-control demonstrates, for the most part
there is plenty of room to manoeuvre. The wholesale sus-
pension of our ordinary allocations of moral responsibility is
therefore quite exceptional. We will be rightly suspicious of those
who attempt to avoid moral responsibility by claiming to be
out of control.

6. Conclusion

In my view, the accounts of evaluation, orthonomy, and
agent-control given in previous chapters, and the distinctions
between recklessness, weakness, and compulsion made here, provide a very precise diagnosis of moral failings, and so underwrite our differential allocations of moral responsibility for
actions. However, while this common-sense moral psychology
deals comfortably with the common cases, it also needs to be
able to deal with the hard cases. In the next and final chapter
I consider the pressures placed upon ordinary notions of
responsibility by agents whose actions are extraordinarily evil.

---

[7] Nevertheless the difficulty of doing so may be great and I have already
said that this mitigates the agent's responsibility. In the case of those suffering depression and other such illnesses, moral responsibility is also to some
extent shared by those around them (and collectively by society). It would
be reprehensible to point the finger of blame at an ill person for neglecting
her obligations while doing nothing to help her. The topic of collective responsibility is important but not something I can do justice to here.

7

Moral Failure and Moral Responsibility: The Problem of Evildoers

Serial killers and paedophiles are surely the criminal equivalent of royalty. They are perennial favourites of the tabloid press,
and there are films and mini-series devoted to their ghastly
exploits. When they are caught, there is often much debate over
their sanity and so, it is assumed, over their candidacy for moral
and legal responsibility.

This is not surprising. When we learn of really appalling acts
we are inclined to think that the perpetrators must be mad,
since not only is what they do horrible, but their motivation
is essentially mysterious to us. We are not inclined to query
the sanity of the vast bulk of wrongdoers, whose motives are
merely of the ignoble and transparent kind that move people
to commit fraud, theft, and sometimes murder. We understand anger, jealousy, selfishness, and the quest for wealth and
power. But we do not readily comprehend the pleasure to be
got out of the aberrant actions of serial killers and paedophiles, for example, and we do not understand the single-
mindedness that can support the re-emergent evil of genocide
or 'ethnic cleansing', with the indifference to suffering that
appears to be entailed by such a project. These are the hard
cases for any theory of moral responsibility to deal with, and
many theorists charitably tend to exempt what they do not
understand. But is such exemption warranted?

In this chapter I want to present four evildoers: two real and
two fictional. The evildoers represent four largely distinct categories. These categories are not intended to exhaust the variety of evildoers that there are; they are chosen because of the
problems that we face in the moral assessment of the agents

who fall into them. My concern here is not with agents who are *clearly* to be exempted from blame, for the reasons widely endorsed in the legal system and by common sense: that their acts were involuntary or forced or compulsive, performed under extraordinary stress, or out of genuine and non-culpable ignorance or delusion. Such excuses map neatly onto the dimensions of judgement and control already discussed, and encompass those cases, such as severe schizophrenia, in which mental illness frees agents of responsibility by its obvious effects on their capacities for judgement and control.[1]

My interest, rather, is in agents who appear, but for the awful nature of their actions, to be uncontroversially the authors of those actions. These are people whose evil actions were conceived by them, planned in advance, and carefully carried out in accordance with those plans, and who were largely aware of the nature and consequences of their actions.

I do not reject out of hand the possibility that agents such as those I will describe are mentally ill: but their actions cannot automatically qualify them as such. I am not in favour of expanding the definition of mental illness to include any action which falls markedly outside accepted norms.[2] I agree with Thomas Szasz that we only succeed in obscuring 'the issue of man's responsibility for his actions by hiding it behind the skirt of an all explaining conception of mental illness' (Szasz,

---

[1] The McNaghten Rules of 1843, broadly interpreted, still serve as the basis of the defence of mental illness to a criminal charge. The American Law Institute's *Model Penal Code* states that 'A person is not responsible for criminal conduct if at the time of such conduct, as a result of mental illness, he lacks substantial capacity either to appreciate the criminality (or wrongfulness) of his conduct or to conform his conduct to the requirement of law' (cited in Ten, 1987: 125). Mental illness, then, excuses because it renders failures of both judgement and control non-culpable. The agent presumably could not have judged or acted better.

[2] Women have been particularly ill-served by the notion that activity outside the established norms of femininity is indicative of mental disorder; and runaway slaves in the American South were thought to suffer from an hereditary illness, drapetomania, whose sole symptom was a propensity to run away from their masters. These examples, while not directly relevant to our discussion of actions which should seem evil at any point in history, do suggest that we should not move too quickly to an illness model to excuse or explain behaviour outside of the norm. I am not, though, denying the existence of mental illness or its tragic and incapacitating effects on sufferers.

1973: 195). Instead I will argue that our tendency to label them as sick or mad is to be explained more by facts about us than by facts about them. We are all too keen to distance ourselves from them.

The measures of moral responsibility argued for in the preceding chapter need not be suspended when the going gets tough. Indeed, my claim is that, when properly explicated, they provide a very precise diagnostic tool for such occasions. By considering our evildoers' conceptions of their actions, and the kinds of control which they did or could have exercised over their actions in the light of the preceding discussions, I suggest that we will find ourselves able to comprehend what at first seem to be incomprehensible failures, and so able to make a principled assessment of the degrees of responsibility which they bear for their actions. But first let us meet the members of the rogues' gallery.

1. A Rogues' Gallery

(i) The Ideologue

Jonathan Bennett (1974) paints a portrait of Heinrich Himmler, who as chief of the SS during Hitler's regime was responsible for the concentration camps in which some four and a half million Jews were murdered. Here is an example of a person whose evil actions flow from a commitment to values that are horribly wrong. The lives, deaths, and sufferings of real people were to Himmler merely instrumental to the greater glory of the Third Reich. The vastness of his crimes, and the rigid persistence of his belief in the rightness of his actions in the face of the obvious and extreme suffering that his policies exacted, must cause us to question Himmler's sanity. Such rigidity suggests an element of compulsiveness in his behaviour. It is not, as Bennett points out, that he had no understanding of or sympathy for the sufferings of his victims; he did, but his sympathies had no impact upon his values. His evaluative beliefs were apparently impervious to both reason and sympathy.

(ii) The Outsider

Our outsider is the self-proclaimed sociopath Raymond, protagonist of the film *The Vanishing* (1988). Raymond, a well-liked and respected teacher and family man, has a history of setting himself challenges. As a youth he wonders why he should not jump off a high balcony: 'Where is it written', he asks himself, 'that I will not jump?' He jumps. As an adult he begins to wonder if he could do the most unlikely thing he can imagine for himself to do. He then, good-humouredly and patiently, plans and executes the abduction and live interment of a young woman, Saskia, and follows this up by satisfying the obsessive desire of Saskia's boyfriend, Rex, to know what has become of her by arranging the same fate for him. While his particular choice of action obliquely reflects his own claustrophobia, his untroubled embrace of the evil which stands at the end of his actions cannot be said to be explained by this minor kink in his psyche. Claustrophobia exempts Raymond from wearing a seat belt; it doesn't exonerate him from burying his victims alive.

Raymond's actions appear to be a model of control, and it is not clear that he is ignorant or mistaken in any way about the nature of his actions. However, the complete absence of principle and ordinary fellow-feeling, combined with the unusual nature of his choices, raise questions about Raymond's sanity. Perhaps we cannot blame him for what he does, since it is not clear that he could have been any different. Raymond seems to lack some essential prerequisite of moral life. Those who fall outside the moral community might fall beyond responsibility as well.

(iii) The Rationalizer

Like the Nazi, this person's values are sick and mistaken, and his actions are evil. However, the kind of person I am thinking of here differs significantly from someone like Himmler. When I was in England some years ago the tabloid press was united in its outrage when it was discovered that a paedophile group had booked a Brighton hotel for a convention. The hotel hastily cancelled the booking; the paedophile spokesman, while choosing to remain anonymous, was unrepentant. Paedophiles, he claimed, had a right to share information and put their point of view about adult–child sex: theirs was a legitimate sexual preference.

Let's imagine a thwarted conference-goer, Peter, a solicitor for a large finance company, keen tennis player, devoted son to his ailing mother, and member of several community organizations including the local youth group. Peter, in consequence of the sexual attraction he feels towards children, subscribes to various paedophile newsgroups on the World Wide Web. He gets bulletins which advertise and provide child pornography and pass on handy hints about good places to make contact with children. Many contributors to the newsgroup also defend the view that paedophilia is a normal and harmless sexual preference. Indeed, they cite psychological studies which indicate that such contact is benign. Peter comes to believe that children enjoy and initiate sexual contact with adults, and that the age of consent should be dramatically lowered. He feels aggrieved when he is charged with indecent assault, and blames his child victims for behaving seductively.[3] Peter acts on the basis of desires that most of us regard as perverse and indicative of psychological unhealth: desires which are not merely to be resisted but eliminated. Does the mere fact that Peter endorses his desires indicate that he is in control? Are his errors of judgement innocent or reckless? Or is it the case that his desires, by their very nature, provide some excuse both for his evaluative judgements and his actions?

(iv) The Pariah

Unlike agents in the previous categories, this agent shares our values and views his own actions as wrong. At his sentencing,

---

[3] Peter is a composite character. *Convicted* paedophiles, with some notable exceptions, usually lack his intelligence, social skills, and position, since it is very difficult to gain a conviction on the uncorroborated evidence of a child unless the offender pleads guilty. Men like Peter would know this. However, he shares a common cluster of attitudes with other paedophiles: that children are sexually knowing, and both invite and expect paedophiles' advances. My thanks here to Liz Bigelow, formerly psychologist in charge of the sex offenders programme at Pentridge Prison, Melbourne, for some very helpful conversations.

Jeffrey Dahmer, the bizarre serial killer and necrophiliac, expressed remorse over his actions. He said that he knew all along that what he was doing was wrong, that he had thought he was evil but had since been convinced by doctors that he was sick. The dichotomy between his mainstream values and his insane desires and behaviour is so marked that we are especially inclined to accept the claim that his actions were compulsive, committed under the press of alien and unwanted desires which were too strong to resist.

If any of our four is to be excused from moral responsibility on the grounds that he could not help himself, surely Jeffrey Dahmer must be the one. Yet there are grounds for thinking that even Jeffrey Dahmer was weak rather than compelled. It might be argued, as it was at the hearing of his insanity plea, that the prudential behaviour required in the planning and execution of his crimes reveals a capacity for self-control, which could and should have been exercised to bring his actions more into line with his proclaimed values. And even if we accept that his desires were irresistible, this may not, on my account, entirely exempt him from responsibility.

2. Detachment, Engagement, and Holding Responsible

These evildoers, as so far described, should seem significantly different from, say, the schizophrenic who kills her parents while in the grip of the delusions which characterize her illness. The schizophrenic is, when ill, both radically ignorant and out of control, with no possibility of addressing either deficiency. Opportunities for diachronic self-control are also greatly restricted for the schizophrenic, since the onset of episodes of such illnesses is accompanied by a loss of insight into one's mental state. The schizophrenic is, for these reasons, plainly not responsible for her terrible actions.[4] It should not be so

---

[4] It was claimed at the trial of Peter Sutcliffe, the Yorkshire Ripper, that he was acting under instructions from voices telling him to kill prostitutes. The jury did not accept this story, and they may have been right. C. L. Ten cites an experiment in the United States in which psychiatrists were deceived into making false diagnoses of schizophrenia (Ten, 1987: 129). However, the

clear that members of our rogues' gallery are to be excused. But, as Szasz (1973) and Wootten (1978) have both noted, there is a tendency to categorize evildoers by the content of their actions rather than by the aetiology of their actions, and this undiscriminating approach often leads to blanket exemptions from responsibility.

More recently, Charles Siragusa, a New York prosecutor, has bemoaned the difficulty of getting juries to abandon their natural belief that anyone capable of gruesome or bizarre acts is insane, and to accept instead that 'the guy knew exactly what he was doing, that he enjoyed it and that he got off on the violence'. He takes the view that 'anybody who takes pleasure in killing is not normal. But that does not mean they are insane' (*The Age*, Melbourne 11 Feb. 1992: 5). Siragusa accepts that in a loose sense it is appropriate to call such offenders mad, but he claims that their madness is not such as to *automatically* invoke the standard excuses and get them off the moral hook.

It is clear that the difficulty we experience in getting a grip on the psychology of the perpetrators of such acts infects our ability to assess properly the level of moral responsibility to be borne by them. We are radically unsure of how to go about apportioning blame in the case of truly atrocious actions, and so we tend to jump all too hastily from the position that anyone who does such things must in some sense be mad to the conclusion that the offender cannot really be responsible for what he did, without even examining the implicit assumption that all such people are the passive or unwilling victims of compulsive desires or benighted beliefs. Yet it seems rather strange to assume that, while the perpetrators of *moderately* bad acts

fact that schizophrenia can be feigned does not show that there are no genuine cases, or that schizophrenia does not excuse. Wendy Holloway appears to wonder why the mere fact, if it was one, that he had such delusions would excuse Sutcliffe, for the content of the delusions could be a projection of Sutcliffe's own hatred for women, and 'derives from a generalized taken-for-granted misogyny' (1987: 127). Misogyny is plainly unreasonable and men should not be excused for acting in accordance with its presumptions about women; nevertheless, if Sutcliffe had really been schizophrenic he would have lacked the capacity to check either his beliefs or his actions, and so could not properly be held responsible.

are properly blamed for what they do, the responsibility of per-petrators of worse acts is somehow erased by the very awful-ness of their deeds. Why is it that we are so often confounded in our ordinary allocations of responsibility when we are con-fronted with cases of extreme evil? Why do we assume that the ordinary measures of moral responsibility described in the pre-ceding chapter will not serve in these cases?

One answer might be to assert with Strawson that holding people responsible for what they do, praising or blaming them for their actions, is something we can *only* do in so far as we occupy the participant stance with regard to them (Strawson, 1982). Within this stance we are equals, with mutual obliga-tions, and so it makes sense to be variously aggrieved, dis-appointed, pleased, or obligated by each other's actions. We respond to each other's demands, we meet each other's ex-pectations, or we fall short. In having these kinds of reactive attitudes we manifest respect for others. For we are assuming that they too are quite generally fit for the give and take of social life, and for the particular commitments and relation-ships they have entered into, and so are capable of respond-ing appropriately to our representations and reproaches. Gary Watson points out that for Strawson the reactive attitudes 'are constitutive of moral responsibility; to regard oneself or another as responsible just is the proneness to react to them in these kinds of ways under certain conditions' (Watson, 1987: 257).

Now, sometimes these assumptions of fitness break down, as when we are confronted with a very young child, or a per-son with a severe intellectual disability; and it is then, the Strawsonian position suggests, that our ordinary practices of praise and blame falter, as we are forced to move from the participant to the objective stance. Resentment is not just inappropriate here: it cannot be sustained. Faced with incon-trovertible evidence of unfitness or unreadiness, the feelings fade. It follows then that actions which fall beyond the pale of ordinary experience and understanding might not be actions for which we can hold agents responsible, precisely because they destroy or tend to destroy assumptions of fitness and so 'pro-foundly modify' our reactive attitudes.

Contrary to Watson, I think that some such idea is pervasive, and is at the root of our ambivalent attitudes towards evildoers. Faced with such people, we do indeed tend to withdraw from the participant stance, and see them instead as 'object[s] of social policy; as a subject for what, in a wide range of sense, might be called treatment; as something certainly to be taken account, perhaps precautionary account, of; to be managed or handled or cured' (Strawson, 1982: 66). This, on Strawson's account, is incompatible with seeing them as responsible. I am not so sure.

I want to argue that the business of allocating moral responsibility is not over once we notice that the evil action was based on the kind of false beliefs and warped desires that render the person unfit for ordinary social relations. The crucial issue in deciding whether a person is responsible for her actions is not the quality of those actions, nor the content of the desires which supported them, no matter how sick or aberrant they appear to us. It is rather, as with any other case, that person's capacity to understand and to control what she was doing. And while the extreme and apparently foreign nature of their actions presses us to think that evil agents must be out of control, either brainwashed, possessed, or driven by compulsive desires too strong to resist, a more careful assessment casts doubt on this comfortable conclusion.

The thought that these people might be relevantly similar to us is profoundly unpalatable—moving to the objective stance is our instinctive denial of the proposition—but it must be entertained.[5] Most men would not identify with brutal rapists. Yet it is well established in the psychological literature that the macho attitudes of convicted rapists towards women, and their propensity to become aroused by depictions of sexual violence, are not discontinuous with attitudes found in sections of the wider population. Indeed, their attitudes and responses are largely indistinguishable from those held by a large minority of normal male college students (Koss and Leonard, 1984; Heilbrun and Seif, 1988; Malamuth and Sockloskie,

---

[5] It has of course been entertained in a number of moral traditions, including Christianity.

1991; Koralewski and Conger, 1992). The difference is, for many of them, not a difference in kind, but only one in degree or circumstance. Our tendency towards dissociation does not reflect the fact of similarity in this case; nevertheless it does not and should not prevent us from holding rapists responsible for their actions.

The argument of the preceding two chapters tends to the conclusion that moral responsibility is in fact extraordinarily difficult to evade. Our practice of holding people responsible for what they do has a more solid foundation than Strawson allows. A close analysis of our evildoers suggests that, while their failings are certainly spectacular, and disastrous in their consequences to others, they are for the most part no different in kind from those which afflict ordinary mortals. Their judgements are unreasonable, or they lack self-control. That is, the evildoers I consider turn out to be reckless or weak or compulsive, and in so far as they share our failings and our capacities, they are proper candidates for moral accountability.

3. Evil Actions, Self-control, and Moral Responsibility

My discussion of self-control has cast the net of responsibility very wide. It suggests that, in general, claims that someone was unable to exercise control over her actions should be treated with scepticism. But where precisely does this leave us with regard to the exceptional members of our rogues' gallery? To what extent are *their* actions the result of failures of self-control, rather than of judgement, and to what extent are these failures culpable? It should be apparent from the thumbnail sketches given above that in many respects these evildoers exercise impressive and sophisticated forms of control over their actions. It is therefore important to take a closer look at the level of agent-control exercised by these agents, and so begin to determine the precise nature of their failings.

(i) Intentional Control and Responsibility

Does the possession of the capacity for intentional control tell us anything about moral responsibility? While agents may sometimes be held responsible for things they do not do with particular intention (e.g. negligent actions, such as running down a pedestrian while daydreaming), it is obvious that one must be a reasonably adept intentional agent before the question of responsibility arises at all. The agents we are considering all meet this threshold. It makes sense to raise the question of their responsibility for their evil deeds. But were their *evil* actions intentional?

Though it is certain that their actions were the result of careful planning, in Jeffrey Dahmer's case at least it is not so clear that there was no loss of intentional control at the point of action. At that point Dahmer is described as 'rocking and chanting . . . in his trance . . . his whole body changed' (Masters, 1993: 19). So described, he sounds insufficiently aware of what he is doing for his behaviour to count as intentional. Nor does it seem that at this point greater awareness is possible for him; he is not like the driver who could have looked before driving through the intersection. But perhaps he is like the drunk driver who could have prevented himself from getting into such a state in the first place. Where intentional agency is voluntarily surrendered, the agent who surrenders it will not be absolved of all responsibility for subsequent events. The question of Dahmer's responsibility remains open.

If the story about intentional agency were a complete account of agent-control, then at least three of our evildoers appear to be models of control; and if this were a sufficient condition for moral responsibility there need be no more debate about their culpability. However, as I have already noted, this capacity is conceptually peripheral to our normatively loaded notions of self-control. Mere intentional self-control may be exercised by Peter and Raymond as efficiently as by Mother Theresa. It tells us almost nothing about their fitness to be called to account for their actions.

(ii) Instrumental Control and Moral Responsibility

The instrumentally self-controlled agent aims to maximize overall satisfaction of her desires given the way the world actually is.[6] She is not misled by mere proximity of pleasure or satisfaction. She has the capacity to delay gratification. Now, this kind of self-control need not be connected to the agent's evaluative beliefs or judgements of desirability. Nevertheless, we must ask whether the capacity for control at this level might not be sufficient to render the agent morally responsible for her actions.

We cannot be sure whether Himmler was acting in accordance with his strongest desires when he ordered the mass slaughter of Jews, or, rather, circumventing them in order to do what he believed to be most valuable. Jeffrey Dahmer, Raymond, and Peter do however exercise instrumental control, though in Peter's case his actions are also nominally in accordance with his values, while in Dahmer's case they contravene his values. But in each case it is clear enough that it is primarily the world which these agents seek to manipulate, not themselves. The world places certain obstacles in the way of the maximal satisfaction of their strongest desires; after all, people most often won't get into cars with strangers who plan to harm them, so they must be forced, manipulated, or tricked. Evil agents, then, may act upon the world in ways which show them to possess considerable ingenuity, foresight, and understanding of the psychology of others.

Suppose, for example, that Jeffrey Dahmer's strongest desire is that he repeatedly kill and mutilate without getting caught. In so far as he is instrumentally rational, therefore, he will not be open about what he intends to do, for he might thereby alert his prospective victims and the police. He waits, he plans, he conceals. He chooses his victims carefully— forlorn figures whose disappearance might pass unnoticed —and befriends them. He endures the present frustration of his simple desire to kill and dismember bodies, but only in order to satisfy the stronger complex of desires that he do this

---

[6] Perhaps some of our evildoers lacked self-control in this respect. Had they thought more carefully about their actual desires, they would have derived from them desires to do something other than they did. Would Dahmer have done so? Implausible. We may suppose that all of our evildoers were competent at serving their actual desires.

without getting caught.[7] This may be a virtuoso display of instrumental rationality, and it appears sufficient to satisfy Charles Siragusa and others that Dahmer and those like him are responsible for what they do. Should it so satisfy us?

Brian Masters, Dahmer's biographer, thinks not. He thinks that Dahmer's own history makes it clear that one can engage in 'logical sane actions towards an illogical insane purpose' (Masters, 1993: 19), and while he thinks that the public's attitude that such crimes have nothing to do with them is a pretence, he appears to hold that laying blame is an inappropriate response to Dahmer's plight. The very content of his desires excuses his actions. Feinberg, too, thinks that mental illness might be an independent ground of exculpation that requires our consideration, even when the standard grounds of compulsion or ignorance do not apply. He argues that 'if we treat the mentally ill criminal in precisely the same way as we treat the normal one, we can only bring him to the point of hopeless despair . . . His bizarre desires will be taken as simply given, as evil impulses with no point and no reward' (Feinberg, 1970b: 291).

There are two responses to be made here. First, I believe that we must not confuse the question of a person's responsibility for their actions with questions about their subsequent treatment. It would, for example, be callous and counterproductive to reproach the depressive for not seeking help, even if it is true that she could have done so. Holding someone responsible, to whatever extent, need not and should not rule out compassion for their plight or an acknowledgement of any contribution made by society to their predicament. Indeed, the suggested move away from the pretence that evildoers are inhuman monsters who are *nothing* like us, which is implicit in holding them responsible, may prevent us from treating them inhumanely.[8]

---

[7] This interpretation may impute too much in the way of prudence to Dahmer. For many such crimes, it is likely that the planning and preparation is exciting in itself. Anticipation offers its own pleasures, and its rituals should not be confused with self-control.

[8] Gary Watson's paper on Robert Harris, the killer who was so indifferent to his crime that he ate the left-over hamburger of his young victim

Second, it is not yet clear that the standard grounds for excuse do not apply in this case, so it is not clear that some extra ground will be needed if we wish to excuse Dahmer. Feinberg's attachment to the idea of mental illness as an independent ground of exculpation appears to be a consequence of his views on compulsion. For Feinberg, the defence of compulsion is not available, since he thinks no desire is literally irresistible. It will always be the case that if the person had tried harder they could have resisted. And while any desire may be difficult to resist if one is in a 'weakened condition', he thinks there is no reason to suppose that 'so-called sick desires' are more difficult to resist than ordinary desires (1970*b*: 283).

But if sick desires are not harder for the agent to resist, it is a mystery why Feinberg wants to excuse those who do not resist them, for surely they are precisely the desires which ought to be resisted. And if certain sick desires are especially hard to resist, as Dahmer's desires may have been, then we don't need to look beyond the dimension of control to find an excuse for the agent who acts on them.

Feinberg here seems to be suggesting that what excuses in these cases is the nexus between the content and the persistence of the agent's desires. While rejecting the notion that 'senseless misunderstood motives' should automatically count as compulsive, he points out that such motives, when persistent, might be considered an unfair burden. A senseless bizarre desire is no harder for the agent 'to restrain on individual occasions, but he must be restraining it *always*; one slip and he is undone' (Feinberg, 1970*b*: 290). This sounds plausible: one would certainly feel sympathy for a person so burdened. But

(Watson, 1987), makes this kind of point, I think. He writes: 'The fact that Harris's cruelty is an intelligible response to his circumstances gives a foothold not only for sympathy, but for the thought that if *I* had been subjected to such circumstances, I might well have become as vile . . . This thought induces not only an ontological shudder, but a sense of equality with the other' (276).

However, this does not mean that Harris was not vile or that anyone in his circumstances would have acted as he did. Harris himself believed that he had chosen his path. I note also that the reports of Harris's execution revealed that his last act was to mouth the word 'sorry' to the father of one of his victims. He was not, after all, outside the moral community.

on closer examination it is hard to sustain. Why would such desires mitigate responsibility unless they are also reasonably strong and intrusive? I might have a very mild recurring desire to drive on the wrong side of the road, but I don't see that its pointless and persistent nature excuses my driving on the wrong side of the road, when it is always easy for me to resist. In any case, persistent *bizarre* desires are not the only desires that we might always need to be restraining. A desire to cheat on one's spouse is not at all bizarre, but it might be persistent; one slip and fidelity is undone. It is clear that what is actually doing the mitigating in the cases Feinberg is thinking of is the *compulsive* nature of the desires.

While Masters and Feinberg are surely right to point out that the mere presence of behaviour which is appropriately designed to fulfil a desire of the agent does not settle the question of her responsibility (after all, a child or even a dog may display such behaviour), neither does their favoured option of excusing those actions designed to serve bizarre desires. I would argue, however, that the sophisticated capacity for instrumental self-control displayed by our evildoers cannot be dismissed as irrelevant. It seems to me that the capacity for instrumental self-control *is* significant when considering the allocation of moral responsibility, in providing good (though not conclusive) evidence that the agent is sufficiently knowledgeable and sufficiently sophisticated in her reasoning to have had the opportunity to form her values in accordance with reason, and to have had some capacity to act according to those values. Thus agents who display a refined capacity for instrumental control may be considered, *prima facie*, responsible for their actions.

This, of course, is not the end of the story. There is another rung on the hierarchy of control that must be consulted. Continent, compulsive, and weak-willed acts are certainly all intentional; and, intuitively at least, they may also be instrumentally rational. But they are not equally culpable, since, according to the distinctions drawn in the preceding chapter, the continent agent succeeds in acting in accordance with a normative judgement, the weak-willed agent fails when it was open to her to succeed, whereas the compulsive agent, at least at the time of action, could not have succeeded. Common sense holds that these distinctions underwrite a differential allocation of responsibility. We must find out, therefore, whether our agents' actions were freely chosen in accordance with their values, or at least with some other norm by which they govern their behaviour. If they were, we must examine the quality of their judgements in order to finally diagnose their failings and their degree of culpability.

(iii) Orthonomous Self-control and Moral Responsibility

The possibility of third-tier control only arises for those agents who recognize or adopt some kind of norm to govern their particular projects, judgements, and actions: who see these norms as exerting a requirement on them which might sometimes conflict with their other projects or desires. The norms of reason, properly explicated, bring agents under the rule of the right (see Chapter 4). Such agents are broadly constrained in their practical judgements by thoughts of what would be good or reasonable, desirable, or at least permissible. When these agents act in accordance with such judgements they act orthonomously. But orthonomy is not always easy to achieve, and agents may need to exercise self-control to bring their actions into line with their judgements.

Initially it looks as though three of our agents—Dahmer, Himmler, and Peter—are in the business of evaluating their deeds in distinctively moral terms. Raymond is not, and will be considered separately. Peter uses the language of rights to justify his actions; Himmler speaks of his obligation to the German people and the future, and regrets the unavoidable suffering involved; and Dahmer makes it clear that he knew all along that what he did was wrong. He killed, he says, 'for my own warped selfish desires for self-gratification . . . I should have stayed with God . . . I tried and failed and created a holocaust' (Melbourne *Herald-Sun*, 18 Feb. 1992: 4).

None of these agents excludes himself from the moral realm; all are apparently committed to judging in accordance with reason. With this in mind, does a consideration of their capacity to conform their actions to their values fix, without remainder, the degree of responsibility they should bear for their actions?

Orthonomous self-control is called for when a gap opens up between an agent's evaluations and her desires. For Dahmer this gap may have been unbridgeable. In Himmler's case the gap, when it opened, was bridgeable. But for Peter the gap never opens at all. What kinds of control did these agents exercise, and what kinds might have been possible for them?

Many of the techniques used to exercise self-control at the moment of temptation are common to both instrumental and orthonomous control. In so far as synchronic self-control just involves focusing on certain facts, we have seen that this can be done in the service of one's strongest complex desires, or in the service of one's values. Therefore, as instrumentally rational agents, all of our evildoers could be presumed to have had some knowledge and experience of restoring, redirecting, or narrowing the focus of their attention as appropriate.

Heinrich Himmler does appear to have exercised control in this way. Acting in accordance with his highest values required him to overcome a felt reluctance to inflict suffering on the Jews, and this I suspect would largely have been done by continual rehearsing and reviewing of the reasons he saw for getting rid of the Jews. He did not relish doing what he thought it was desirable that he do, and it looks obvious that if he had believed some other course of action was prescribed by his values, he would have had no independent pleasure in, or inclination toward, mass murder. According to Bennett (1974: 128–9), Himmler paid a physical and emotional price for keeping his sympathies firmly subordinate to his values. His actions, though not *broadly* orthonomous, because the judgements from which they flowed were not appropriately re-sponsive to the reasons available to him, were at least *strictly* orthonomous. He had the capacity for synchronic self-control, and therefore must be held fully responsible for his actions, unless it can be shown that the mistakes he made at the level of judge-ment were innocent or excusable.

Jeffrey Dahmer did not exercise synchronic control, and it seems most probable that he could not have. For we can imag-ine that his desires were so salient that no attempt at redirecting or narrowing the focus of his attention would have succeeded in supplanting them. A successful exercise of synchronic self-control through the technique of expansion and aggregation of motives would also have been beyond him, since that is largely contingent upon the agent having an adequate range of interests, values, and desires. Earlier, I claimed that it is a rare agent indeed who has no such resources to call upon in situations of temptation. But Jeffrey Dahmer *is* rare indeed. Feinberg suggests that what distinguishes the motives of some mentally ill wrongdoers is that 'their motives do not fit together and make a coherent whole because one kind of desire, conspicuous as a sore thumb, keeps getting in the way' (Feinberg, 1970*b*: 287). In Dahmer's case, however, it seems that his ordinary values were the sore thumb, and his dreadful desires were the organizing principle of his life. He had 'compensated for a deprivation of affective contact by constructing a secret alternative life into which strayed people who . . . were reduced to being nothing more than props in his private fantasies' (Masters, 1993: 19). This suggests that, at the time of action at least, Dahmer had no other desires and interests with which to oppose his obsession with dead bodies. Synchronic self-control was quite beyond him. He was in fact acting compulsively.

Does this mean that he should be excused from all responsibility? This will depend on whether we think that Dahmer could have done something in advance to forestall his evil actions. It should be apparent from our earlier discussion that the techniques of diachronic self-control are *especially* useful—indeed necessary—for people subject to compulsive or repulsive desires which they do not value.

Given this, the capacity for self-control across time will be crucial to determining the level of moral responsibility to be borne by those who have performed evil acts under the press of desires too strong to resist. Perhaps their evil desires are both overriding and ever-present; if this is so, they deserve sympathy not blame. But any such claims must be treated with great caution. On the analysis given in Chapter 5, opportunities to exercise self-control are so abundant that it will be an extraordinary person who can truthfully claim that at no point could she have done other than exactly what she did. Evildoers who, at the time that they did so, could not but have performed their evil action may still be held responsible for past failures to exercise control when such exercise was possible, and could have had a material impact on whether or not the evil action was eventually performed.

Of course, the successful exercise of self-control, whether synchronic or diachronic, does require a bit of know-how, and agents should not be held responsible for failures which rest on ignorance—either of the *need* to exercise self-control in the circumstances, or of the *ways* in which it may be done. But, to provide excuse, such ignorance must not itself be culpable or simply unbelievable. It is no excuse for the alcoholic to say that she didn't know that she would have a drink if she went to the party, and therefore didn't realize that diachronic self-control was called for, if she has been to many parties and has drunk to excess at all of them. For his part, Jeffrey Dahmer, at least after committing several murders, could not excuse his subsequent offences by saying that he did not foresee that the temptations would arise again, and that he therefore did not see any reason to take steps to ensure that they could not be acted upon.

Dahmer believed that his desires were evil, and he took great care to hide them. Why did he not bend his efforts towards getting rid of them instead? Perhaps there was nothing he could do short of confessing his state to someone; and perhaps this would have been very difficult. But, given the gravity of his offences, the attempt should have been made. Wherever there is room to manoeuvre, there is an accrual of moral responsibility. *If* Jeffrey Dahmer had room to manoeuvre, it is both intelligible and appropriate to hold him at least partially responsible for the consequences of not doing so.[9]

What about Peter? Perhaps he is like Himmler. He has no visible problem with self-control, so presumably his failings

---

[9] This is a big 'if'. In Dahmer's case it appears that his sexual obsession with dead bodies began in early adolescence. It seems unreasonable to expect that *he* could have foreseen the outcome of such an interest while still a child or have reported his feelings and sought help for them when such help might have been effective. Perhaps the responsibility lies as much with those who may have suspected the direction of his interests.

are confined to the level of judgement. His manifest failings in judgement will be discussed shortly. For the moment I want to explore a bit further the question of Peter's capacity for self-control.

In my discussion of compulsion I noted that it is possible for someone to value an activity which she in fact performs compulsively. What makes it the case that a desire is compulsive is the truth of certain counterfactuals. Desires and values *should* vary, if not actually then at least counterfactually. Under certain conditions a gap should appear between an agent's judgement and her desires. In Peter's case, we can safely assume that, had he judged that it was undesirable that he have sex with children, some such gap would have opened, since it is unlikely that his desires would have evaporated completely upon the reflection that such actions are wrong. If we also think that he would have been unable to resist these desires, then his responsibility for his actions may be much reduced.

But Peter's circumstances are in no way as extreme as Jeffrey Dahmer's. His interests are varied; he is intelligent, respected, and well paid. His desire for sex with children is his sore thumb, though, in the actual world, he does not recognize it as such. Techniques of both synchronic and diachronic control are abundantly available to him. Were he to judge that he ought not act on his desires, he could call upon his fear of losing his job and reputation, and remind himself of the distress exposure would cause his mother. He could reflect on the hurt to his young victims. He could resign his positions in youth groups, and immerse himself in activities which did not involve contact with children. And he has both the knowledge and the means to seek professional help to control or eliminate his desires.

We must conclude that Peter's desires are not irresistible, though he may be dispositionally weak-willed. But, in the event that he acknowledges that self-control is called for, he has the skills and resources necessary to exercise synchronic as well as diachronic self-control, and so on this dimension he appears to possess all the qualifications for being held responsible for his actions.

So far, only Jeffrey Dahmer's responsibility is mitigated by considerations of our evildoers' capacities for self-control. As his judgement that his actions were wrong is undoubtedly correct, it is not necessary to consider him further. For our other evildoers, however, an examination of the quality of their judgements is crucial to determining their responsibility.

4. *Freedom, Recklessness, and Responsibility*

(i) The Rationalizer

Consider a person who claims to value honesty but then finds herself in a situation where it would be to her advantage to tell a lie, and so wants to tell a lie. We would expect the gap between judgement and desire to open in this circumstance, so signalling to the agent the need to exercise self-control. But suppose there turns out to be no gap, or suppose that it is invariably closed by a shift in the agent's judgements. Then there is subjectively no occasion for this person to exercise self-control when she wants to lie, for it will turn out that *this* lie is always permissible.

Peter's values seem to be rather like this, i.e. unduly, if not entirely, influenced and maintained by his actual desires. He believes it is permissible for him to have sex with children, because they have consented and he does not hurt them. But these beliefs are more responsive to his desires than to the evidence, and we can test this counterfactually. If Peter did not desire sex with children, would he find the arguments supporting such actions at all persuasive? Now, it is highly improbable that any adult who did not independently desire to have sexual relations with small children would come to believe that this was a good or permissible thing—that children wanted or were in any way benefited by such contact with adults. It is unlikely that they could be so blind to the power imbalance between adults and children as to imagine that children are the choosers and initiators of such transactions. Yet this is just what Peter does think. And Peter is, in other areas of his life, perfectly amenable to the evidence when forming his beliefs. If we think his obnoxious beliefs could not survive the loss of the relevant desires, we must conclude that Peter is simply engaging in wishful thinking, and that the harmony between his judgements and his actions displays, at best, mere narrow orthonomy.[10]

Peter's values are shaped behind his back by his desires, but this is no excuse for them. His ignorance is not innocent. For we are each of us responsible for scrutinizing our values and ensuring that they are responsive to the evidence, and susceptible of justification to those affected. This Peter does not do. He is not guided by the standards of reason to which he pays lip service when justifying his actions.

It would be hard to believe that such reflection is altogether beyond him. Agents such as Peter might well be forced by certain rational requirements, such as consistency, to extend their judgements, and thus expand the area within which the need to exercise self-control can present itself. For example, if Peter's judgement that he ought not to steal his client's money is motivated in part by the thought that it is a violation of trust, then it should be possible for him to come to see that abuse of children is a violation of trust too, and so that he ought not to do that either. If agents will not extend or modify their judgements in the face of sound evidence or good argument, they are properly subject to censure. If their ignorance of right values or appropriate action stems from an insensitivity to the concerns of others, from a failure to listen to, reflect upon, and respond to evidence and criticism, or from a selective response to evidence and criticism, then their ignorance is culpable, and will not exempt them from responsibility for their evil actions. If they had known better they might have acted differently. And it seems possible that they could indeed have known better.

It would be hard, in any event, to believe that Peter was not aware of the dissonance between the very deliberate actions he undertook in order to win the trust of parents and children alike at the local youth group, and the plans he had to abuse that trust once it was secured. And if he noticed the dissonance, the question would arise as to whether he could have exercised self-control to conform his actions to his more firmly

---

[10] It is of course no *coincidence* that this concordance exists. See Chs. 4 and 5 for the distinction between narrow and strict orthonomy.

grounded values. We have answered that question in the affirmative, though Peter's laxness in forming some of his values suggests that he might be equally lax in acting on them. Peter's failures are Peter's responsibility, and while we may pity him for his aberrant desires, we have every right to blame him for his evil actions and to demand that he do better.

(ii) The Ideologue

Himmler, like Peter, is clearly responsible for his evil deeds. He too acted on the basis of evil values, but in his case the fault is not that he was weak, or given to rationalization: it is that he was arrogant. While he exercised rigid control over his actions, he failed to ensure that the appropriate checks and balances were in place to regulate his values. Our evaluative beliefs tell us about what we have reason to do; in forming these beliefs, then, we need to attend to the relevant evidence, or we may end up being mistaken about what we have reason to do.

Our values are subject to pressure from both our sympathies and other contrary desires. Most often the contrary desires are a cue to us to exercise self-control. But often enough, when our sympathies run counter to our antecedently held values, we should take a second look at the values themselves, for the circumstances which trigger the need for self-control are phenomenologically very similar to the circumstances which cue the need for value revision. A wise agent will know the difference, or should discover it in the course of revisiting her reasons. Himmler's error was not in failing to have sympathy for his victims, but in failing to heed his sympathies in the way he should have done, so displaying a culpable lack of humility with regard to his evaluative beliefs.

It will not do to defend Himmler by speaking of the atmosphere of the times. Of course it would have been difficult to resist the anti-Semitic propaganda, and the vision splendid of the thousand-year Reich. Of course, any one of us might have fallen under its spell. But that would not have excused us, and it does not excuse him, of the responsibility for the organized suffering and deaths of concentration camp inmates, though it should of course induce in us a certain humility, and a sharp awareness of our moral luck. Himmler was not an impressionable child, with no access to information other than official propaganda, and no contact with Jewish people to contradict its gruesome lies. He chose to sacrifice Jews and Russians to the greater glory of the Fatherland with his eyes open. We might excuse the members of the Hitler Youth, but not the members of Hitler's inner circle.

(iii) The Outsider

To the extent that we hold Jeffrey Dahmer, Peter, and Himmler morally responsible for their values and their actions, we are reacting to them, in Watson's words, as moral selves. But where does Raymond fit in this discussion? Do the dimensions of judgement and control allow us to categorize his actions as actions for which he can be held responsible? For Raymond does not seem to belong at all. Unlike our other rogues, he does not acknowledge any moral constraints on action; he explicitly places himself outside the boundaries of moral address. Having no values as we have described them, he can apparently neither succeed nor fail in orthonomous control. Of all our evildoers he seems the most alien, the most unreachable.

But Raymond is no wanton. He is apparently neither particularly impulsive nor compulsively driven. He is not at the mercy of passing desire. Rather he claims for himself a kind of existential freedom which is incompatible with both wantonness and orthonomy. He is perfectly capable of selecting a project and sticking to it: it is just that he does not base his choices in reason. Arguably, he might adopt the Frankfurtian norm of identification described in the preceding chapter; but in so far as any governing norm can be attributed to Raymond I think it is closer to a Sartrean norm of authenticity.[11] In any case he is, in Frankfurt's terms, a free agent since he is moved only by those desires he most wants to be moved by. Raymond is autonomous, though not of course

---

[11] See Ch. 4. I acknowledge that Sartre thinks the use of any norms to govern choice is a denial of freedom, and as such is in bad faith. See Sartre (1956), also Sartre (1992: ch. 4). But he does seem to set up some governing principle of action in his insistence on freedom, and his critique of bad faith.

orthonomous, since he rejects or is in some sense impervious to the broad constraints of reason.[12] But autonomy is, for Frankfurt, sufficient for moral responsibility. Is he right?

I have argued that moral responsibility is to be measured along the dimensions of control and judgement. When we look along the dimension of control, in Raymond's case the results are inconclusive. We can be confident that, if Raymond had decided to take up hang-gliding rather than abduction and murder, he would have had no difficulty in acting on his decisions. Perhaps the world in which he does take up hang-gliding is not a very distant world. But what can we say about Raymond's capacity for self-control in the world where he decides that he *ought not* to abduct others: in the world where he decides that their interests provide an unassailable reason for him to refrain?

I think we are left with nothing to say, because in that world Raymond is unrecognizably different from the way he actually is; it is unimaginable that *Raymond* would make such a judgement, so we simply cannot guess how his desires and actions might be affected. In all near worlds, Raymond conforms to social and moral conventions to suit himself. Where there are good instrumental reasons for conforming to them, as there often are, where conforming will contribute to his well-being, as it often will, he can conform. But we suppose too much when we suppose that Raymond's actions might be governable by these other kinds of considerations, because first we have to think that Raymond is capable of responding to these considerations at the level of judgement.[13] So the question of his responsibility centres upon a consideration of the nature of his failures at the level of judgement.

---

[12] On the Humean model endorsed by Dreier and Foot, Raymond is, of course, lacking nothing in the way of rationality.

[13] I said at the beginning that Raymond is a family man, and so the question arises as to whether he has non-instrumental, non-self-centred concern for his wife and daughters. Certainly he behaves affectionately towards them. But one gets the feeling that a man like Raymond might really be *playing* at being the family man. He enjoys the lifestyle; he finds their affection amusing and pleasurable; he has some fondness for them. It is revealing of the reflexive and shallow nature of his affections, however, that he is able to find amusement in practising a technique he will use in the abduction on one of his daughters.

When we look at the nature of his failures rather than at the content of his judgements, we might conclude that Raymond's indifference to moral claims in forming his particular judgements is not really so unusual. His motivation in fact differs little from that of individuals who are moved exclusively by intellectual curiosity, or who go skydiving or mountain climbing just to see if they can. Like them, Raymond enjoys a challenge; like many of them he is thoroughly self-centred. He is aware of the interests of his victims, just as the scientist might be aware of the claims of his family, but they carry no weight in his deliberations. The primary motivation for his actions seems to be a kind of curiosity: what would it be like to do something evil? Could *he* do something really evil? This keen, experimental interest in evil may be rare, but why should Raymond not be considered just as good a candidate for moral responsibility as the person who challenges herself to sail solo round the world on a raft, or to climb Mt Everest, for no other reason than that she wonders if she can?

A retrospective glance at the breathtakingly amoral and self-centred tycoons of the final decades of the twentieth century might also help to convince us that Raymond falls into a well-populated category of evildoers, though few of them would be able to articulate the philosophical underpinnings of their rejection of ordinary constraints. Their judgements and actions are unreasonable, not because they misrepresent the legitimate concerns of others, as Peter does, but because they are deeply indifferent to them. The indifference which Raymond displays is at the extreme end of even this spectrum, to be sure. But indifference itself is not beyond our comprehension; it is not such as to confound us in our moral responses to amoral tycoons. If they are to be held responsible for their failures along the dimension of judgement, then why not Raymond?

However, this is too quick a conclusion. Raymond is unique in that his indifference is global, not particular—as the athlete's indifference to family claims or the tycoon's indifference to societal good might be. These agents, like Peter, might display moral allegiances or moral sensitivities in other areas of their lives, which, however primitive, make remonstration and

argument possible, and so may serve to reveal their indifference as unreasonable, even by their own lights.

For such people there is, in Bernard Williams' words, 'no
bottomless gulf between this state [the capacity to think at least
sometimes in terms of other people's interests] and the basic
dispositions of morality . . . if we grant a man with even a
minimal concern for others, then we do not have to ascribe to
him any fundamentally new kind of thought or experience to
include him in the world of morality, but only what is recognizably an extension of what he already has' (Williams, 1972:
23–4).

If Raymond constitutively lacks this entrée into the moral
realm—if he simply cannot recognize the interests of others as
reason-giving—then there is no possibility of his coming to be
moved by moral concerns and moral reasons. He really is an
outsider among us, and it would be as pointless to blame him
for failing to be moved by moral concerns as it would be to
upbraid a blind person for failing to appreciate a Van Gogh.
He is the person for whom moral language is, in Korsgaard's
terms, 'mere noise'.

This does not mean, though, that we are helpless in the face
of the Raymonds of this world. Although they cannot be held
morally responsible for what they do, they are, after all, perfectly rational in the sophisticated Humean sense. Although
they cannot internalize moral and legal standards, they do know
what these are. How else could Raymond so effectively set his
face against them? He uses these very standards, along with
the ordinary goodwill and trust of others, to achieve his evil
ends. Raymond is a rational calculator of the likely costs and
benefits of his actions; and he is quite capable of deciding to
desist if the cost, and the probability of detection, are made
high enough. For example, when he drives across the border
into France, with Saskia's boyfriend in the car, he calmly tells
him that if they are required to show their passports the
deal is off. Rex will not find out what happened to Saskia.
Raymond does what he does with his eyes open. He thus fulfils
the requirements for *legal* responsibility, which, I suggest, are
lower than those for moral responsibility.

Here are some well-accepted examples which highlight this
distinction. It might be better if we obeyed the rules of the road

out of co-operative concern for the safety of all, but the law is indifferent as to whether we obey them for those reasons or out of a desire to avoid the sanctions that are placed on breaking them. It is also indifferent as to our reasons for breaking the rules; very few excuses are accepted in this area. Strict liability applies to most traffic offences, and the probability of being caught and punished has proved a very effective deterrent. Likewise, it would certainly be better if people refrained from murder because murder is wrong, but the law is largely unconcerned with people's reasons for refraining from murder. It cares only that they do refrain, though here the standard excuses are accepted: the accused must have had the capacity and fair opportunity to conform her actions to the law.

I am not suggesting that strict liability should apply in the criminal law. But we don't need strict liability to hold Raymond legally responsible for his actions, for they were not performed inadvertently, or in ignorance of the law, or under duress. If we know the rules, and are capable of making the calculations and of being deterred by the prospect of punishment, then that should be sufficient for our being held responsible, in this lesser sense, and treated accordingly.

Joel Feinberg agrees that 'from the point of view of what punishment can achieve for others, it is a perfectly appropriate mode of treatment for rationally competent, non-compulsive mentally ill offenders' (1970*b*: 291). However, he thinks that this represents an unenlightened approach, which achieves nothing for the offender himself. He argues instead for the period of incarceration to be given over to sympathetic attempts to help the offender to achieve self-understanding, in the hope that this will 'permit him to become a responsible citizen' (292).

But Raymond is not like the rather pathetic offenders Feinberg considers. He is not lacking in insight, and he is not being violated by his own desires. He is well aware that he is different from other people; but nothing can be done about that. Sympathy, reproach, and paternalistic treatment are all equally out of place. Indeed, placing Raymond in rehabilitation and counselling programmes may even show a lack of respect for him. This is not to say, of course, that punishment beyond the deprivation of liberty is warranted, for Raymond or for anyone else. It is just to argue that in such unusual cases legal address, not welfarism, properly replaces moral address.[14] Raymond voluntarily takes a calculated risk: he plays a game which he knows he may lose, and he enjoys playing it. Thus he cannot entirely escape responsibility for the consequences of his actions, and we are able to reconcile our recognition of his status as a moral outsider with the intuition that he merits punishment.

5. Conclusion

I have argued for the conclusion that all of our evildoers bear some responsibility for their evil actions, though Raymond cannot be held *morally* responsible, and Dahmer's moral responsibility is quite limited. The insistence on at least partial responsibility in the case of Dahmer, and full responsibility for Peter and Himmler, may seem harsh. Holding Himmler responsible is surely being wise after the event. Holding Dahmer and Peter responsible rubs salt in the wounds of lives already damaged by grotesque desires. But, as I have already argued, holding people responsible is not incompatible with compassionate treatment or with forgiveness, and holding *ourselves* responsible is very often done in hindsight. We realize that a decision was too hasty, or that it didn't take proper account

---

[14] Of course some forms of punishment may not themselves be morally justified. If the punishment proposed was cruel and unusual then we would not be morally justified in demanding that someone be punished according to law. Likewise if the law itself was morally obnoxious in prohibiting some behaviour, say, the admission of Aborigines to public swimming pools, we would not be morally justified in demanding that violations be punished according to law. But I am assuming that it is not the case that the prohibition on murder is unjustified or that the punishment is excessive, so it will not be morally offensive to hold Raymond legally responsible.

Raymond is the only one of our selection of evildoers for whom legal and moral address come apart. Dahmer to a considerable extent lacked the capacity to conform his actions to the law, and so ought largely to escape legal as well as moral responsibility, and Peter has both the knowledge and the capacity to obey the law. Himmler's actions did indeed conform to the law of Nazi Germany, but the law itself was clearly morally reprehensible, so Himmler cannot escape moral responsibility. The question of our moral responsibility to obey the law is, of course, a large one which I cannot address more fully here.

of someone else's viewpoint; we realize that an action was un-
kind, and that we could have controlled our anger by leaving
the room. These are proper matters for regret and self-
reproach (though of course not *excessive* self-reproach). No one
is less admirable than a person who finds endless excuses for
her own deficiencies. No one is less likely to behave responsibly in the future. By holding ourselves responsible for past
actions, we make ourselves responsible for our future actions.

If it is appropriate for us to take responsibility for our own
actions, then it is in principle appropriate to hold others
responsible for their failures. This is not just to be seen as a
strategy for drawing others into the moral community—as a
way of making them responsible by *holding* them responsible.[15]
That is indeed a way of instilling or teaching responsibility, of
bringing agents to see themselves as responsible, but it will be
completely inappropriate unless there is real scope for the
agent to exercise judgement and control over her actions.

We can't make a ten year old *truly* responsible for the running of Microsoft by appointing her managing director, and
announcing that she will be blamed for any company losses.
We can't even make her responsible by somehow inducing her
to *believe* that she is responsible. Holding people responsible
must make the right connections to their capacities. Nevertheless, finding endless excuses for others is as bad as making
endless excuses for ourselves, and is usually just as misplaced.
Of course we need a certain humility in approaching questions
of moral responsibility; our knowledge of other people's
circumstances is bound to be limited, so we should not rush
to judgement. But neither should we be paralysed, when the
conditions for responsibility appear to be met, because of the
unpleasant or even horrific nature of the action the agent
performs.

---

[15] This has been suggested in the case of trust. Trusting someone can make
them trustworthy (Gambetta, 1988: 234). Similarly, giving someone responsibility might make them behave responsibly. But here the term 'responsible' has a quite different connotation from the way in which I have used it
to discuss blameworthiness. As a character trait, responsibleness is not far
removed from trustworthiness. However, someone who is not at all trustworthy may well be blameworthy for what she does.

Attributions of moral responsibility, then, are not just made from a participant stance, and do not always depend upon our assessment of someone's present capacity to engage with us and respond to our reproaches from within that stance. The prerequisites for responsibility are, rather, the prerequisites for reason; moral failures are always failures to be, in the broad sense given in Chapter 4, reasonable.

So, though at first glance the actions of our evildoers seemed to be beyond comprehension, and therefore beyond rational assessment and criticism, a close examination has indicated that for the most part their failures are depressingly commonplace. They are weak, reckless, or compulsive. They have not invented any new categories of error; they are just worst cases in those categories. We can locate their failings in the same places as we find our own. Even Raymond, the outsider, serves to remind us of the dangers and unreasonableness of undue self-centredness and indifference to the concerns of others.[16] In holding these agents responsible for their evaluative beliefs, their actions, and even to some extent for their desires, we admit our own responsibility to do what we do on the basis of a set of broadly reasonable beliefs, to be responsive to our sympathies and to the legitimate interests of others, and to develop our capacities for control over excessive or manifestly unreasonable desires.

---

[16] He also shows, I think, the absurdity of imagining that morality could be based on self-interest alone.

BIBLIOGRAPHY

ARISTOTLE (*NE*), *Nichomachean Ethics*, trans. David Ross (Oxford: Oxford University Press, 1980).
—— *Politics*, trans. T. A. Sinclair, revd. Trevor J. Saunders (Harmondsworth: Penguin, 1992).
BAIER, Annette (1987), 'The Need for More than Justice', *Canadian Journal of Philosophy*, suppl. vol. 13: 41–56.
BARON, Marcia (1984), 'The Alleged Moral Repugnance of Acting from Duty', *Journal of Philosophy*, 81: 197–220.
BENNETT, Jonathan (1974), 'The Conscience of Huckleberry Finn', *Philosophy*, 49: 123–34.
BERKELEY, George (1710), *The Principles of Human Knowledge*, ed. G. J. Warnock (London: Fontana, 1962).
BERLIN, Isaiah (1969), *Four Essays on Liberty* (Oxford: Oxford University Press).
BIGELOW, John, Dodds, Susan M., and Pargetter, Robert (1990), 'Temptation and the Will', *American Philosophical Quarterly*, 27: 39–49.
BISHOP, John (1989), *Natural Agency: An Essay on the Causal Theory of Action* (Cambridge: Cambridge University Press).
BOSWELL, James (1791), *The Life of Samuel Johnson*, ed. E. Malone (Oxford: Oxford University Press, 1946).
BRINK, David O. (1997), 'Moral Motivation', *Ethics*, 108: 4–32.
CHARLES, D. (1982–3), 'Rationality and Irrationality', *Proceedings of the Aristotelian Society*, 83: 191–212.
CHURCHLAND, Patricia (1986), *Neurophilosophy* (Cambridge, Mass.: MIT Press).
CHURCHLAND, Paul (1988), *Matter and Consciousness: A Contemporary Introduction to the Philosophy of Mind*, revd. edn. (Cambridge, Mass.: MIT Press).
COCKING, Dean, and Oakley, Justin (1995), 'Indirect Consequentialism, Friendship, and the Problem of Alienation', *Ethics*, 106: 86–111.
COHEN, Daniel (1999), 'Free Will Hunting', unpub. B.A. honours research paper (Monash University).
COHON, Rachel (1986), 'Are External Reasons Impossible?', *Ethics*, 96: 545–56.

COPP, David (1997), 'Belief, Reason, and Motivation: Michael Smith's *The Moral Problem*', *Ethics*, 108: 33–54.

CORDNER, Christopher (1985), 'Jackson on Weakness of Will', *Mind*, 94: 273–80.

CULLITY, Garrett, and Gaut, Berys (1997) (eds.), *Ethics and Practical Reason* (Oxford: Clarendon Press).

DALGARNO, Melvin, and Matthews, Eric (1989) (eds.), *The Philosophy of Thomas Reid* (Boston: Kluwer Academic Publishers).

DAVIDSON, Donald (1969), 'How is Weakness of the Will Possible?', in Joel Feinberg (ed.), *Moral Concepts* (Oxford: Oxford University Press), 93–113.

—— (1980*a*), 'Actions, Reasons and Causes', in Davidson (1980*b*), 3–19; 1st publ. in *Journal of Philosophy*, 60 (1963), 685–99.

—— (1980*b*), *Essays on Actions and Events* (Oxford: Clarendon Press).

—— (1980*c*), 'Freedom to Act', in Davidson (1980*b*), 63–81; 1st publ. in Ted Honderich (ed.), *Essays on Freedom of Action* (London: Routledge & Kegan Paul, 1973), 137–56.

DEIGH, John (1995), 'Empathy and Universalizability', *Ethics*, 105: 743–63.

DREIER, James (1997), 'Humean Doubts about the Practical Justification of Morality', in Cullity and Gaut (1997), 81–99.

DWORKIN, Gerald (1988), *The Theory and Practice of Autonomy* (Cambridge: Cambridge University Press).

ELSTER, Jon (1979), *Ulysses and the Sirens: Studies in Rationality and Irrationality* (Cambridge: Cambridge University Press).

—— (1983), *Sour Grapes: Studies in the Subversion of Rationality* (Cambridge: Cambridge University Press).

FEINBERG, Joel (1970*a*), *Doing and Deserving* (Princeton, NJ: Princeton University Press).

—— (1970*b*), 'What is so Special about Mental Illness?', in Feinberg (1970*a*), 272–92.

FESTINGER, Leon (1957), *A Theory of Cognitive Dissonance* (Evanston, Ill.: Row, Peterson and Co.).

—— (1964), *Conflict, Decision and Dissonance* (London: Tavistock).

FISCHER, John Martin, and Ravizza, Mark (1993) (eds.), *Perspectives on Moral Responsibility* (Ithaca, NY: Cornell University Press).

FLANAGAN, Owen, and Rorty, Amelie Oksenberg (1990) (eds), *Identity, Character and Morality: Essays in Moral Psychology* (Cambridge, Mass.: MIT Press).

FOOT, Philippa (1978*a*), 'Morality as a System of Hypothetical Imperatives', in Foot (1978*c*), 157–73; 1st publ. in *Philosophical Review*, 81 (1972): 305–16.

—— (1978*b*), 'Reasons for Action and Desires', in Foot (1978*c*), 148–56; 1st publ. in *Proceedings of the Aristotelian Society*, suppl. vol. 46 (1972), 203–10.

—— (1978*c*), *Virtues and Vices and Other Essays in Moral Philosophy* (Oxford: Basil Blackwell).

FRANKFURT, Harry G. (1971), 'Freedom of the Will and the Concept of a Person', *Journal of Philosophy*, 68: 5–20.

GAMBETTA, Diego (1988), 'Can We Trust Trust?', in D. Gambetta (ed.), *Trust: Making and Breaking Cooperative Relations* (New York: Basil Blackwell), 213–37.

GILLIGAN, C. (1982), *In a Different Voice: Psychological Theory and Women's Development* (Cambridge, Mass.: Harvard University Press).

GILOVICH, T. (1991), *How We Know What Isn't So* (New York: Macmillan).

GROSSBERG, S., and Gutowski, W. (1987), 'Neural Dynamics of Decision Making under Risk: Affective Balance and Cognitive Emotional Interactions', *Psychological Review*, 94: 300–18.

GULLEY, Norman (1968), *The Philosophy of Socrates* (London: MacMillan).

GUTMANN, Amy (1993), 'The Challenge of Multiculturalism in Political Ethics', *Philosophy and Public Affairs*, 22: 171–206.

HARE, R. M. (1981), *Moral Reasoning* (Oxford: Clarendon Press).

HEILBRUN, A. B., and Seif, D. T. (1988), 'Erotic Value of Female Distress in Sexually Explicit Photographs', *Journal of Sex Research*, 24: 47–57.

HELD, Virginia (1990), 'Feminist Transformations of Moral Theory', *Philosophy and Phenomenological Research*, suppl. vol. 50: 321–44.

HERMAN, Barbara (1981), 'On the Value of Acting from the Motive of Duty', *Philosophical Review*, 90: 359–82.

—— (1984*a*), 'Mutual Aid and Respect for Persons', *Ethics*, 94: 577–602.

—— (1984*b*), 'Rules, Motives and Helping Actions', *Philosophical Studies*, 45: 369–77.

—— (1991), 'Agency, Attachment, and Difference', *Ethics*, 101: 775–89.

—— (1993), *The Practice of Moral Judgement* (Cambridge, Mass.: Harvard University Press).

HOBBES, Thomas (1651), *Leviathan*, ed. Richard Tuck (Cambridge: Cambridge University Press, 1991).

HOGARTH, R. M. (1981), 'Beyond Discrete Biases: Functional and Dysfunctional Aspects of Judgemental Heuristics', *Psychological Bulletin*, 90: 197–217.

HOLLOWAY, Wendy (1987), ' "I Just Wanted to Kill a Woman". Why? The Ripper and Male Sexuality', in *Feminist Review* (ed.), *Sexuality: A Reader* (London: Virago Press), 123–33.

HUME, David (1739), *A Treatise of Human Nature*, ed. D. G. C. MacNabb (Glasgow: Fontana-Collins, 1978).

HURLEY, Susan L. (1985–6), 'Conflict, Akrasia and Cognitivism', *Proceedings of the Aristotelian Society*, 86: 23–49.

—— (1989), *Natural Reasons: Persons and Polity* (New York: Oxford University Press).

JACKSON, Frank (1984), 'Weakness of Will', *Mind*, 93: 1–18.

—— (1991), 'Decision-theoretic Consequentialism and the Nearest and Dearest Objection', *Ethics*, 101: 461–82.

JEFFREY, Richard C. (1974), 'Preference among Preferences', *Journal of Philosophy*, 71: 377–91.

JOHNSTON, Mark (1988), 'Self-deception and the Nature of Mind', in Brian P. McLaughlin and Amelie Oksenberg Rorty (eds.), *Perspectives on Self-Deception* (Berkeley, Calif.: University of California Press), 63–91.

—— (1989), 'Dispositional Theories of Value', *Proceedings of the Aristotelian Society*, suppl. vol. 63: 139–74.

JOWETT, B. (1953) (tr.), *The Dialogues of Plato*, 4th edn. (Oxford: Clarendon Press).

KANT, Immanuel (*Groundwork*), *Groundwork of the Metaphysic of Morals*, trans. H. J. Paton in *The Moral Law* (London: Hutchinson, 1948).

KENNETT, Jeanette (1991), 'Decision Theory and Weakness of Will', *Pacific Philosophical Quarterly*, 72: 113–30.

—— (1993), 'Mixed Motives', *Australasian Journal of Philosophy*, 71: 256–69.

—— and Smith, Michael (1994), 'Philosophy and Commonsense: The Case of Weakness of Will', in Michaelis Michael and John O'Leary-Hawthorne (eds.), *Philosophy in Mind: The Place of Philosophy in the Study of Mind* (Boston: Kluwer Academic Publishers), 141–57.

────── (1996), 'Frog and Toad Lose Control', *Analysis*, 56: 63–73.

────── (1997), 'Synchronic Self-control is Always Non-actional', *Analysis*, 57: 123–31.

KORALEWSKI, Mary A., and Conger, Judith Cohen (1992), 'The Assessment of Social Skills among Sexually Coercive College Males', *Journal of Sex Research*, 29: 169–88.

KORSGAARD, Christine M. (1986), 'Skepticism about Practical Reason', *Journal of Philosophy*, 83: 5–25.

────── (1996), *The Sources of Normativity*, ed. Onora O'Neill (Cambridge, Mass.: Cambridge University Press).

────── (1997), 'The Normativity of Instrumental Reason', in Cullity and Gaut (1997), 215–54

KOSS, Mary, and Leonard, Kenneth (1984), 'Sexually Aggressive Men', in Neil Malamuth and Edward Donnerstein (eds.), *Pornography and Sexual Aggression* (London: Academic Press), 211–32.

LENAMAN, James (1999), 'Michael Smith and the Daleks: Reason, Morality and Contingency', *Utilitas*, 11: 164–77.

LILLEHAMMER, Hallvard (1997), 'Smith on Moral Fetishism', *Analysis*, 57: 187–95.

LIND, Marcia (1990), 'Hume and Moral Emotions', in Flanagan and Rorty (1990), 133–47.

LLOYD, Genevieve (1984), *The Man of Reason: 'Male' and 'Female' in Western Philosophy* (Minneapolis: University of Minnesota Press).

MCDOWELL, John (1978), 'Are Moral Requirements Hypothetical Imperatives?', *Proceedings of the Aristotelian Society*, suppl. vol. 52: 13–29.

────── (1979), 'Virtue and Reason', *Monist*, 62: 331–50.

MCINTYRE, Alison (1990), 'Is Akratic Action Always Irrational?', in Flanagan and Rorty (1990), 379–401.

MACKIE, J. (1977), *Ethics: Inventing Right and Wrong* (London: Penguin).

MCNAUGHTON, David (1988), *Moral Vision: An Introduction to Ethics* (New York: Basil Blackwell).

MALAMUTH, Neil M., and Sockloskie, Robert J. (1991), 'Characteristics of Aggressors against Women: Testing a Model Using a National Sample of College Students', *Journal of Consulting and Clinical Psychology*, 59: 670–81.

MASTERS, Brian (1993), extract from *The Shrine of Jeffrey Dahmer* (n.p.: Hodder and Stoughton, 1993), repr. in *The Australian*, 20–1 Feb.

MELE, Alfred R. (1987), *Irrationality: An Essay on Akrasia, Self-deception, and Self-control* (New York: Oxford University Press).

—— (1988), 'Irrationality: A Précis', *Philosophical Psychology*, 1: 173–7.

—— (1990), 'Errant Self-control and the Self-controlled Person', *Pacific Philosophical Quarterly*, 71: 47–59.

MELE, Alfred R. (1992), 'Akrasia, Self-control, and Second-order Desires', *Nous*, 26: 281–302.

—— (1995), *Autonomous Agents: From Self-control to Autonomy* (New York: Oxford University Press).

—— (1996), 'Internalist Moral Cognitivism and Listlessness', *Ethics*, 106: 727–53.

—— (1997), 'Underestimating Self-control: Kennett and Smith on Frog and Toad', *Analysis*, 57: 119–23.

—— (1998), 'Motivated Belief and Agency', *Philosophical Psychology*, 11: 353–69.

MILLER, Alexander (1996), 'An Objection to Smith's Argument for Internalism', *Analysis*, 56: 169–74.

NAGEL, Thomas (1970), *The Possibility of Altruism* (Oxford: Clarendon Press).

—— (1986), *The View from Nowhere* (Oxford: Oxford University Press).

PEACOCKE, Christopher (1985), 'Intention and Akrasia', in Bruce Vermazen and Merril B. Hintikka (eds.), *Essays on Davidson: Actions and Events* (Oxford: Oxford University Press), 51–73.

PETTIT, Philip, and Smith, Michael (1990), 'Backgrounding Desire', *Philosophical Review*, 99: 565–92.

—— —— (1993), 'Practical Unreason', *Mind*, 102: 53–79.

—— —— (1996), 'Freedom in Belief and Desire', *Journal of Philosophy*, 93: 429–49.

PLATO, *Phaedrus*, in Jowett (1953), iii. 107–89.

—— *Protagoras*, in Jowett (1953), i.: 119–191.

—— *Symposium*, in Jowett (1953), i.: 479–555.

RACHELS, J. (1991), 'Subjectivism', in Peter Singer (ed.), *A Companion to Ethics* (Oxford: Blackwell), 432–41.

RACHLINS, Howard (1974), 'Self-control', *Behaviourism*, 2: 94–107.

RAILTON, Peter (1987), 'On the Hypothetical and Non-hypothetical in Reasoning about Belief and Action', in Cullity and Gaut (1997), 53–79.

—— (1988), 'Alienation, Consequentialism, and the Demands of Morality', in Samuel Scheffler (ed.), *Consequentialism and its Critics*

(Oxford: Oxford University Press), 93–133; 1st publ. in *Philosophy and Public Affairs*, 13 (1984): 134–71.

RAWLS, J. (1972), *A Theory of Justice* (Oxford: Oxford University Press).

SANTAS, Gerasimos (1966), 'Plato's *Protagoras* and Explanations of Weakness', *Philosophical Review*, 75: 3–33.

SARTRE, Jean-Paul (1992), *Being and Nothingness*, trans. Hazel Barnes (New York: Washington Square Press, 1956).

—— (1956), 'Existentialism is a Humanism', trans. Philip Mairet, in Walter Arnold Kaufmann (ed.), *Existentialism from Dostoevsky to Sartre* (New York: Meridian Books), 287–311.

SAYRE-McCORD, Geoffrey (1997), 'The Meta-ethical Problem', *Ethics*, 108: 55–83.

SCANLON, T. M. (1998), *What We Owe to Each Other* (Cambridge, Mass.: Belknap Press, Cambridge University Press).

SHERMAN, Nancy (1990), 'The Place of Emotions in Kantian Morality', in Flanagan and Rorty (1990), 149–70.

SMITH, Michael (1987), 'The Humean Theory of Motivation', *Mind*, 96: 36–61.

—— (1992), 'Valuing: Desiring or Believing?', in David Charles and Kathleen Lennon (eds.), *Reduction, Explanation and Realism* (Oxford: Oxford University Press), 323–59.

—— (1994), *The Moral Problem* (Oxford: Basil Blackwell).

—— (1996), 'The Argument for Internalism: Reply to Miller', *Analysis*, 56: 175–84.

—— (1997a), 'In Defense of *The Moral Problem*: A Reply to Brink, Copp, and Sayre-McCord', *Ethics*, 108: 84–119.

—— (1997b), 'A Theory of Freedom and Responsibility', in Cullity and Gaut (1997), 293–319.

STOCKER, Michael (1976), 'The Schizophrenia of Modern Ethical Theories', *Journal of Philosophy*, 73: 453–66.

—— (1979), 'Desiring the Bad: An Essay in Moral Psychology', *Journal of Philosophy*, 76: 738–53.

—— (1990), *Plural and Conflicting Values* (Oxford: Oxford University Press).

STRAWSON, Peter (1982), 'Freedom and Resentment', in Watson (1982), 59–80; 1st publ. in *Proceedings of the British Academy*, 48 (1962): 1–25.

SZASZ, Thomas S. (1973), 'The Myth of Mental Illness', in Jeffrey G. Murphy (ed.), *Punishment and Rehabilitation* (Belmont, Calif.: Wadsworth), 186–96.

TEN, C. L. (1987), *Crime, Guilt and Punishment* (Oxford: Clarendon Press).

THOMAS, Laurence (1990), 'Trust, Affirmation, and Moral Character', in Flanagan and Rorty (1990), 235–57.

—— (1992), 'Morality and Human Diversity', *Ethics*, 103: 117–34.

VELLEMAN, J. D. (1989), *Practical Reflection* (Princeton, NJ: Princeton University Press).

VELLEMAN, J. D. (1992), 'What Happens When Someone Acts?', *Mind*, 101: 461–81.

—— (1996), 'The Possibility of Practical Reason', *Ethics*, 106: 694–726.

—— (1997), 'Deciding How to Decide', in Cullity and Gaut (1997), 29–52.

—— (1999), 'The Voice of Conscience', *Proceedings of the Aristotelian Society*, 99: 57–76.

WALLACE, R. Jay (1994), *Responsibility and the Moral Sentiments* (Cambridge, Mass.: Harvard University Press, 1994).

—— (1997), 'Reason and Responsibility', in Cullity and Gaut (1997), 321–44.

WALSH, J. J. (1963), *Aristotle's Conception of Moral Weakness* (New York: Columbia University Press).

WATSON, Gary (1977), 'Skepticism about Weakness of Will', *Philosophical Review*, 86: 316–39.

—— (1982*a*), 'Free Agency', in Watson (1982*b*), 96–110; 1st publ. in *Journal of Philosophy*, 72 (1975): 205–20.

—— (1982*b*) (ed.), *Free Will* (Oxford: Oxford University Press).

—— (1987), 'Responsibility and the Limits of Evil: Variations on a Strawsonian theme', in F. Schoeman (ed.), *Responsibility, Character, and the Emotions: New Essays in Moral Psychology* (Cambridge: Cambridge University Press), 256–86.

WILLIAMS, Bernard (1972), *Morality: An Introduction to Ethics* (Cambridge: Cambridge University Press).

—— (1981*a*), 'Internal and External Reasons', in Williams (1981*c*), 101–13; 1st publ. in Ross Harrison (ed.), *Rational Action* (Cambridge: Cambridge University Press, 1979), 17–28.

—— (1981*b*), 'Moral Luck', in Williams (1981*c*), 20–39; 1st publ. in *Proceedings of the Aristotelian Society*, suppl. vol. 50 (1976), 115–35.

—— (1981*c*), *Moral Luck: Philosophical Papers 1973–1980* (Cambridge: Cambridge University Press, 1981).

—— (1981*d*), 'Persons, Character and Morality', in Williams (1981*c*), 1–19; 1st publ. in A. O. Rorty (ed.), *The Identities of Persons* (Berkeley, Calif.: University of California Press, 1976).

—— (1985), *Ethics and the Limits of Philosophy* (London: Collins).

WOLF, Susan (1982), 'Moral Saints', *Journal of Philosophy*, 79 (1982): 419–39.

—— (1990), *Freedom Within Reason* (Oxford: Oxford University Press).

—— (1992), 'Two Levels of Pluralism', *Ethics*, 102: 785–98.

WOLLSTONECRAFT, Mary (1790), 'A Vindication of the Rights of Women', in Mary Wollstonecraft, *Political Writings*, ed. Janet Todd (London: William Pickering, 1993), 67–296.

WOODS, Michael (1972), 'Reasons for Action and Desires', *Proceedings of the Aristotelian Society*, suppl. vol. 46: 189–201.

WOOTTEN, Barbara (1978), *Crime and Penal Policy* (London: Allen & Unwin).

INDEX